Environmental Law in the Russian Federation

Authored by

Aleksey Anisimov

Department of Environmental and Natural Resource Law
Kutafin Moscow State Law University (MSAL)
Moscow, Russia

&

Anatoliy Ryzhenkov

Department of Civil Law and Procedure
Kalmyk State University
Moscow, Russia

Environmental Law in the Russian Federation

Editors: Aleksey Anisimov, Anatoliy Ryzhenkov

ISBN (Online): 978-981-5049-16-9

ISBN (Print): 978-981-5049-17-6

ISBN (Paperback): 978-981-5049-18-3

First published in 2022.

Bentham Science Publishers Pte. Ltd.
80 Robinson Road #02-00
Singapore 068898
Singapore
Email: subscriptions@benthamscience.net

BENTHAM SCIENCE

CONTENTS

FOREWORD

The state of the environment and the efficiency of protecting environmental human and civil rights leave much to be desired in the last years. The low level of environmental legal culture and environmental education of citizens, civil servants, and representatives of the business community is among the numerous reasons for this phenomenon. Meanwhile, it cannot be said that the state and the scientific community do not take any steps to remedy this situation. The textbook under review written by scholars renowned in Russia is an example of the scientific community's concern over the current environmental problems. The textbook is written in accordance with the requirements of the Russian state standard for jurisprudence.

It should be noted that the book under review is written in simple and clear, legally literate literary language and can certainly be successfully used in the educational process. In addition to the analysis of the current legislation and clarification of the provisions of the scientific doctrine, the authors try to familiarize readers with the procedural issues of the exercise of their environmental rights (or, accordingly, the duties of public authorities) in the field of natural resource management and environmental protection. This methodical approach can be found in all chapters of the textbook.

The textbook includes a total of 10 chapters grouped into three parts. The first (general) part considers the general provisions on environmental law, its scope, sources, problems of the exercise of environmental human rights, the system of environmental management authorities, economic incentives of environmental protection, and liability issues. In the second (special) part, the authors consider the distinctive features of environmental protection in individual areas of human activity (industry, agriculture, defense, *etc.*), specific features of the protection of particular natural resources (land, water, subsoil, *etc.*) as well as the concept and peculiarities of the legal regime of areas with a special environmental legal status. The third (specialized) part includes the study of the distinctive features of international cooperation in environmental protection and the experience of a range of foreign countries.

It appears that being original and innovative both by its idea and structure, this textbook is full of interesting facts and contains valuable information on a wide range of current problems of the theory and practice of environmental law. The textbook encourages thinking about the prospects of environmental legal science development and can be useful to readers from other countries – businessmen, the public, students, and scholars in conducting comparative studies.

E.S. Navasardova
Doctor of Juridical Sciences
The Professor of the Department of Environmental,
Land and Labor Law of North-Caucasus Federal University,
Stavropol
Russia

PREFACE

This textbook is written on the basis of a course of lectures given by the authors at Russian higher education institutions. This textbook includes all necessary sections reflecting the fundamental institutions of Russian environmental law.

The general part of the textbook deals with issues of the subject of environmental law, its systems, environmental human and civil rights, and clarifies the peculiarities and functions of environmental management in Russia, the regulation of environmental protection, and issues of the liability for committed environmental offences.

The special part deals with environmental requirements to certain types of activity (in agriculture, transport, waste management, *etc.*), the peculiarities of protection of some natural objects (water, forests, land, *etc.*), and the procedure for creation of specially protected natural areas (national parks, natural monuments, *etc.*). Particular attention is paid to protecting environmentally disadvantaged areas (ecological disaster zones) affected by human economic activity.

The specialized part deals with issues of international environmental cooperation as well as the peculiarities of environmental legislation of certain countries of the world (Kazakhstan, Belarus, USA, China).

The textbook will be of interest in terms of scientific studies and can be used in the educational process by students taking courses in comparative law and comparative environmental law. In addition, the book contains information about the scope of environmental requirements, prohibitions, and restrictions that can be useful to representatives of commercial organizations planning business in Russia and to public environmental associations intending to implement joint projects with representatives of Russian civil society in Russia.

While writing this textbook, the authors tried not to limit themselves to retelling Russian environmental legislation but to show the complexity and consistency of environmental problems, their universality for all countries of the world, to generalize the valuable experience of other countries, which can be useful for the Russian legislator. In its turn, Russian environmental law contains a number of successful rulemaking decisions that can be of interest to legislative bodies of various countries of the world.

CONSENT FOR PUBLICATION

Not applicable.

CONFLICT OF INTEREST

The author declares no conflict of interest, financial or otherwise.

ACKNOWLEDGEMENT

Declared none.

Aleksey Anisimov
Department of Environmental and Natural Resource Law
Kutafin Moscow State Law University (MSAL)
Moscow, Russia

&

Anatoliy Ryzhenkov
Department of Civil Law and Procedure
Kalmyk State University
Moscow, Russia, and Honored Scientist of the Republic of Kalmykia

CHAPTER 1

Environmental Law as a Branch of Russian Law

Abstract: This chapter begins with considering the basic concepts of the interaction between nature and society that underlie the legal regulation of conservation of nature. The authors review the concepts of sustainable development, circular economy, climate change, and environmental law and draw attention to the methods (ways) of legal regulation of environmental relations. Generally speaking, a method of legal regulation is understood as a set of ways (techniques and means) enshrined in legal rules to impact peoples behavior and their social relations governed by law. There are two methods of legal regulation that function in environmental law: imperative and dispositive. The imperative method in environmental law means the establishment of prescriptions, permissions, prohibitions for the subjects of environmental legal relations and manifests itself in the possibility of applying state coercion to the execution of legal prescriptions by legal entities, citizens, including foreign ones, as well as by officials. The dispositive method is based on the equality of the parties to legal relations and their possibility to choose the particular behavior patterns independently. The citizens right to establish public and other environmental associations is a typical example here.

The main stages of development of Russian environmental legislation are analyzed and six levels of the sources of environmental law are distinguished subsequently in the textbook. The principles of environmental law are also considered; these are the basic ideas that underlie environmental law as a branch of law, determine its content and areas for further development and are used in law enforcement practice in case there are gaps in law. The authors distinguish generally accepted principles, interbranch, branch principles and principles of institutions of law in the system of principles of environmental law. A separate section in the textbook is dedicated to the system of environmental law – its internal structure. It is followed by the section dedicated to environmental legal relations –types of social relations regulated by rules of environmental law of Russia. This chapter concludes with a section on ownership of some natural resources.

Keywords: Actions, Climate, Environmental law, Environmental legal regime, Events, Facts, Field of activity, Industry, Institutions, Legal relations, Man, Method, Natural objects, Natural resources, Omissions, Principles, Right of ownership, Sources of law, Subject, System of law.

Aleksey Anisimov and Anatoliy Ryzhenkov

CONCEPTS OF INTERACTION BETWEEN NATURE AND SOCIETY

Consideration of this issue, which goes beyond the scope of law itself, is traditional in the study of environmental law. Discussion of these concepts is necessary because the law only reflects economic, political, social, environmental and other processes occurring in society. Accordingly, the philosophical concepts perceived by the legislator become rules of law. We will try to show the said dynamics in terms of several such concepts.

Concept of Sustainable Development

The concept of sustainable development was first mentioned in the report of the International Commission on Environment and Development (Gro Harlem Brundtland Commission) in 1987; however, it is finalized in the resolutions of the United Nations Conference on Environment and Development, which was held in Rio de Janeiro in 1992. Sustainable development is understood as the progressive development of the state and society, which ensures a balance of the economic, environmental, and social needs of all private and public entities in the present and future generations. Before the emergence of the concept of sustainable development, different countries had used the concept of rational use of natural resources, which involved finding a balance of economic and environmental interests.

Adopting the concept of sustainable development means the next step – the addition of social interests. In Russian science, in the discussion of sustainable development, the emphasis is usually placed only on environmental interests, but its study inevitably leads us to the conclusion that there is an equivalence of three groups of interests, which must be brought to a "common denominator". For this purpose, special criteria and indicators show the degree of compliance of legislation and the condition of three groups of interests with the goals stated in the concept.

In Russia, the most developed criteria and indicators of sustainable development are observed in forestry, to a lesser extent – in the field of use and protection of the fauna. In many other sectors of social life (agriculture, cities, waste management, *etc.*), criteria and indicators exist only in scientific studies and are still to be introduced in practice in the future. At the same time, even though a full-fledged mechanism for implementing the concept of sustainable development is still being formed, the courts often apply this concept in practice.

For example, considering a claim of Rosprirodnadzor (Federal Service for Supervision of Natural Resources) for suspension of the activities of a livestock breeding complex that caused harm to the environment, the district court stated that the suspension of its work would lead to serious social consequences (unemployment) and undermine the economic foundations of the local government (since this is the only effective enterprise in the municipal district). As a result, a penalty was imposed on the owner of the livestock breeding complex. Though the very concept of sustainable development is not mentioned in the court decision, it was actually applied.

Concept of Circular Economy

This concept emerged in 2010, and Ken Webster is its most famous supporter (Webster, 2013). Supporters of this concept distinguish between two economic models – a linear economy, which entails mass production, consumption, and waste disposal, and a closed-loop economy, in which the amount of generated waste tends to zero. Generally speaking, this is the next step in developing the existing approach to separate waste collection.

The main essence of the concept of "circular economy" is a new approach to waste management: materials of biological origin (which must return to the biosphere as raw materials, for example, as fertilizers for agricultural production) as well as technical waste that does not decompose and enters the biosphere (for example, plastics). The latter must become raw materials and be further reused in production cycles as well. As a result, there will be a saving of non-renewable natural resources, which will not be extracted and processed due to the longer service life of manufactured goods and production of new items from the remains of the old ones. Implementing this concept will make it possible to reduce the negative impact on nature, obtain an economic effect from the decrease in extraction and processing of natural resources, and create new job markets.

Supporters of the concept of circular economy pay much attention to consideration of the interrelation of human, social, natural, and economic capital. Studying the drawbacks of the modern economic model, they draw parallels with the life of the forest, which includes effective interaction of water, energy, plants, animals, bacteria, and fungi. Waste of one biological species becomes the food of another one, and waste of another species is food for the third one: therefore, the entire forest ecosystem not only survives but also flourishes. This is why the linear economy has no future. This future exists in the circular economy based on another system of values.

This concept is implemented in developed European countries with varying degrees of success. For example, in Sweden, 99 percent of household waste is processed completely, and they even buy waste in the neighboring countries (Norway, England) to provide stock to their waste treatment plants. However, full-fledged implementation of this concept in Russia and many other countries is hampered by economic reasons (the transition to circular economy standards requires significant public and private investments and tax benefits), legal reasons (the lack of adequate legislation on waste), cultural reasons (the low level of the environmental legal culture of Russian citizens), the lack of political will and a number of other reasons. Meanwhile, implementing this concept will make it possible to eliminate acute social problems of the creation of new landfills close to Moscow and in Arkhangelsk Region and even derive an economic benefit from waste processing.

The implementation of this concept will influence not only the environment but also related branches of legislation. For example, in civil law, it will entail the emergence of new models of joint and shared ownership as well as new types of civil law contracts.

Concept of Climate Change

The problem of climate change has started gaining attention only in 1988, with the creation of the UN Intergovernmental Group of Experts on Climate Change. It prepared the first conclusions and recommendations on this issue. There are still debates among representatives of various technical sciences (meteorology, climatology) as to whether the climate changes and at which rate. This issue is not relevant for lawyers since the Russian Federation signed and ratified the 2015 Paris Climate Agreement (adopted instead of the Kyoto Protocol, which expired). Therefore, Russia made legally binding commitments to reduce CO_2 emissions into the atmosphere. This implies the objective of legal science to develop a mechanism for the implementation of the Agreement.

Why is this problem discussed?

The problem of climate change is a problem of increasing average annual temperatures, which entails a complex of economic, political, social, and other consequences. The economic consequences include droughts, tornadoes and other unfavorable weather phenomena, which occur in places where they have never been observed before (as was the case in the Volga-Akhtuba floodplain in 2015, when it all dried up). Forests burn, and animals unable to survive in the new conditions die.

Increasing average annual temperatures lead to the rising level of the World Ocean, and many islands go under. Their residents become environmental refugees, and their number will soon reach millions. The changes in average annual temperatures lead to an increase in human mortality from diseases and changes in the habitats of some insects that carry diseases. Despite all this, large multinational companies continue to be the main opponents of the concept of global climate change. They do not want to decrease their profit because of the introduction of new nature protection technologies and conduct the corresponding information campaign against the UN policy to reduce CO_2 emissions through the controlled media.

Global climate change poses two main survival strategies for humankind: the strategy of adaptation to climate change and the strategy of mitigation of such effects. Mitigation is a state policy aimed at reducing the sources or emissions of greenhouse gases. In its turn, adaptation is a measure aimed at stimulating the survival of natural or human-modified ecological systems under rising average annual temperatures (Parker-Flynn, 2014). Measures to mitigate the consequences of climate change are often preventive as they focus on the sources of climate change – industrial facilities, while adaptation is a measure to respond to the effects of an already changing climate. There are several options for climate change mitigation: production of energy with fewer greenhouse gas emissions than traditional fossil fuel; development of technology to remove greenhouse gases from the atmosphere; adoption of new agricultural and forestry practices that reduce the volume of greenhouse gases in the atmosphere. At the same time, there are no contradictions between mitigation and adaptation strategies, and they are interrelated and interdependent.

In a purely legal context, the attorneys general of eight US states first tried to solve the problem of climate change in the courts in 2004, when they commenced the first legal proceedings on a public nuisance in connection with global warming. The plaintiffs stated that the defendants (five largest electric power companies) managed electric power stations that burned fossil fuel and produced CO_2 emissions, which contributed to the "public nuisance" due to global warming; that the citizens had already suffered significant harm from global warming and would face harm also in the future. The plaintiffs did not claim for pecuniary damage but sought an injunction for the defendants to reduce their future emissions by a certain percentage every year for at least a decade. The US district court dismissed the claim in September 2005.

All subsequent claims of this kind were dismissed by US courts as well. The courts stated that the plaintiffs had arbitrarily chosen a number of industries (oil, electric utility, and automotive industries) which allegedly emitted too much CO_2 and other greenhouse gases but this did not give them grounds to claim multi-billion-dollar compensation for violations of legitimate rights of citizens and to demand that their emissions be reduced by some arbitrary amount. US federal courts do not possess the necessary institutional expertise or authority to make such complex policy determinations. To adjudicate a "public nuisance" claim based on global warming, the courts would be required to sort through and balance an array of competing interests — including environmental, industrial, commercial, foreign policy, security, and consumer choice concerns — and decide how much CO_2 and other greenhouse gases the targeted industries should be allowed to emit into the atmosphere. However, all this does not belong to the authorities of the courts (Boutrous, T.J. and Lanza, D. 2008). This is why the attempt to transfer this concept to the legal field failed.

Russia almost completely lacks the necessary legal tools to overcome the effects of global climate change. Today "climate" in different contexts is mentioned only in a range of bylaws aimed at the implementation of international obligations of Russia to reduce CO_2 emissions. Climate itself is not mentioned as an object of environmental legal relations either in the Federal Law "On Environmental Protection" or in any other acts of environmental legislation (in contrast to environmental laws of Belarus or Kazakhstan, which already provide for such an object).

Therefore, the concept of global climate change is implemented in practice at different rates in different countries, and the Russian Federation now gradually joins this legal process.

Concept of a Shift from Anthropocentric to an Ecocentric Perception of the World

The consumer attitude of society to nature and its resources has been dominant for centuries (if not in word then in deed) both in states with market economies and with planned ones. In practical terms, the essence of the concept of consumer attitude to nature is that nature is perceived as a storeroom from which resources must be extracted to develop material production and create societys wealth.

This concept was most vividly expressed by I.V. Michurin: "We cannot wait for favors from Nature. To take them from it – that is our task". The main character of the novel by Ivan Turgenev titled "Fathers and Sons" (1862) mentions the same: "Nature is not a temple but a workshop, and a man is a workman in it". Natures depletion and degradation are an expected result of the consumer attitude to it, which affects people and society correspondingly. The philosophical justification of the consumer attitude to nature has received the politically correct name "anthropocentric model of interaction between nature and society". This means that man is in the center of the Universe, all processes occurring in nature, and all living organisms are created by God exclusively for a man and his consumption. A typical manifestation of this approach is environmental quality regulations aimed at ensuring the sanitary and epidemiological well-being of the population rather than at comprehensive environmental protection in general.

These regulations reduce the harmful impact on nature up to the volumes that are harmless to humans. Meanwhile, the Earth is also inhabited by other organisms, which have a different threshold of requirements for the quality of the environment necessary for their survival. For example, people made bonfires in caves from ancient times and acquired some immunity to smoke over time. However, other living organisms do not have such immunity, and the current environmental legislation has little regard for their interests and does not stipulate measures for their protection. That is why they become extinct due to pollution of air with harmful emissions. The only measure to protect them is the Red Data Book of animals and plants, but it fights against the consequences rather than the causes of the extinction of flora and fauna. There are many other examples of human ignoring of the interests of flora and fauna, from the partial flow transfer of the northern rivers to the southern republics of the USSR for irrigation of fields that failed in the late 80s of the last century to the blocking of the rivers and the construction of hydroelectric power plants on them, which led to the extinction of the sturgeon population, which was not able to spawn in the upper reaches of the river. In addition, the water quality appeared to be incompatible with the life of these and other species of fish because of the industrial discharges.

Understanding this problem on a global scale led to the emergence of the Report of the United Nations Secretary-General "Harmony with Nature" of July 19, 2017. It appears that this report is not a routine statement of current environmental problems but a breakthrough in the ideology of environmental protection, suggesting a range of new areas for the formation of an ecocentric worldview (*i.e.*, which focuses on the interests of nature itself rather than humans) of a fundamentally new type, fitting in with many philosophical and legal concepts that have been discussed by the leading world scientific centers for many years.

The report suggests changing the generally accepted terminologies, proposing completely new legal categories, mentioning "legal philosophy of the Earth" or the principles of "Earth-centred law". The new legal structure of "the Earth's right to a healthy environment" (the Earth but not a person or a state) should be pointed out separately. Its central idea is that human rights depend on the rights of nature, and the implementation of the 2030 Agenda for Sustainable Development – on the observance of the principles of existence in harmony with nature. Legislative recognition of natures inherent rights shifts the debate on environmental protection into a different field, where responsibility and sustainability issues are discussed. A change in the perception of nature is a condition for its preservation and conservation: it should be considered not just legal property but the holder of legal personality and inherent rights as a healthy natural ecosystem. The implementation of provisions of the new concept should lead to a radical change in environmental legislation. The report includes particular examples from the legislation and judicial practice of a number of foreign countries, which have already taken the first step towards the transition to this new philosophical concept.

In particular, on November 10, 2016, the Constitutional Court of Colombia recognized the Atrato River and its basin and tributaries as having rights. In Ecuador, the nation's Constitution was amended to include rights of nature in 2008. In at least five cases, court decisions have recognized those rights, and a number of regulatory actions have enforced that provision. The Plurinational State of Bolivia has enacted two national laws that address the rights of nature, and Argentina and Brazil also have trends in that regard.

From the perspective of Russian legal culture and mentality, many provisions of this report seem strange and unacceptable. However, if we refer to the analysis of Russian environmental legislation, we will find that there are already certain manifestations of the ecocentric approach. The concept of animal rights, which was spontaneously implemented in Russia, can be mentioned as an example. For example, Article 245 of the Criminal Code of the Russian Federation provides for liability for violation of the rules of humane treatment of animals; it is forbidden to kill rare animals included in the Red Data Book; The Federal Law "On Responsible Treatment of Animals" of December 27, 2018, in Article 4 mentions the principle of "treatment of animals as creatures capable of experiencing emotions and physical suffering".

Therefore, the gradual transition to the ecocentric perception of nature also occurs in Russia, though more slowly than in other countries. Nevertheless, a new ecological worldview has already emerged, and in 50-70 years, it will be taken for granted and seem something natural to everyone.

SUBJECT AND METHOD OF ENVIRONMENTAL LAW AS A BRANCH OF RUSSIAN LAW

Any branch of law has its subject. The subject of a branch of law provides an answer to the question: what its rules govern social relations.

In contrast to civil or criminal law, in which the formation of the legal regulation subject has already finished, environmental law is a young branch of law, and there are two points of view regarding its legal regulation. Within the framework of the first of them (it is called "environmental law in a broad sense"), environmental law regulates relations in the use of natural resources and environmental protection. Within the framework of the second point of view ("environmental law in a narrow sense"), the subject of environmental law includes only relations in environmental protection, and the issues of ownership and other rights to natural resources are governed by the rules of natural resources law (land, water, mining, forest, fauna law) as well as by the rules of civil law. Each of these points of view has its own advantages and disadvantages; however, given that the Federal Law "On Environmental Protection" is built according to the "narrow model" and does not regulate relations of ownership of natural resources, it appears reasonable to further adhere to the "narrow approach" of the subject of environmental law. In this case, the analysis of environmental legislation makes it possible to conclude that its rules regulate three groups of social relations.

The first group includes the relations arising in regard to the human impact on the condition of the environment in various areas of activity, *i.e.*, industry, transport, power sector, agriculture, *etc*. This activity can have a harmful impact on several or even all types of natural objects and systems, for example, the violations committed during the operation of the Chernobyl Nuclear Power Plant and the accident that resulted in an unauthorized release of radioactive substances. Radiation have a harmful impact on the condition of all-natural resources – forests, land, water, *etc*. – in the radioactive contamination area. Environmental requirements for the power industry are intended to prevent such an impact on nature.

The second group includes relations arising regarding the protection of certain types of natural objects. For example, the Law on Environmental Protection stipulates measures for the protection of soil (Art. 62), the green fund of settlements (Art. 61), fauna (Art. 60), *etc*. Moreover, all laws related to natural resources (the Water Code, the Land Code, the Forest Code, *etc*.) contain special chapters dedicated to the issues of protection of the relevant natural objects (water, forests, land, fauna, *etc*.). Protection measures for each type of such natural object have their peculiarities (measures for protecting forests from fires are of little use for the protection of water).

The third group includes relations regarding establishing a special environmental legal regime in certain areas. In some cases, this regime aims to preserve (conservation) of unique and rare natural objects in their natural state, and specially protected natural areas are created for this purpose: state nature reserves, wildlife sanctuaries, national parks, natural monuments, *etc*. In other cases, the special regime involves a particular range of measures to restore degraded ecological systems, and the relevant areas are given a special status – ecological disaster zones (unfortunately, they have not been created yet due to the lack of a clear legal basis).

Being an independent branch in the system of Russian law, environmental law is closely interrelated with other branches of law. No branches of Russian law exist in isolation from each other.

1. **Environmental and administrative law:** They are interrelated in two aspects. First, the rules of administrative law determine the system of state administrative bodies, including in the field of environmental protection. Second, the rules of administrative law (the Code of Administrative Offenses of the Russian Federation) provide for administrative liability for various offenses, including in the field of environmental protection.

2. **Environmental and civil law:** They have two areas of interaction as well. First, the rules of civil law provide grounds and the procedure for compensating harm, including cases where this harm is caused to the life, health, or property of citizens by an environmental offense. Second, in the field of nature protection, the legislation provides for a number of incentive measures that are regulated by the rules of both civil and environmental law (for example, environmental insurance tourism).

3. **Environmental and financial law:** The rules of financial law provide for the amount of financing of environmental measures for a calendar year (in laws on the budget), the procedure for credit of payments and penalties for environmental pollution to the budgets of different levels, as well as the mechanism for the establishment of the amounts of payments for the impact on nature.

4. **Environmental and urban development law:** The Urban Development Code provides for developing territorial planning documents at the federal, regional, and local levels (general layouts). These documents set the planned changes in the use of the territories. For example, the maps included in them must reflect the planned creation of specially protected natural areas, locations of industrial facilities that negatively affect the environment, *etc*. Documents of urban development zoning (they are called land use and development rules) determine possible parameters of the use of the territory that falls into different territorial zones. For example, they mention special zones of specially protected areas, recreational zones, *etc*. They establish a range of restrictions and prohibitions.

Therefore, environmental law is an independent branch of Russian law that regulates social relations in the field of interaction between nature and socicty through the establishment of environmental requirements, regulations, and other rules restricting or prohibiting particular types of economic and other activities of citizens and legal entities to ensure a favorable environmental quality.

Closing the issue of the subject of environmental law, we should note that its rules regulate only the relations in the protection of natural objects that are part of the environment. This is why the rules of environmental law do not regulate the protection of animals and birds (they are a subject of civil law), water in the water supply systems or soil in flower pots. Another difficult question is whether stray animals fall within the scope of the rules of environmental law. On the one hand, they are not wild but domestic animals; on the other hand, they are in the state of natural freedom, *i.e.*, they are not controlled by humans. It appears that it will be appropriate to attribute to the subject of environmental law only those stray animals that have completely gone wild and live in natural conditions (forest parks, wastelands, suburban steppes, and ravines).

METHODS OF ENVIRONMENTAL LAW

Generally speaking, a method of legal regulation is understood as a set of ways (techniques and means) enshrined in legal rules to impact the behavior of people participating in social relations governed by law. There are two methods of legal regulation that function in environmental law: imperative and dispositive.

The imperative method in environmental law means establishing prescriptions, permissions, and prohibitions for the subjects of environmental legal relations and manifests itself in applying state coercion to the execution of legal prescriptions by legal entities and citizens, including foreign ones, as well as by officials. The distinguishing feature of this method is the obligatory participation of the state represented by specially authorized agencies or local government bodies in such legal relations. In this regard, the parties to these legal relations are in an unequal position – in the relationship of power and subordination.

This method in environmental law manifests itself, for example, in the establishment of regulations for maximum permissible concentrations for harmful substances or in the case of bringing persons to liability.

The dispositive method is based on the equality of the parties to legal relations and their possibility to choose independently particular behavior patterns. The citizens right to establish public and other environmental associations is a typical example here.

The imperative and dispositive methods are involved in dynamic interaction. Some dominance of the imperative method is justified by the public nature of environmental relations, the role and responsibility of the state for maintaining favorable living conditions for the population. However, it is impossible to say that it prevails in environmental law.

It is necessary to distinguish between environmental law as a branch of law, science, and academic discipline. When we speak of the branch of law, we discuss legal rules and institutions. When we speak of the science of environmental law, we list the ideas discussed by scholars and make it possible to improve legal regulation of environmental relations (if the legislator agrees with them). When we speak of the academic discipline, we consider only a small part of the science and the branch of environmental law, only the part included in the state educational standards for law faculties.

MAIN STAGES OF DEVELOPMENT OF ENVIRONMENTAL LEGISLATION

Some authors try to find the origins of environmental legal rules in their modern understanding, even in the times of Kievan Rus. We do not share this approach since the history of Russia, although regulations containing objective nature protection requirements were adopted, they pursued the goals and objectives that are different from the comprehensive protection of ecological systems and natural objects.

In most cases, these rules were aimed at the protection of ownership relations of the state (for example, protection of the royal hunting grounds or "forests for shipbuilding" necessary to build the fleet).

There are three stages of the formation of environmental legislation.

The first stage (from the middle of the 19th century to 1917) is the stage of conservative environmental protection. In this period, the legislator pursued two environmentally significant goals: to establish prohibitions on certain types of natural resource management (forest use, hunting, *etc*.), and to withdraw certain natural areas from economic use, giving them the status of special protection. At this stage, the first nature reserve, Barguzinsky, appeared in 1916. It should be noted that there are also some prerequisites for forming sanitary legislation.

In this period, an event that can be regarded as the first step to the formation of international cooperation in the field of environmental protection took place, in particular, the international conference for the protection of nature held in Bern in

1913, which was attended by representatives of 17 states, including the Russian Empire. At this conference, for the first time in history, the idea was expressed that nature does not know national borders, and its effective protection can be ensured only by joint efforts of all states of the planet. To coordinate these activities, it was proposed to find a World Nature Protection Committee, which was a completely revolutionary idea. The Committee was founded, but its work was terminated by World War I. The next time the international community returned to this idea only in 1972, when the United Nations Environment Programme, UNEP, was created as an agency.

The first (not implemented) draft Law of the Russian Empire on Nature Protection was developed in 1915-1916 under the leadership of the academician I.P. Borodin, the pioneer of serious scientific nature protection activity in Russia. The next time this idea was reconsidered in the USSR in 1960.

Indeed, two world wars postponed the process of the formation of environmental legislation in Russia and the world by 50-60 years.

The second stage (1917-1991) is the stage of nature protection focused on natural resources. This period is marked by the transition from protecting certain natural objects and systems to protecting natural resources.

Decrees and then basic laws and codes regulating the peculiarities of using the main types of natural resources were adopted in the first years of the Soviet power. The USSR carried out several codifications of legislation on natural resources. For example, the 1970 Land Code of the RSFSR, the 1972 Water Code of the RSFSR, the 1978 Forest Code of the RSFSR, the 1978 Law of the RSFSR "On Protection and Use of Fauna", *etc*. were adopted.

The Law of the RSFSR of October 27, 1960 "On Protection of Nature in the RSFSR" was dedicated directly to the protection of natural resources. It included articles on the protection of land, water, flora, forests, fauna; however, it did not play a significant role in the regulation of nature protection relations. The law did not include effective nature protection measures, mechanisms for their implementation, and liability for violation of its provisions. The trend of the creation of specially protected natural areas, which was started at the end of the first stage, continued at this stage. Several hundreds of them were created in the USSR during the second stage.

The third stage (from 1991 up to now) is the environmental stage of nature protection. It commenced with adopting the Law of the RSFSR "On Protection of the Natural Environment" of December 19, 1991. It established not only the ecological condition of natural resources or certain objects of flora and fauna but also the condition of the natural environment in general as an object of legal protection as well as provided for legal requirements for human activities in various branches of the economy – in the industry, power sector, agriculture, defense, specially protected natural areas, *etc*. The law distinguished three categories of objects of environmental legal relations: integrated: natural ecological systems, the natural environment in general and the ozone layer; differentiated: land, water, subsoil, forests, air, fauna, genetic fund; specially protected: state nature reserves, natural monuments, *etc*. This approach is preserved in the current Law on Environmental Protection.

The sources of environmental law are traditionally classified according to three criteria: according to the legal force, the subject of regulation, and the subjects of lawmaking. If we combine these criteria, then the system of the sources of environmental law will have the following hierarchy.

The first level includes the Constitution of the Russian Federation.

Article 36 of the Constitution is dedicated to the issues of environmental protection. It establishes restrictions of rights of the owners of land plots – the owners freely own, use and dispose of the land and other natural resources if this does not cause harm to the environment. Article 42 relates to the right of every person and citizen to a favorable environment, reliable information about its condition, and compensation for the damage caused to their health or property by an environmental offense. Article 72 attributes legislation on environmental protection and environmental safety to the joint jurisdiction of the Russian Federation and its constituent entities. This is why after the adoption of the Constitution, environmental legislation is further formed at two levels: of the Russian Federation and its constituent entities. Along with the provision of legal rights, Article 58 of the Constitution of the Russian Federation imposes the duty to protect nature and the environment on every citizen.

The second level includes a set of generally accepted principles and rules of international law.

The sources of international law are usually divided into two groups:

a. International instruments containing mandatory legal rules – the Convention on Biological Diversity (Rio de Janeiro, June 5, 1992); the Convention on Long-Range Transboundary Air Pollution (Geneva, November 13, 1979), *etc.*

b. International instruments containing advisory rules – the Declaration of the United Nations Conference on Environment and Development (Rio de Janeiro,

June 14, 1992); the Stockholm Declaration of the United Nations Conference on the Human Environment (Stockholm, June 16, 1972). The instruments of this group are implemented by states because of the higher authority of the UN recommendations rather than because of their legal bindingness.

It is not allowed to apply rules of international agreements of the Russian Federation in the interpretation that conflicts with the Constitution of the Russian Federation.

The third level is federal constitutional laws and federal laws. No federal constitutional laws directly regulating environmental relations have been adopted.

The federal laws regulating environmental relations include Federal Law No. 7-FZ of January 10, 2002 "On Environmental Protection," which continues to be the conceptual approaches to the nature protection organization established in 1991. The law preserves and develops the rules governing environmental standardization, establishing the rights and duties of citizens and public associations, requirements in the field of environmental protection during economic and other activities (including requirements in the field of environmental protection during privatization and nationalization of property, design, construction, and operation of oil and gas production facilities, *etc.*).

At the same time, the law also has its drawbacks.

A characteristic feature of the law is the abundance of the rules referring to other laws (some of them have not been adopted yet, for example, the federal law on ecological disaster zones). Consequently, before these regulatory legal acts are adopted, particular rules of the law do not operate. Also the definition of "environment" itself is not optimal; it includes "man-modified objects", which are created by man to meet the social needs and do not have the properties of natural objects, as well as the mention of "environmental auditing" among the basic concepts, meanwhile, there is no separate article regulating this type of activities. Finally, it does not reflect any current problems and approaches to environmental protection relevant to the 21st century (climate protection, protection of nature from biotechnology or nanotechnology, *etc.*).

Several laws specifying certain provisions of the head act of environmental legislation in three main areas have been adopted at the federal level since 1991.

First, these are the laws establishing or specifying environmental requirements for certain types of economic or other human activities. They include the Federal Law "On Production and Consumption Waste" of June 24, 1998, the Federal Law "On the Industrial Safety of Hazardous Production Facilities" of July 21, 1997, the Federal Law "On Environmental Expert Reviews" of November 23, 1995, and other laws.

Second, these are environmental laws that, along with the rules related to the use of the corresponding natural resources, also include the rules aimed at their protection. They include the Water Code of the Russian Federation of June 3, 2006, the Forest Code of the Russian Federation of December 4, 2006, the Land Code of the Russian Federation of October 25, 2001, the Federal Law "On Subsoil" of February 21, 1992, Federal Law "On Fauna" of April 24, 1995, and several other laws.

It should be specially noted that the Air Code is not the source of environmental law since it regulates only the issues of the organization of air transport. The Federal Law "On Air Protection" of May 4, 1999, is the source of environmental law.

Third, these are the laws establishing the procedure for creating areas with a special environmental legal regime for their preservation and restoration for the present and future generations. They include the Federal Law "On Specially Protected Natural Areas" of March 14, 1995.

The fourth level includes by-laws of the federal government and administrative authorities. They include Decrees of the President of the Russian Federation, Decrees of the Government of the Russian Federation, and acts of federal executive authorities. These legal acts can be classified according to three criteria: specifying provisions of law; adopted to determine the powers of state authority; approving the program goals and objectives of the state environmental management.

Decree of the Government of the Russian Federation No. 469 of July 23, 2007 "On the Procedure for Approval of Regulations for Permissible Discharges of Substances and Microorganisms into Water Bodies for Water Users" can be mentioned as an example of the first type of the bylaws.

The Decree of the Government of the Russian Federation of November 11, 2015, "On Approval of the Provision on the Ministry of Natural Resources and Environment of the Russian Federation" is an example of the second type of by-laws.

The Decree of the President of the Russian Federation of April 19, 2017, "On the Environmental Security Strategy of the Russian Federation until 2025" is an example of the third type of by-laws.

The fifth level includes regulations of constituent entities of the Russian Federation. The constitution attributes environmental legislation to the subjects under the joint jurisdiction of the Russian Federation and constituent entities of the Russian Federation. According to this, government and administrative authorities of constituent entities of the Russian Federation have contributed to the regulation of environmental relations in the corresponding territories since 1994.

It is possible to distinguish three main areas in environmental rulemaking of constituent entities of the Russian Federation: specifying and detailing federal environmental requirements for certain types of activities; creating the legal basis for the functioning of areas with a special environmental legal regime; establishing peculiarities of protection of certain types of natural objects.

The sixth level includes acts of local government bodies.

These acts can be adopted regarding waste management issues, greening and improvement of areas, creation of specially protected natural areas of local significance, *etc*.

PRINCIPLES OF ENVIRONMENTAL LAW

The principles of environmental law are the basic ideas that underlie environmental law as a branch of law, determine its content and areas for further development, and are used in law enforcement practice in case there are gaps in law.

The principles can be classified according to various criteria. The approach according to which they are classified by the subject of legal regulation is the most common. As a result, generally accepted principles, interbranch, branch principles, and principles of institutions of law are distinguished in the system of principles of environmental law.

1) In environmental law, the system of principles is headed by generally accepted principles of international law enshrined in various documents of the United Nations as well as resolutions of other international organizations. There is no exhaustive and clearly defined list of internationally recognized environmental principles at the moment, though the analysis of the declarations and other documents adopted at the summits of the United Nations makes it possible to doctrinally distinguish, for example, the principle of formation of the green economy in the context of sustainable development and poverty eradication. Many of the generally accepted international environmental principles formulated before have been included in the national legal systems and reflected in the

Constitutions and laws. The most well-known such case is the principle of sustainable development proposed at the International United Nations Conference on Environment and Development held in Rio de Janeiro in 1992 reproduced in the Constitutions of several foreign countries (Kenya, Nicaragua, Qatar, Sudan, *etc.*) as well as in Russias Federal Law "On Environmental Protection" of January 10, 2002.

The generally accepted principles of international law are closely related to Russian general principles of law, formulated in the Constitution of Russia (legality, responsibility, independence of courts, *etc.*). However, these principles are not associated with the environment.

2) An interbranch principle of environmental law is understood as the main idea common for two or more branches of law, reflecting the patterns of development of social relations within nature protection and enshrined in the rules of two or more branches of Russian law.

Such principles include ensuring favorable conditions for human activity, responsibility for violation of environmental legislation requirements, payable natural resource management, compensation for environmental harm, *etc.* These principles are interbranch because their implementation is impossible only within the framework of environmental legislation; this is why this process involves rules of constitutional, administrative, urban development, financial, criminal, and other legislation.

3) Branch principles. This type of principle is enshrined and implemented within one branch of law. With respect to environmental law, branch principles include the principle of independence of state environmental supervision, the principle of the presumption of environmental hazard of planned economic and other activities, the principle of mandatory environmental impact assessment in making decisions on economic and other activities, as well as a range of other principles.

4) Environmental legal principles of the level of certain institutions. In contrast to branch and interbranch principles, institutional principles are usually included in specialized environmental laws. For example, waste management principles can be found in the Federal Law "On Production and Consumption Waste", and environmental expert review principles – in the Law of the Russian Federation "On Environmental Expert Reviews".

The second common classification of environmental law principles is based on the criteria of the scope and the mechanism of implementation of the principles, including humanitarian, administrative and economic principles of environmental law. Humanitarian principles include the principle of ensuring favorable conditions for human activity; economic – the principle of payable natural resource management and compensation for environmental harm; and administrative – the principle of mandatory participation of state authorities of the of the Russian Federation, and local government bodies in nature protection activities.

Along with statutory principles, there are doctrinal principles of environmental law, *i.e.*, the principles proposed by scholars but have not been added in the law text yet. Such discussed principles of environmental law include the principle of counteraction to climate change, the principle of development of environmental entrepreneurship, the principle of greening, and a range of other principles.

It should be noted that the Land Code of the Russian Federation prohibits the establishment of additional principles of land law through laws of constituent entities of the Russian Federation. Meanwhile, Article 3 of the Federal Law "On Environmental Protection" does not prohibit constituent entities of the Russian Federation from extending the list of principles of environmental law. In this regard, it appears that constituent entities of the Russian Federation can use this possibility more widely, enshrining the system of principles that reflect the environmental conditions of the corresponding region in regional laws.

As already mentioned above, the courts often refer to the principles of environmental law since their observance ensures normal and uniform development and functioning of the entire Russian legal system in general. Meanwhile, the question is relevant whether there can be principles of law that are not enshrined in the rules of legislation but formulated in judicial practice. There is every reason for this conclusion; they arise from the analysis of the current judicial practice in environmental cases. For example, in the course of consideration of cases, the courts often conclude that payment for environmental harm is compensatory in nature and must be established on the basis of the principle of equivalence according to the type and volume of the negative impact on the environment.

Meanwhile, the "principle of equivalence" is not mentioned in Article 3 of the Federal Law "On Environmental Protection", which refers only to the principle of "payable natural resource management and compensation for environmental harm" as well as the principle of "responsibility for violation of legislation in the field of environmental protection". Therefore, the specification of two principles of environmental law occurred in judicial practice.

Hence it follows that new principles of environmental law can emerge not only as a result of supplementing environmental legislation but also using their formulation in judicial practice.

SYSTEM OF ENVIRONMENTAL LAW

The system of environmental law is understood as a scientifically substantiated sequence of order of environmental legal institutions and rules according to their importance, role and content, on the basis of the nature of regulated social relations. We should remind that a legal institution is a relatively small, stable group of legal rules that regulate a particular variety of social relations.

The general part of environmental law consists of the institutions containing general provisions applying to all or most regulated environmental relations.

They include the following institutions:

- Environmental rights and duties of citizens and their associations;
- State and municipal management of environmental protection (including standardization, monitoring, and environmental supervision);
- Environmental education;
- Economic regulation in the area of environmental protection;
- Responsibility for violation of environmental legislation.

The special part of environmental law consists of the institutions that contain requirements for the subjects of environmental law in certain areas of activity or in particular territories and establish:

- environmental requirements for certain types of activities (agricultural, industrial activities, requirements for construction and operation of power engineering facilities, defense, *etc*.);
- the legal position of specially protected natural areas and ecological disaster zones;
- peculiarities of the legal protection of certain types of natural objects (forests, water, land, air, subsoil, fauna).

The special part of environmental law includes the international mechanism for cooperation between Russia and other countries in the field of environmental protection.

ENVIRONMENTAL LEGAL RELATIONS

The study of the category of legal relations is necessary not only for static consideration of environmental law as a set of legal rules but also for dynamic consideration to show the mechanism of functioning of rules of law. For example, in family law, it is necessary to file an application with a civil registry office to enter into a marriage. It is impossible to get married without this action fact, which is associated with the occurrence of legal consequences by rules of law. Similar rules apply to environmental law.

Environmental legal relations are social relations, regulated by rules of the environmental and other branches of law, in the field of interaction between nature and society regarding fulfillment and observance of environmental requirements and regulations by users of natural resources, creation of specially protected natural areas, and protection of certain natural objects as well as use by citizens of measures to protect their right to a favorable environment. Environmental legal relations can be classified according to several criteria.

1. Based on the nature of the impact on social relations, regulatory and protective legal relations are distinguished. Regulatory environmental legal relations are related to environmental standardization, expert review, licensing, certification, auditing, monitoring, *etc*. Protective legal relations include legal relations aimed at protecting the environmental rights of individuals and legal entities and bringing to liability for environmental offenses.

2. According to the degree of definition of the subjects, environmental legal relations are divided into absolute and relative. In absolute environmental legal relations, only one party is defined clearly – the holder of the legal right, for example, the right to a favorable environment, to reliable information on the state of the environment. The other party to legal relations, which is obliged to respect these rights, is not defined personally. In relative environmental legal relations, the parties are defined personally, for example, in environmental auditing or eco insurance contracts.

Environmental legal relations include the object, the subject, and the content (rights and duties of the participants) of environmental legal relations.

Subjects of environmental legal relations. Among the subjects of environmental legal relations, we should mention citizens, legal entities (commercial and non-commercial, including foreign ones), the Russian Federation, constituent entities of the Russian Federation, and municipalities. Public legal entities perform their environmental function through the activity of representative, executive, and judicial authorities.

The first characteristic feature of the subjects of environmental legal relations is almost constant participation of the state (the Russian Federation, constituent entities of the Russian Federation), and less often – of municipalities.

The second characteristic feature is the different scope of environmental rights and duties of legal entities. The matter is not even that public environmental associations do not have special duties since they do not produce a negative impact on the environment. There are fundamental differences among commercial legal entities, depending on the nature and types of their negative impact on the environment. For example, the Federal Law "On the Industrial Safety of Hazardous Production Facilities" of July 21, 1997 establishes a number of additional prohibitions and restrictions for the owners of these facilities (if they produce explosive, toxic or other environmentally hazardous substances specified in the appendix to the Law).

"Future generations", referred to in many international instruments, are a particular debatable subject of environmental legal relations. The responsibility before "the present and future generations" is mentioned in the preamble of the Constitution of the Russian Federation. Future generations in different contexts are mentioned in Article 1 of the Urban Development Code of the Russian Federation (within the framework of the principle of sustainable development of the territory), the Federal Law "On Environmental Protection" (the preamble and Article 63.1), Article 35 of the Law of the Russian Federation "On Subsoil", Article 3 of the Federal Law "On Air Protection", and several other federal environmental legislative acts. However, environmental legislation still stipulates no clear criteria or procedures for exercising the rights of this variety of subjects.

Object of environmental legal relations.

The object of any branch legal relations is the benefit for which people enter into social relations (legal relations) regulated by rules of law. Given that environmental law is a new branch of law, many issues are still discussed.

One of them relates to the category of objects of environmental legal relations. Most scholars are of the opinion that objects of environmental legal relations include only objects of the material world – components of the natural environment, natural objects, and systems (land, water, subsoil, specially protected natural areas, *etc*.). However, representatives of another scientific field believe that in addition to objects of the material world, environmental legal relations can include particular activities of citizens, legal entities, and public authorities. For example, when citizens send requests to state authorities for the provision of environmental information, actions of officials rather than specific natural objects are the object of such legal relations.

The debatable question of whether people themselves are the object of environmental legal relations should be mentioned separately. Supporters of this concept think that man is part of nature and not only the subject of legal relations, and this inclusion of man in the list of environmental protection objects does not contradict the essence of environmental legislation. Opponents of this concept point out that if a man is part of nature, man does not need law, including environmental law. Nature does not live under law. In nature, everything happens according to objective rules of the material world. Meanwhile, man, thanks to the inherent ability to think and work effectively, has withdrawn from the natural environment and formed society. Man has learned to control his behavior rationally, due to which man needs knowledge of the laws of nature, the patterns of interaction between society and nature, and social tools based on this knowledge, in particular, law, to manage the development of society in harmony with nature (Kolbasov, 1999). It appears that man cannot be considered as an object of environmental law within the framework of the current legislation. However, with the shift from an anthropocentric to an ecocentric worldview, this will happen sooner or later.

The content of environmental legal relations comprises interdependent legal rights and duties of their participants. In legal science, a legal right is understood as a measure of possible behavior assigned to an authorized person to satisfy this persons interests, secured by the imposition of duties on the counterparties.

A legal duty is the type and measure of due conduct imposed on the obligated person, securing the right of the other party and guaranteed by the state. Legal duties can be active (for example, the need to take measures to prevent the loss of fauna during agricultural works) or passive (the need to refrain from actions, for example, from making fires in forests, storing chemicals in inappropriate places).

The content of environmental legal relations depends on the object in connection with which they arise. From this point of view, we can distinguish rights and duties related to a certain natural object (water, land); rights and duties in territorial legal relations (in specially protected natural areas); rights and duties in the field of observance and fulfillment of environmental requirements in certain areas of human activity.

Legislation establishes the limits of the exercise of environmental rights and freedoms by citizens and legal entities, restricting their possibility to enter into particular categories of environmental legal relations. For example, draft technical documentation for new military equipment or technology containing state secrets is not provided to public environmental associations for public environmental expert reviews. The content of environmental legal relations depends on the peculiarities of the subjects of specific legal relations, for example, we find completely different sets of environmental rights and duties of a commercial legal entity (for instance, a subsoil user) and a public environmental organization. We can observe significant differences in the sets of rights and duties of citizens and public authorities of any levels.

The content of environmental duties will gradually change upward since the consequences of global climate change, and the crisis of the traditional consumption pattern are obvious, and the concept of circular economy pays much attention to the change of this pattern.

Legal facts in environmental law.

Today there is no established understanding of the term “legal facts in environmental law”, but this category itself is widely discussed in legal science. The following definition can be proposed: legal facts in environmental law are life circumstances that are due to the current level of legal regulation of nature protection relations, the availability or lack of these circumstances is associated by rules of law with the emergence, change, or termination of legal relations concerning the preservation of the environment (biosphere) in general as well as protection and restoration of certain natural objects and systems, with mandatory participation of public authorities in these legal relations. However, it should be noted that in environmental law certain legal facts rarely entail the emergence, change, or termination of environmental legal relations. Far more often, environmental legal relations give rise to sets of legal facts that are different in nature (events, actions), and these legal relations are interbranch quite often.

General classification of operative facts

Operative facts can be classified according to several criteria. Three classifications are of greatest interest for the theory of environmental law: according to the nature of the consequences (establishing, changing and terminating rights), according to the criterion of human will (events and actions: lawful, wrongful, or omissions); according to the time factor (facts of states, facts of single actions). Moreover, environmental law distinguishes simple and complex sets of facts, and the factor of gradual accumulation of compositional elements is important within the framework of the latter.

1) Classification according to the criterion of the nature of the consequences

Facts that establish rights in environmental law are traditionally divided into acts of public authorities, which give rise to environmental legal relations and civil law contracts. The vast majority of operative facts that establish rights comprise acts of public authorities. Such acts can be classified into three groups. First, these are acts permitting economic activities related to the negative impact on the environment. For example, environmental legislation provides the duty of legal entities and individual entrepreneurs to carry out economic and (or) other activities at the facilities of category I to obtain a complex environmental permit. Second, acts of public authorities entail the creation of specially protected natural areas (reserves, national parks). Third, discharges (emissions) and other types of negative impact on certain natural objects are produced on the basis of resolutions of public authorities. For example, this operative fact gives rise to legal relations concerning the discharge of wastewater into water bodies.

Contracts as a ground for the emergence of environmental legal relations are not common; there are environmental insurance contracts, environmental auditing contracts, as well as a range of other contracts.

Facts that change rights aim to change subjects, objects, or content of environmental legal relations. These changes can occur for various reasons. For example, a complex environmental permit is subject to revision in part or in full in cases of changes in the technological processes of the main production facilities, replacement of equipment or raw materials, which lead to changes in the established volume or mass of emissions or discharges of pollutants, limits for disposal of production and consumption waste.

Operative facts that terminate rights mean the specific circumstances of objective reality that terminate legal relations, rights, and duties. Environmental legal relations can be terminated at the will of an economic entity (refusal to use water bodies or other natural resources leads to termination of duties to protect them) or occur at the will of public authorities. An example of the latter is complete cessation of placement, design, construction, reconstruction, commissioning, operation, conservation, and liquidation of buildings, structures, and other facilities in case of violation of requirements in the field of environmental protection on the basis of (commercial) court decisions. Licenses for transportation, processing, utilization, neutralization, placement of waste of hazard classes I-IV can also be canceled by court decisions.

2) Classification of operative facts according to the criterion of human will

As mentioned above, this common classification includes events and actions that have environmental legal distinguishing features. Legal events are specific external life circumstances that are independent of the will and consciousness of people and lead to environmental legal consequences. Scientific and technological progress has expanded the human capability to impact natural phenomena.

This circumstance gave rise to the proposal to distinguish between absolute and relative events. The difference between them is that the former is completely independent of the will of people (earthquakes, floods), and the latter is indirectly caused by human activity but take place beyond human will, for example, destruction of the ozone layer, climate change, *etc*. The accident at the Japanese nuclear power plant Fukushima-1, which occurred on March 11, 2011, is a typical example of an absolute event that led to an environmental disaster. It was caused by a terrible earthquake of magnitude 9.1, followed by a tsunami that raised the ocean waves by 40 meters.

Such a variety of operative facts of events are quite common in environmental law. Time periods are a variety of absolute events; they have the initial and final points and are often mentioned in different nature protection laws. In addition, time periods can be indefinite or clearly definite. However, time periods themselves do not lead to the emergence, change, or termination of environmental legal relations; they are elements of sets of facts, as we observe this in other branches of law also.

Actions as various operative facts in environmental law can be lawful, carried out within the framework of legal rules, and illegal, meaning an environmental offense committed by a person. Lawful actions are divided into legal acts and legal actions. Legal acts are external forms of expression of human will to achieve a lawful result. They are divided into transactions (conclusion of environmental auditing contracts), individual acts of state authorities or local government bodies – administrative acts (for example, resolutions on the creation of forest green belts and their area or resolutions on refusal to create them are adopted by state legislative (representative) authorities of constituent entities of the Russian Federation) as well as court decisions (for example, on the provision of environmental information to a public environmental association). Contracts as operative facts are not very common in environmental law. “Legal actions” include lawful actions which are performed unintentionally. They are not aimed directly at achieving a specific result or the the emergence of rights and duties related to it. The lack of a special purpose to cause legal consequences distinguishes them from legal acts.

An omission is a persons particular form of conduct, which manifests itself in the lack of clearly expressed behavioral responses. In addition, the wrongful nature of this inactive conduct is not obligatory since the omission does not always mean failure to fulfill the assigned duty. An example of a wrongful omission is the failure of legal entities to fulfill the assigned duties, which cause pollution or another negative impact on the environment (par. 3, Art. 6.35 of the Code of Administrative Offenses of the Russian Federation). Another example of illegal omissions is an evasion of provision of information to the state register of facilities having a negative impact on the environment. As a lawful omission, we can mention the non-extension of a fixed-term voluntary environmental insurance contract which entails the termination of its validity.

Illegal actions as operative facts are characterized by the following attributes: they exist at a particular point in space and time; violate rules and regulations; damage legal rights and legitimate interests; mean non-fulfillment of duties; cause negative legal consequences stipulated by law or contracts. Classification of illegal actions usually includes criminal offenses, administrative offenses, civil offenses, and disciplinary offenses. In addition, also conduct without fault can be illegal; for example, harm caused to nature by a source of increased danger entails liability regardless of fault.

An example of illegal penal actions is the pollution of the atmosphere (Art. 251 of the Criminal Code of the Russian Federation), and administrative ones – the violation of sanitary safety rules in forests (Art. 8.31 of the Code of Administrative Offenses of the Russian Federation).

Illegal actions in environmental law have particular distinguishing features: most environmental offenses are latent in nature, and many of the negative environmental consequences are characterized by slow (gradual) accumulation. It is this circumstance that led to the emergence of such a framework as “accumulated harm to the environment” in environmental law (Chapter XIV.1 of the Federal Law “On Environmental Protection” of January 10, 2002).

3) Classification of operative facts according to the time factor

Legal science reasonably distinguishes between single operative action facts (for example, in retail sales) and long-term (multiple) action facts (events) that are characterized by lasting existence (marriage, citizenship). The latter is known as operative facts of states. Operative facts of states cannot be included in the same group with events and actions since they are characterized by stability and a long period of existence, during which they can repeatedly cause legal consequences. Peculiarities of this type of operative facts in environmental law can be shown in the following examples. Suppose a public environmental organization files an application for an environmental demonstration in accordance with Articles 11-12 of the Federal Law “On Environmental Protection”. In that case, this is a single action that does not have long-term consequences. A resolution of a public authority to create a specially protected natural area (for example, a reserve or a national park) gives rise to the emergence of lasting environmental legal relations, both for residents of the settlements included in specially protected natural areas (or directorates of such specially protected natural areas) and for third parties. Since specially protected natural areas are created for an indefinite term, all parties related to them begin to have continuing duties for their “special protection", which means a set of sufficiently strict restrictions and prohibitions on the implementation of economic and other types of activities.

The status of hunters can be mentioned as another example of operative facts of states in environmental law. The rights and duties arising out of it are not limited in time. Similarly, the status of a "citizen exposed to radiation as a result of the Chernobyl accident" means the right to receive a lifetime monetary payment.

Sets of operative facts in environmental law

At the moment, many branches of law (including environmental law) are characterized by the fact that several operative facts (a set of facts) rather than one are necessary for the emergence or termination of legal relations. At the same time, we can talk about simple sets of facts, for which a certain number of actions or events are sufficient, and complex sets of facts, distinguished by the gradual accumulation of the facts indicated in the hypothesis of the legal rule of facts.

Examples of simple sets of facts are filing applications, registration of public environmental organizations, the performance of actions to identify, assess and record sites of accumulated harm to the environment. We see a simple set of actions giving rise to the corresponding legal relations in both cases. A complex set of facts in environmental law involves the consistent accumulation of a number of various operative facts (events and actions), which can belong to various branches.

For example, the construction and operation of oil and gas production facilities are allowed if there is a project to restore the contaminated land in zones of temporary and (or) permanent use of land and approval as a result of the state expert examination of the project documentation. Construction of these facilities will also require a lease of a land plot, a permit for the construction of these production facilities, and a number of other authorization documents. In addition, we can observe a consistent accumulation of operative facts, where lack of one of them makes it impossible to move on to the next stage of the construction process of these environmentally hazardous production facilities. These procedures are governed by regulatory legal acts belonging to various branches: environmental, land, urban development, and civil law.

OWNERSHIP OF NATURAL RESOURCES AND THE RIGHT OF NATURAL RESOURCE MANAGEMENT

The need to consider natural resource management issues within the framework of the educational course in environmental law is due to the fact that the issues of the use of natural resources and environmental protection are closely related. Components of the natural environment can have both environmental and economic significance and be used in economic and other human activities. In this case, it becomes necessary to assign a specific natural resource (or its part) to a private or public owner as well as to establish the procedure for its transfer for permanent or temporary possession (use). Rules on ownership of natural resources are enshrined in Article 9 of the Constitution of the Russian Federation, according to which land and other natural resources can be in private, state, municipal, and other forms of ownership.

Six types of natural resources are distinguished traditionally: land, water, mountain, forest, fauna, air. There are relevant federal laws adopted for each type of natural resource and regulating their ownership issues. Does a real variety of types and forms of ownership of all-natural resources follow from these laws?

1. **Land:** Chapter III of the Land Code of the Russian Federation (Articles 15-19) establishes that land plots may be in private, state (of the Russian Federation and its constituent entities), and municipal ownership, which fully corresponds to the provisions of the Constitution of the Russian Federation.

2. **Forests:** Forests as a natural object and a natural resource can grow on the land of the forest fund and land of other categories. Under Article 8 of the Forest Code of the Russian Federation, forest areas that are part of the land of the forest fund are in federal ownership. In addition, it should be noted that forests can also grow on the land of other categories (for example, within the boundaries of national parks or other specially protected natural areas), but in these cases, they fall within the legal regime of other categories of land. For example, forests can grow within the boundaries of nature parks that are in ownership of constituent entities of the Russian Federation, and in this case, they will belong to the constituent entities of the Russian Federation. However, this and similar exceptions to the rules only confirm the dominance of federal ownership of forests.

3. **Water:** According to Article 8 of the Water Code of the Russian Federation, water bodies are in federal ownership, excluding ponds and flooded quarries, which may be in private and municipal ownership as well as in ownership of constituent entities of the Russian Federation.

4. **Subsoil:** Under Article 1.2 of the Law of the Russian Federation "On Subsoil", subsoil is in state ownership, *i.e.*, in ownership of the Russian Federation and its constituent entities. The law does not stipulate municipal and private ownership of subsoil and mineral resources contained in it.

5. **Fauna:** According to Article 4 of the Federal Law "On Fauna", fauna within the boundaries of Russia is in state ownership, *i.e.*, in ownership of the Russian Federation and its constituent entities.

6. **Air:** Issues of ownership of air in Russia (in contrast to China) are not settled, though the state performs functions of disposing of it, for example, establishing emission limits.

The overview above shows that only land legislation fully complies with Article 9 of the Constitution of Russia; we can mention partial compliance of water legislation (in terms of ponds and flooded quarries – an extremely small part of water bodies) and forest legislation (in case of forests located on land not included in the category of land of the forest fund). As for the other three types of natural resources (subsoil, fauna, and air), there is a definite contradiction between legislation on them and Article 9 of the Constitution of the Russian Federation stipulating a variety of types and forms of ownership of all natural resources and not establishing any exceptions.

It should be noted that Article 9 of the Constitution of the Russian Federation refers to (but does not clarify) "other forms of ownership". There is no interpretation of this form of ownership in legislation on natural resources; however, it can be assumed that the legislator understands "other forms of ownership" as common shared and common joint ownership, which can emerge only concerning land plots but not other natural resources.

The right of natural resource management is exercised in relation to all types of natural resources regardless of their types and forms of ownership of them. Natural resource management is the use of natural resources and (or) impact on the environment in everyday human life, in economic or other activities of individuals and legal entities. Natural resource management is divided into common and special. Common natural resource management is permanent and free for the satisfaction of the vital needs of the population without providing natural resources for use and obtaining permits. Restriction of common natural resource management is allowed in accordance with the procedure provided for by the laws of the Russian Federation.

The right of common natural resource management is enshrined in legislation because the use of many natural resources (water, air) is an essential condition for human life, an element of the right to a favorable environment. The main guarantees of the right of common natural resource management are enshrined in the Constitution of the Russian Federation (freedom of movement, environmental rights, *etc*.). Article 262 of the Civil Code of the Russian Federation establishes that citizens have the right to stay on land plots not closed to public access which are in state or municipal ownership freely, without any permits, and to use natural objects available on these plots within limits allowed by law and other legal acts, as well as by the owner of the corresponding land plot. Suppose a plot is not fenced or its owner has not otherwise clearly indicated that entry to the plot is not allowed without the owners permission. In that case, any person may pass through the plot, provided that this does not cause any damage or disturbance to the owner. By virtue of Article 221 of the Civil Code of the Russian Federation, in cases where, in accordance with the law, the general permission given by the owner, or in accordance with a local custom in a particular territory, it is allowed to pick berries, catch fish and other aquatic biological resources, collect or catch other public things and animals, ownership the corresponding things is acquired by the person who collects or catches them.

We find similar legal frameworks also in land legislation. The Land Code of the Russian Federation often uses the terms "common land plots" and "common territories". According to paragraph 12 of Article 85 of the Land Code of the Russian Federation, common land plots occupied by squares, streets, lanes, roads, embankments, public gardens, boulevards, water bodies, beaches and other objects may be included in various territorial zones and are not subject to privatization. Article 1 of the Urban Development Code of the Russian Federation contains a similar rule. According to it, common territories are the territories that are freely used by an unlimited range of persons (including squares, streets, lanes, embankments, the waterside of common water bodies, public gardens, boulevards).

Citizens have the right to visit forests and to gather wild fruits, berries, nuts, mushrooms, other edible forest resources (food forest resources), as well as non-timber forest resources for their own needs freely and without any charge (Art. 11 of the Forest Code of the Russian Federation). Every citizen has the right to have access to common water bodies and use them free of charge for personal and domestic needs. Every citizen has the right to use (without mechanical vehicles) the waterside of common water bodies for moving and staying close to them, including for recreational fishing and mooring of floating structures (Article 6 of the Water Code of the Russian Federation).

According to Article 19 of the Federal Law "On Subsoil", the owners of land plots, land users, land possessors, lessees of land plots have the right to use common mineral resources available within the boundaries of the land plots and not recorded as state assets, within the boundaries of these land plots, without blasting operations, for their own needs, to use groundwater, the volume of extraction of which should be no more than 100 cubic meters per day, from aquifers that are not sources of the centralized water supply and are located above aquifers that are sources of the centralized water supply, as well as to construct underground structures to a depth of five meters according to the procedure established by laws and other regulations of constituent entities of the Russian Federation.

Citizens of the Russian Federation do recreational fishing freely and without any charge in common water bodies (Article 6 of Federal Law No. 475-FZ of December 25, 2018 "On Recreational Fishing and Amendments to Certain Legislative Acts of the Russian Federation").

This type of common natural resource management can be continued.

In addition, it should be noted that the right of common natural resource management is not absolute. Its exercise must not violate other persons rights and interests protected by law and public interests. This is why all acts on natural resources regulating common natural resource management also contain a range of special restrictions of this right. For example, citizens are obliged to observe fire and sanitary safety rules in forests; they are prohibited from gathering mushrooms and wild plants, the species of which are included in the Red Data Book of the Russian Federation or constituent entities of the Russian Federation; in common water bodies, withdrawal of water resources for drinking and domestic water supply, bathing, use of small vessels, jet skis and other technical means intended for recreation in water bodies, *etc.* may be prohibited; recreational fishing restrictions are established both in terms of the volume of the capture of aquatic biological resources and the methods of fishing (use of nets).

Special natural resource management is the activity of individuals or legal entities that use natural resources or produce emissions (charges or perform waste disposal) to the environment on a paid basis. In most cases, special natural resource management is carried out by persons engaged in entrepreneurial activity. Users of natural resources can include Russian and foreign individuals and legal entities temporarily or permanently staying in the territory of the Russian Federation, with some exceptions (for example, foreigners may not be the owners of agricultural lands).

Users of natural resources can be as follows:

a. Permanent (the right of natural resource management is perpetual) and temporary (when this right is limited to a certain period);

b. Primary (the right of natural resource management is acquired from the state or other primary users of natural resources by way of alienation of this right or universal succession) and secondary (the right of temporary natural resource management is acquired on a contract basis from the primary user of natural resources retaining this status).

The right of special natural resource management emerges on the following grounds:

1. Licenses (in case of subsoil use) or other permits for use and withdrawal of natural resources, as well as for certain types of activities in the field of environmental protection;

2. Resolutions of executive authorities of the Russian Federation or constituent entities of the Russian Federation, local government bodies on the provision of natural resources for use;

3. Contracts for certain types of natural resource management.

Individuals and legal entities that acquire the right of special natural resource management may not dispose it off, except for the cases provided for by the federal laws. The right of special natural resource management can be limited or prohibited following the laws of the Russian Federation to ensure the security of the state and environmental protection. Special natural resource management can include one or several types of natural resource management as a whole. Types of natural resource management are as follows:

1. **Land use:** Land plots can be used based on the right of private ownership as well as the right of permanent (perpetual) use, the right of lifetime ownership with hereditary succession, the right of the lease, the right of easement, and the right of gratuitous use. Land plots can be used for agriculture, construction, recreational activities, as well as for other purposes, according to the attribution of a specific land plot to one of seven categories of land in the land fund of the Russian Federation, as well as the type of permitted use of the land plot within one (individual) category of land.

2. **Water use:** On the basis of water use agreements, the right to use surface water bodies that are in federal ownership, ownership of constituent entities of the Russian Federation, or ownership of municipalities is acquired for the purpose of withdrawal of water resources from water bodies; use of the water area of water bodies; production of electrical energy without withdrawal of water resources from water bodies. On the basis of resolutions on the provision of water bodies for use, the right to use surface water bodies that are in federal ownership, ownership of constituent entities of the Russian Federation, or ownership of municipalities is acquired for support of the countrys defense and state security; discharge of wastewater; construction and reconstruction of hydraulic structures; creation of fixed or floating drilling rigs (platforms), floating (mobile) offshore platforms, fixed offshore platforms, and artificial islands; construction and reconstruction of bridges, underwater crossings, pipelines, and other linear facilities, if such construction and reconstruction are related to changes of the bottom and banks of surface water bodies; mineral exploration and mining, *etc*. (Article 11 of the Water Code of the Russian Federation).

3. **Forest use:** Land legislation provides for the following types of forest use: wood harvesting; resin harvesting; harvesting and collection of non-timber forest resources; harvesting of food forest resources and collection of medicinal plants; game management and hunting activities; agriculture; research activities, training, and education activities; recreational activities; establishment and use of forest plantations; cultivation of forest fruit, berry, ornamental plants, medicinal plants; cultivation of plant materials (seedlings), *etc*. Forest areas that are in state or municipal ownership are provided on the basis of resolutions of authorized state authorities or local government bodies in case the forest areas are provided for permanent (perpetual) use, lease agreements in case the forest areas are leased; gratuitous use agreements in case the forest areas are provided for gratuitous use. Forest plantations located on the land that is in state or municipal ownership are sold under contracts for the sale of forest plantations (Article 75 of the Forest Code of the Russian Federation).

4. **Subsoil use:** Subsoil is provided for use for the regional geological survey; geological survey, including prospecting and evaluation of mineral deposits as well as geological survey and evaluation of the suitability of subsoil areas for construction and operation of underground structures not related to mining; mineral exploration and mining, including use of waste from mining and related processing facilities; construction and operation of underground structures not related to mining; establishment of specially protected geological

sites of scientific, cultural, aesthetic, sanitary, therapeutic and other significance; the gathering of mineralogical, paleontological and other geological collection materials.

Subsoil may be provided for use simultaneously for geological survey, mineral exploration, and mining.

5. **Fauna use:** The types of fauna use that legal entities and citizens may carry out are as follows: hunting; fishing, including the capture of aquatic invertebrates and marine mammals; capture of animals not attributed to hunting resources and aquatic biological resources; use of useful properties of vital functions of animals; study and other use of fauna for scientific, cultural, educational, recreational, aesthetic purposes without their withdrawal from the habitat; extraction of useful properties of vital functions of animals; obtaining of products of vital functions of animals.

6. **Air use:** Since air has no boundaries, it is not provided for use for any type of economic activity. However, it is used for air transport movement, for emission of harmful substances, and other purposes.

CONCLUSION

Thus, environmental law regulates three spheres of social relations: concerning human impact on the state of the environment in various spheres of activity, the protection of certain types of natural objects; and the establishment of a special environmental legal regime in certain territories. The main method of regulating environmental relations is imperative, consisting of obligatory prescriptions. Environmental law as a branch of law consists of three parts and is regulated by various legal acts, the main of which is the Federal Law "On Environmental Protection". The ownership of most natural resources is vested in the federal centre.

QUESTIONS AND TASKS FOR SELF-CONTROL

1. What are the main concepts of interaction between nature and society?

2. Define environmental law as a branch of law, science, and academic discipline. What rules of environmental law regulate groups of social relations?

3. Describe the similarity and differences between the subjects of environmental and natural resources law. What methods of legal regulation are used in environmental law?

4. What are the principles of environmental law?

5. What are the stages of the formation of environmental law?

6. List the main sources of environmental law.

7. Define the system of environmental law. What institutions are included in the general and special parts of environmental law?

8. Define environmental legal relations. What is their difference from legal relations of other branches of law?

9. Define operative facts in environmental law. What classifications of them do you know?

10. What are the main types and forms of ownership of natural resources? What is the difference between common and special natural resource management rights?

REFERENCES

Boutrous, T.J., Lanza, D. (2008). Global Warming Tort Litigation: The Real "Public Nuisance". *Ecology Law Currents, 35*, 82-87.

Kolbasov, O.S. (1999). Terminological Wandering in Ecology. *State and Law, 10*, 34.

Parker-Flynn, J.E. (2014). Global Warming Tort Litigation: The Real "Public Nuisance". *Ecology Law Currents*

Webster, K. (2013). Missing the wood for the trees: systemic defects and the future of education for sustainable development. *Curric. J., 24*(2), 301.
[http://dx.doi.org/10.1080/09585176.2013.802585]

CHAPTER 2

Human and Civil Right to a Favorable Environment

Abstract: This chapter deals with the main stages of the formation of environmental rights in international law. The authors define the human right to a favorable environment as the possibility for every person, people, and the whole humankind to live with such a state of the Earths biosphere that ensures the maximum level of physical and mental health, as well as means eliminating global threats to the biosphere caused by human activity.

It is stated that further development of the system of environmental rights will inevitably affect human rights and the environment, and the rights of environmental refugees. The main authorities of Russian citizens and public associations in the field of environmental protection are studied in terms of Russian legislation. These include right to establish public associations and non-commercial organizations which carry out activities in the area of environmental protection; the right to participate in assemblies, rallies, pickets, processions and demonstrations, referendums and other activities relating to environmental protection that are not contrary to legislation; the right of citizens to require state authorities, local government bodies and other organizations to provide timely, complete and reliable environmental information; the right to propose organization of a public environmental expert review and participate in it; the right to file complaints, applications and proposals concerning nature protection issues and the negative impact of it on state authorities, local government bodies and other organizations and to obtain timely and substantiated responses; the right of citizens to file claims in court for compensation for harm caused to the environment, as well as to their life, health and property, and the right to provide assistance to public authorities in settlement of environmental protection issues. Further, the authors consider environmental duties of citizens and their associations as well as state guarantees of citizens rights (*i.e.*, a set of Russian conditions for the exercise of environmental rights and means of their protection in case of encroachment on them by the state or third parties).

Keywords: Citizens, Climate, Complaints, Demonstrations, Duties, Environmental information, Expert review, Guarantees, Harm, Human rights, International cooperation, Judicial practice, Law, Public associations, Pickets, Rallies, Refugees, Stages, State authorities, UN.

Aleksey Anisimov and Anatoliy Ryzhenkov

HUMAN RIGHT TO A FAVORABLE ENVIRONMENT

Several decades ago, the human right to a favorable environment was formed in international law. Some stages can be distinguished in this process.

1. **1948-1972:** During the first stage, the UN Charter (1945), the Universal Declaration of Human Rights (1948), and the International Covenants on Human Rights (1966) do not mention the “right to a favorable environment” but refer to the connection between the quality of the “standards of life” and the quality of the environment as well as specify the “standard of living” adequate for a dignified human existence. Other international documents of this period focus on the protection of certain categories of subjects from some types of negative impact.

2. **1972-1992:** This stage is attributable to the resolutions of the United Nations Conference on the Human Environment, held in Stockholm in June 1972. The outcome of the conference was the adoption of a declaration on the environment, a declaration of principles and an action plan combined into a single document titled “Stockholm Declaration”. The declaration of principles formulates the concept of the human right to a favorable environment for the first time in international law. The Stockholm Conference (1972) is followed by the beginning of the process of the greening of international law, which was not observed earlier. This manifests itself in reference to the need to preserve the environment even in specialized documents in the field of human rights, which are dedicated to entirely different issues, for example, in Article 9 of the Universal Declaration on the Eradication of Hunger and Malnutrition (1974). According to this rule, to assure the proper conservation of natural resources being utilized, or which might be utilized, for food production, all countries must collaborate to facilitate the preservation of the environment, including the marine environment.

During this period, the United Nations General Assembly adopted the World Charter for Nature (1982), which determines the number of essential areas of international cooperation in the field of environmental protection, including measures to maintain genetic diversity; rational use of natural resources; protection of nature from the consequences of military activities.

Since the mid-1970s, international cooperation in environmental rights at UN has gained prominence. Special attention should be paid to the CSCE activities (now the OSCE) and, in particular, the Final Act of the Conference on Security and Cooperation in Europe of 1975. This document states the impossibility to ensure high quality of the environment only at the domestic level; therefore, a system of measures was proposed to resolve this problem on a global scale. For example, it was stated that it was necessary to take measures to combat pollution of air, water, and land, to intensify the efforts for further development of reserve management and studies, improvement of the state of the environment in settlements, scientific studies, monitoring and assessment of changes in the environment as well as legal cooperation.

These recommendations influenced the subsequent international instruments and were reflected in the 1979 Convention on Long-Range Transboundary Air Pollution. The Vienna meeting of representatives of the CSCE member states, which was held in the period from November 1986 to January 1989, provided recommendations in the field of reduction of emissions of sulphur, hydrogen sulphide, and other pollutants, development of new methods of waste burial instead of dumping it at sea, studies of the phenomena of global climate warming, protection of the ozone layer, *etc*. It was proposed to strengthen international cooperation and improve the exchange of environmental information to achieve these goals.

3. **1992-2002:** This stage is distinguished by implementing the resolutions of the United Nations Conference on Environment and Development, held in Rio de Janeiro in 1992. Since 1992, a favorable environmental quality has been considered as an element of sustainable development of society. The principle of sustainable development means the state duty to preserve all ecosystems and ecological processes vital for the functioning of the biosphere, maintain biological diversity, and observe the principle of optimal sustainability in the exploitation of biological resources and living ecosystems. In other words, sustainable development is stable social and economic development that does not destroy its natural basis and ensures uninterrupted progress in social development.

The declaration adopted at the Rio de Janeiro Conference on Environment and Development points out a range of new elements of the human right to a favorable environment, including the human right to require reduction and elimination of unsustainable patterns of production and consumption; the human right to access international information concerning the environment that is held by various states; the human right to participate in settlement of international issues relating to the environment; the human right to effective judicial and administrative proceedings, including redress and remedy; the human right to participate in making decisions that affect the biosphere.

In 1998, the Convention on Access to Information, Public Participation in Decision-Making, and Access to Justice in Environmental Matters was adopted

(Aarhus, June 25, 1998). It has not been ratified yet by the Russian Federation. The Convention understands the right of every person to a favorable environment as the right "to live in an environment adequate to his or her health and well-being". Along with eliminating the negative impact on peoples health, the convention also distinguishes such a criterion of environmental quality as "adequateness to human well-being" but does not describe it in detail. The convention mentions not only the people of this age but also future generations as subjects, and their right to a favorable environment. As follows from Art. 1 of the Convention, the right to a favorable environment is guaranteed by other environmental rights – the right to public participation in decision-making, access to information, and access to justice in environmental matters.

4. **2002-2012:** The beginning of this stage of development of environmental human rights is associated with resolutions of the World Summit on Sustainable Development in Johannesburg in 2002. The Johannesburg Declaration on Sustainable Development focuses on the issues of poverty eradication, change of consumption and production patterns, as well as protection and rational use of natural resources as the main objectives and requirements for sustainable development considered in the declaration in the context of globalization processes in the world. The conference resolutions emphasize the difference in the possibilities of development for developed and developing countries propose measures to ensure sustainable development of countries of Africa, Latin America, and some other regions. It is noteworthy that paragraph 169 of the Plan of Implementation of the World Summit on Sustainable Development emphasizes the necessity for further consideration of the relationship between environment and human rights, including the right to development.

The conference addressed several other important environmental issues related to the gradual reduction of the number of people without access to safe drinking water; restoration of fish resources of the World Ocean; change of the attitude of business to the problems of ensuring sustainable development; reduction of the production of chemicals harmful to health; substantiation of the role of energy for sustainable development, *etc*. The need for further development of "environmental justice" was also suggested at the conference.

5. **Since 2012 till now:** The beginning of this stage is associated with resolutions of the United Nations Conference on Sustainable Development, Rio+20, which was held in Rio de Janeiro in 2012. The conference focused on the discussion of issues of poverty eradication and measures to ensure sustainable development. The term "green economy" was first used in the resolutions of

the conference. Building a green economy in countries of the world means ensuring rational use of natural resources with minimum losses for thc environment, increasing the efficiency of their use, and reducing the volume of production and consumption waste.

Considering international cooperation in the field of protection of environmental human rights makes it possible to formulate the following definition.

The human right to a favorable environment is the possibility for every person, people, and the whole of humankind to live with such a state of the Earths biosphere that ensures the maximum level of physical and mental health, as well as to use the system of means eliminating global threats to the biosphere caused by human activity. In the generally accepted international classification of human (personal, political, social, economic, cultural) rights, the human right to a favorable environment should be attributed to social rights.

Further development of the environment and human rights will inevitably affect other two important fields that are actively discussed in foreign legal science. They are the issue of formation of the climate and human rights and the issue of rights of environmental refugees. These issues are closely interrelated, and in both cases, they have not been reflected yet in official international instruments.

In recent years, reports about natural disasters – incredible droughts, floods, typhoons and tsunamis — have become more common in the news feed. Undoubtedly, they can be declared as "mysterious natural phenomena", an occurrence that is not connected with human activity, and their consequences do not affect human rights. However, there is also another point of view, which has more and more supporters. The issue of climate and human rights was first raised in 2005, when some Native American Indians (Inuit) living in the Arctic filed a petition claiming compensation from the U.S. government for its failure to take measures to reduce the level of greenhouse gases, as a result of which the climate in the places where they live changed. Rising average annual temperatures led to melting permafrost, their houses collapsed, and common animals, objects of hunting, began to vanish. The petition of the tribe representatives was dismissed then, but this problem drew attention, and its public discussion began (Knox, 2009).

In 2007, the island country of the Maldives convened an international meeting to draw the attention of the international community to issues of climate and the rising level of the World Ocean. If this trend continues, a number of island states will disappear underwater, and their residents will become migrants.

Opponents of the idea of climate and human rights assert that the contribution of a state (or furthermore, an enterprise) to global climate change cannot be well-proven; therefore, it is impossible to sue for compensation from anyone for climate change, even if it caused harm to citizens of the country. On the one hand, it is really so. On the other hand, the complexity of proving causal links between greenhouse gas emissions, climate change, and violations of human rights should not justify the inaction of states regarding insufficient protection of human rights or poor cooperation on environmental protection, including overcoming the consequences of climate change. This is why the existing problem must be reflected in international legal acts. In the meantime, rising water temperatures pose a threat of permanent loss of a number of countries underwater. These problems are not discussed in Russia, and climate is not mentioned in any context in the Federal Law "On Environmental Protection". References to it can be observed in laws of other countries of the CIS, for example, Kazakhstan and Belarus, and their experiences are of interest also to Russia. Therefore, climate and human rights are still forming a variety of environmental rights in international environmental law due to global climate change processes.

Climate change inevitably raises another issue of human rights related to the growth of environmental migration. All definitions and classifications existing in international public law take into account political or economic migrants; however, environmental migration, because of its peculiarities, is poorly reflected in the 1951 Refugee Convention. Meanwhile, there are reasonable assumptions that the number of environmental refugees will reach 200 million by 2050. At the same time, the main paradox of this situation is that the countries with minimal contribution to environmental pollution are most affected by climate change. In our view, to mitigate this problem, the international community has to take the following measures. First, to determine the terminology by enshrining the concept of "environmental refugee", its attributes and elements in the Refugee Convention or another international instrument. We propose the following definition: environmental refugees are persons that had to leave the places of their permanent residence and to stay permanently or temporarily in the territory of another state as a result of anthropogenic or natural causes of environmental change that pose a serious threat to their life or means of living.

Second, the international community must establish clear procedures for the assignment of environmental refugee status to people. In our view, the most optimal solution will be to enshrine the new category of international law, "ecological disaster zone", in a special international agreement. In fact, in the territory of any state, there are objectively natural objects and systems that have a different value and vulnerability to environmental threats. The concept of cultural and natural heritage site is developed for highly valuable ecological systems in international law. Moreover, many states of the world create networks of reserves, national parks, and specially protected natural areas of other categories in their territories. Nevertheless, ecological systems cannot only be with a plus sign (*i.e.*, have unique and valuable features) but also with a minus sign, *i.e.*, differ from the general ecological state of the territory of a country for the worse.

For example, special legal regimes, the regime of ecological disaster zones, can be stipulated for such areas at the national level. They are not available in Russia yet, but such environmentally disadvantaged areas are within the field of legal regulation in the legislation of other countries of the CIS. This is why creating this legal structure (international ecological disaster zone) in international law would make it possible to clearly answer whether a person is an environmental refugee. To confirm this status, it will be enough to prove the residence of a person in a certain area at a certain time, for example, at the moment of the accident at the Chernobyl Nuclear Power Plant in Pripyat.

CIVIL RIGHT TO A FAVORABLE ENVIRONMENT

The "human right" and the "civil right" to a favorable environment are mentioned in various international and national regulations. Use of both of these terms raises the question of how they correlate. In the most general way, we can give the following answer to this question. Human rights are enshrined in international legal acts; they can exist irrespective of their national and legislative recognition and regardless of the connection of their holder with a particular state. Therefore, they are natural, inalienable rights belonging to everyone from birth. The civil rights of citizens are under the protection of the state where they have their citizenship. Many people do not have the status of a citizen (they are stateless persons), and, therefore, they are formally holders of human rights but do not have civil rights. The human and the civil rights to a favorable environment differ in their objects and subjects. While the object of the human right is the state of the Earths biosphere in general, and its favorable quality determines the health of the whole population of the planet, the object of the civil right is a particular qualitative state of the biosphere of only the Russian Federation as one of the parts of the international community. Consequently, the subjects of these rights will be different as well.

The subjects of the human right are all people of the planet, irrespective of their nationality, race, citizenship, residence, *etc*. The subjects of the civil right are only citizens of the Russian Federation and persons staying in its territory (foreign citizens stateless persons).

The human and civil rights to a favorable environment are fundamentally different also in the means of protection. While the right of citizens to a favorable environment is protected in judicial or administrative proceedings with the help of the system of law enforcement agencies of the Russian Federation, for protection of the human right, there is not only this system but also a very complex system of international human rights organizations.

Finally, in contrast to the human right enshrined primarily in the Declarations and other international documents, the civil right to a favorable environment is enshrined in the Constitution and specified in environmental branch legislation of the Russian Federation and its constituent entities.

Speaking of the civil right to a favorable environment, it is necessary to briefly discuss some terminological issues.

1. The civil right to a favorable environment is the main but not the only type of environmental rights of citizens. For its exercise, the legislator provides for the right of citizens to access environmental information, compensation for harm caused by an environmental offense, and some other rights. All of them are the means of achieving the main goal – ensuring a favorable environmental quality in Russia.

2. The "right to a healthy environment" is often mentioned in international legal acts. What is the difference between a "healthy" and a "favorable" environment? The concept of a "favorable" environment is a broader concept that includes a "healthy" environment. The latter is usually understood as compliance of the environment with the sanitation and hygiene regulations established for different types of pollution.

3. The concept of a "favorable environment" in the Federal Law "On Environmental Protection" is formulated in a narrow sense. The law understands it as the environment the quality of which ensures the sustainable functioning of natural ecological systems and combined natural and man-modified natural objects. A "favorable environment" in a broad sense should be understood as the state of the environment of citizens which complies with the regulations relating to its cleanness, resource capacity, environmental sustainability, species diversity, possibility to meet the citizens needs for recreation, tourism, treatment, as well as to include standard natural zones untouched by human activity. This right includes the possibility for citizens to use original goods (the right of common natural resource management) but excludes the relations of ownership of natural objects and possibilities of their commercial use (the right of special natural resource management).

Considering the interconnection and interdependence of rights and duties, it is important to point out the duties of public authorities arising out of paragraphs 1 and 2 of Article 11 of the Law on Environmental Protection and necessary for the exercise of the right of citizens to a favorable environment. These duties of authorities, in particular, include developing environmental regulations; bringing those guilty of a violation of environmental instructions to legal liability; financing environmental measures and programs from budgets of all levels; the duty of relevant officials to provide environmental information; taking into account environmental requirements in the course of territorial planning and urban development zoning of areas; state environmental supervision, state environmental expert reviews, *etc.*

A number of specific authorities of citizens in the field of environmental protection follow the Constitution and environmental legislation. In terms of the logic of the legislator, the use of these authorities by citizens will allow them to exercise their constitutional right to a favorable environment. All authorities of citizens can be classified in two large groups according to the criterion of the protection method: independent protection of their environmental rights and protection with the help of state authorities. The first group includes authorities of citizens to hold demonstrations, picketing, and other similar activities, and the second group – inquiries to state authorities with applications, complaints, proposals, claims, *etc.* Let us consider both of the above groups of environmental rights of citizens.

1. The right to establish public associations and non-commercial organizations that carry out activities in environmental protection. The procedure for the creation of such non-commercial organizations is stipulated by the Civil Code of the Russian Federation and other federal laws. Three founding citizens are enough to establish a public organization (Art. 123.5 of the Civil Code of the Russian Federation). Upon the state registration, these non-commercial public associations acquire the full range of rights and obligations stipulated by environmental legislation, including the right to conduct a public environmental expert review, file claims in court and carry out environmental educational activities.

All public environmental organizations can be conveniently divided into two groups. The first one includes organizations engaged in educational and other non-legal activities. The second one is focused on protecting the environmental rights of citizens, including in court. They conduct public environmental expert reviews, participate in public hearings, public environmental control, *etc.* Both groups can have different numbers of members, territorial coverage, and a narrow (only protection of animals) or broad specialization.

Foreign public environmental organizations can operate in the territory of Russia as well. Greenpeace is the best known of them.

Political parties are one of the types of public associations (Art. 7 of Federal Law of May 19, 1995 "On Public Associations"). In European countries and the USA public environmental associations are an impressive political force, winning elections and obtaining a significant number of seats in representative state authorities and local government bodies. We begin to observe similar processes also in Russia. For example, there are large and interesting environmental sections in the programs of two political parties – Yabloko and A Just Russia.

2. Citizens have the right to participate in assemblies, rallies, pickets, processions and demonstrations, referendums, and other activities relating to environmental protection that are not contrary to legislation.

This rule specifies Art. 31 of the Constitution of the Russian Federation that provides citizens with the possibility of peaceful assembly without weapons, organization of assemblies, rallies and demonstrations, processions, and pickets. Exercise of this right does not allow violation of rights and freedoms of other persons as well as the use of this right to forcibly change the constitutional order, incite racial, national, class, religious hatred, promote violence and war. The organization of these activities is stipulated in detail by Federal Law No. 54-FZ of June 19, 2004 "On Assemblies, Rallies, Demonstrations, Processions and Pickets". As follows from Art. 7 of this law, the notice of a public activity shall be submitted in writing by its organizer to an executive authority of a constituent entity of the Russian Federation or a local government body no earlier than 15 and no later than 10 days before the day of the public activity. Public activities cannot be organized everywhere. For example, it is prohibited to organize them in the territories directly adjacent to hazardous production facilities or other facilities, the operation of which requires compliance with special safety regulations (Art. 8). In recent years, the practical implementation of this environmental authority by citizens has developed quite unevenly. In the 80 and 90s of the last century, these forms of expression of citizens will be massive (especially after the accident at the Chernobyl Nuclear Power Plant – against the construction of a nuclear power plant and the diversion of the northern rivers to the south). This authority was used extremely rarely during almost the entire period of the 2000s. In the 2010s, the interest of citizens in the organization of environmental rallies, processions, and demonstrations gradually revives.

Another form of protection by citizens of their environmental rights is their participation in referendums on environmental issues. According to par. 3, Art. 3 of the Constitution, referendums and free elections are the highest direct expression of the peoples power. The right to participate in referendums is also stipulated by par. 2, Art. 32 of the Constitution. Referendums can be of three levels – federal, regional (of a constituent entity of the Russian Federation), and local. In compliance with Art. 1 of Federal Constitutional Law No. 5-FKZ of June 28, 2004 "On Referendums in the Russian Federation", the referendum is a nationwide vote of citizens of the Russian Federation, possessing the right to participate in referendums on issues of national importance. Environmental protection can also be one of these issues of national importance.

Organization of a federal referendum implies the creation of an initiative group consisting of subgroups covering at least half of constituent entities of the Russian Federation. The initiative group of the referendum is obliged to collect at least two million signatures of referendum participants in support of the referendum. In addition, per one constituent entity of the Russian Federation, there must be a maximum of 50 thousand signatures of referendum participants residing in the territory of the corresponding constituent entity of the Russian Federation.

Fulfillment of these requirements is a rather difficult task. This is why among the best-known initiatives to organize a federal environmental referendum, it is possible to point out only the collection of signatures for the referendum on the possibility of importing spent nuclear materials and nuclear fuel of foreign nuclear power plants to Russia for the purposes of burial and processing in the territory of the Russian Federation (a bill that allowed this possibility was passed at the first reading by the State Duma in December 2000), it took place in several constituent entities of the Russian Federation at the beginning of 2001. However, this public initiative was not implemented, and soon the Law on Environmental Protection, which entered into force, settled this procedure and ended the discussion. Nevertheless, even when constituent entities of the Russian Federation organized regional environmental referendums, there were difficulties recognizing their results. For example, a referendum on constructing a nuclear plant was held in Kostroma Region in 1996. The Ministry for Atomic Energy of the Russian Federation (MinAtom) appealed against the negative result of the referendum to the Supreme Court of the Russian Federation, which agreed with its contentions about the legality of the construction of this plant. The fact is that it is impossible to organize a regional referendum on nuclear power issues (for example, bans on the construction of nuclear power plants), since, under Art. 12 of Federal Law No. 67-FZ of June 12, 2002 "On the Basic Guarantees of Electoral Rights and the Right to Participate in Referendums of Citizens of the Russian Federation", referendums of constituent entities of the Russian Federation or local referendums can be held on issues which are under the jurisdiction of the corresponding constituent entity of the Russian Federation or a local government body. Under Art. 71 of the Constitution of the Russian Federation, the federal energy systems and the nuclear power industry are under the jurisdiction of the Russian Federation. Issues of the nuclear power industry are not under the jurisdiction of constituent entities of the Russian Federation or the joint jurisdiction of the Russian Federation and constituent entities of the Russian Federation.

3. The right of citizens to require state authorities, local government bodies, and other organizations to provide timely, complete, and reliable environmental information. Information on the state of the environment (environmental information) is data (reports, information) irrespective of their form of the environment presentation, in particular, on the historical, current, and estimated state of the environment, its pollution, the processes, and phenomena occurring in it as well as the impact of the actual and planned economic and other activities on the environment and actions that are taken or planned in the field of environmental protection. Therefore, this definition places emphasis on three important features of environmental information: it is not only data on the state of the environment (for example, on the level of air pollution in an individual city) but also on the activity of economic entities that have or can have a negative impact on nature as well as environmental protection measures taken by the pollutants and state authorities. By the direct indication of the law, public authorities are obliged to publish the following information on the state of the environment on official websites on the Internet (or using state and municipal information systems): on the state and pollution of the environment, including air, surface water bodies, soil; on the radiation situation; on stationary sources, on the level and (or) the amount or the mass of emissions and discharges of pollutants; on the management of production and consumption waste; on activities for the reduction of the negative impact on the environment.

The right of citizens to obtain environmental information is enshrined not only directly in the Federal Law “On Environmental Protection” but also in many other regulatory legal acts. For example, par. 2, Art. 24 of the Constitution provides for the duty of state authorities, local governments, and their officials to provide everyone with the possibility to familiarize themselves with documents and materials directly relating to their rights and freedoms. A similar rule is specified in par. 4, Art. 29 of the Constitution, according to which everyone has the right to freely search for the information necessary for them and obtain it (including that in the field of ecology). There are many references to the right of citizens to access environmental information also in other federal environmental laws. For example, Art. 29 of the Federal Law “On Air Protection” establishes the right of citizens and their associations to obtain information on the state of the atmosphere.

The information necessary for citizens and public environmental associations is primarily at the disposal of state authorities specially authorized in the field of environmental protection (Roshydromet). They receive this information on the state of the environment through monitoring (observation over the qualitative state of the environment). However, in case of the extent and the nature of the harmful impact of economic entities, their managers are obliged to provide the corresponding information at the request of public environmental associations.

Despite the establishment of the right of citizens and their associations to obtain environmental information in the Constitution and federal laws, as well as the availability of provisions approved by the Government of the Russian Federation and relating to specially authorized federal bodies in the field of environmental protection, which are obliged to provide citizens with environmental information, obtainment of the latter is often associated with a range of problems, for example, illegal classification of information on the state of nature. Meanwhile, in compliance with Art. 7 of Law of the Russian Federation No. 5485-1 of July 21, 1993 "On State Secrets", information on the state of the environment does not belong to the data which is a state secret.

It should be noted that executive authorities of both federal and regional levels try to solve the problem of the citizens access to the obtainment of environmental information through publication of various data on the activity of these bodies, hotline numbers, *etc.* on their websites (for example, on the website of the Ministry of Natural Resources and Environment (Minprirody) of the Russian Federation). There are special public reception offices in some regions under nature protection authorities, which receive citizens.

Special attention should be paid to the activity of the Ministry of Natural Resources and Environment (Minprirody) of the Russian Federation at the publication of the annual state report on the state of the environment that contains a lot of data on pollution of the atmosphere, water resources and other components of the natural environment, thus making it possible to inform both public authorities and citizens of the state of the environment, types of current environmentally hazardous activities, *etc.* Finally, the Code of Administrative Offenses of the Russian Federation includes Art. 8.5, which stipulates administrative liability for withholding, deliberate distortion, or untimely provision of complete and reliable information on the state of the environment and natural resources, on the sources of pollution or another harmful impact on them, on the radiation situation, as well as distortion of data on the state of land, water and other environmental objects by persons obliged to provide this information. There is the corresponding judicial practice relating to this article.

There is a range of problems associated with interpreting the criteria of environmental information used in Art. 11 of the Federal Law "On Environmental Protection": it must be complete, timely, and reliable. The criterion of "timeliness" means that public authorities are obliged to respond to citizens inquiries within the period established by law (one month in most cases). The criterion of reliability in legislation is determined by contradiction through the wording of unreliability of information. Unreliable information is considered deliberately false data on the state of the environment that does not correspond to reality. The Chernobyl Nuclear Power Plant accident was a typical example; citizens knew the truth about it very late. Before the Party bodies reported that nothing special had happened at the Chernobyl Nuclear Power Plant, *i.e.*, they provided unreliable environmental information.

The category of "complete" information is of an evaluative nature. Evaluation of completeness of the provided data depends on the content and accuracy of the subject of the informational request formulated by citizens and their associations. There are subjective difficulties associated with the fact that citizens do not always possess the required knowledge to formulate a legally correct question to the relevant officials in this regard. Consequently, "completeness" or "non-completeness" of the response of the relevant officials to the inquiries of the citizens are subject to individual evaluation, which can contain elements of subjectivity since the law does not set the "completeness" criteria for this information.

It is necessary to note that citizens and public environmental associations are not only consumers of environmental information; they also collect and distribute it, thus being the source of environmental information for public authorities (for example, notifying them of places of unauthorized dumps).

4. Citizens have the right to propose the organization of a public environmental expert review and participate in it. The Federal Law "On Environmental Expert Reviews" provides the necessity to establish compliance of documents and (or) documentation substantiating planned economic or other activities with environmental requirements using the organization of state and public environmental expert reviews of these documents or types of activities. This expert review can be organized, for example, in relation to draft technical documentation for new equipment and technology, the use of which can impact the environment, and technical documentation for new substances that can enter the environment. Public expert reviews are conducted regarding the same objects as state environmental expert reviews with some exceptions (for example, they cannot be conducted regarding facilities with the state-secret regime). This expert review is conducted by public environmental associations.

5. Citizens have the right to file complaints, applications, and proposals concerning environmental protection issues and the negative impact on the environment with state authorities, local government bodies, and other organizations to obtain timely and substantiated responses. This rule complies with provisions of Art. 33 of the Constitution, according to which citizens of the Russian Federation shall have the right to address personally and submit individual or collective appeals to state authorities and local government bodies. The right of citizens to appeal corresponds with the duty of bodies and officials to consider citizens appeals according to the established procedure within a particular period of time and notify them of the results. The current legislation provides for three forms of appeals.

Proposals of citizens can relate to the enhancement of the operation of nature protection authorities, their structure, or ways to solve particular environmental problems. Through applications, citizens ask a specific office for assistance in exercising their constitutional right to a favorable environment. Filing complaints, citizens may require the elimination of violations of their environmental rights committed due to decision-making or other actions (omissions) of the corresponding officials. Proposals and applications are filed with the officials who are in charge of the settlement of the relevant environmental issue. Complaints are filed with the officials who have authority over the person that decided appeal.

The subject of complaints can be decisions of public authorities on change of the boundaries of reserves, refusal to provide environmental information, lack of the report of an environmental expert review, *etc*.

Such a kind of the right to appeal as the right to file electronic petitions on environmental issues will be further developed in the near future. In fact, this form of interaction between the government and society already exists. The website of the Russian Public Initiative is created for this purpose. If a petition of citizens collects 100,000 votes, it will be considered by the authorities. However, examination of this website concludes that it contains few environmental petitions (both by quantity and popularity), and their subject is usually limited to problems of waste management, deforestation, and protection of wild animals. Therefore, an e-petition is a collective complaint, application, and proposal submitted to the authorized public authority *via* the Internet.

6. Citizens have the right to file claims in court for compensation for harm caused to the environment and their life, health, and property. The right of citizens to claim compensation for damage caused to their health or property by environmental offenses as stipulated by Article 42 of the Constitution of the Russian Federation. The right of citizens to file claims for compensation for harm

to the environment is enshrined in Art. 11 of the Federal Law "On Environmental Protection". The close interrelation between the state of health and the state of the environment follows directly from par. 2, Art. 18 of Federal Law No. 323-FZ of November 21, 2011 "On the Fundamentals of Protection of the Health of Citizens in the Russian Federation". According to it, the right to health protection is also secured by environmental protection. Under Art. 46 of the Civil Procedure Code of the Russian Federation, citizens and organizations, shall have the right to apply to the court for protection of rights, freedoms, and legitimate interests of other persons upon their request, or protection of rights of an indefinite range of persons.

Therefore, this authority of citizens has a sufficiently detailed mechanism of implementation. In addition, attention should be given to the following circumstance. Environmental law distinguishes two types of harm: harm caused to the environment or its individual components and harm to the health and property of citizens (property of legal entities). Harm to the life and health of citizens is often called "echogenic harm", *i.e.*, harm caused by environmental factors. These two types of harm cannot be connected with each other directly. In other words, harm caused to nature does not necessarily entail harm to the health of citizens. For example, millions of hectares of forest burned in Siberia and the Russian Far East in summer 2019. The harm caused to forests as a natural object is obvious. The harm caused to the health of citizens, especially those who were not in the immediate vicinity of it at the time of the fire, is unobvious. This harm requires particular evidence.

There are numerous examples where citizens and their associations exercise their constitutional right to compensation for harm caused by an environmental offense by applying to courts of general jurisdiction and the Constitutional Court of the Russian Federation. For example, according to Resolution of the Constitutional Court of the Russian Federation No. 18-P of December 1, 1997 "In the Case Concerning the Review of the Constitutionality of Certain Provisions of Article 1 of Federal Law No. 179-FZ of November 24, 1995. On Introduction of Amendments to the Law of the Russian Federation. On Social Protection of Citizens Exposed to Radiation as a Result of the Accident at the Chernobyl NPP, the provisions of the above Federal Law on reduction of the number of payments and benefits for citizens affected by radiation were recognized as unconstitutional, the group of persons receiving these benefits was limited. The court pointed out that it was unacceptable to reduce the scope of obligations previously assumed by the state about citizens.

In recent years there has also been the formation of the practice of protection of environmental rights at the international level, since the Russian Federation joined the Convention for the Protection of Human Rights and Fundamental Freedoms (Rome, December 4, 1950). Consequently, Russian citizens and legal entities can apply to the ECHR to protect their environmental rights and freedoms when domestic possibilities for their protection are exhausted. The Constitutional Court of the Russian Federation also refers to various judgements of the ECHR in environmental cases. Although the Convention for the Protection of Human Rights and Fundamental Freedoms does not contain an article dedicated to environmental rights, this does not impede the protection of the latter with the use of other articles of the convention. The following cases can be mentioned among the most interesting ones related to the protection of environmental human rights with the participation of Russians in the practice of the ECHR.

The Case of Fadeyeva v. Russia (Application No. 55723/00). The applicant alleged that living in the sanitary security zone of Severstal PLC in the city of Cherepovets caused significant harm to her health. Consequently, there had been a violation of Art. 8 of the Convention for the Protection of Human Rights and Fundamental Freedoms about her as the state failed to perform its duty to protect her private life and home from severe environmental nuisance arising from the industrial activities of the Severstal steel plant. In Judgment of June 9, 2005, the ECHR held that there had been a violation of Art. 8 of the Convention for the Protection of Human Rights and Fundamental Freedoms and that the Russian Federation was to pay the applicant EUR 6,000 in respect of non-pecuniary damage.

The Case of Ledyayeva and others v. Russia *(*Application No. 53157/99*)*. The applicants, residents of the city of Cherepovets living close to the steel plant, applied to the ECHR and alleged that the pollution of the environment violated their right to privacy protection and inviolability of the home. This contradicts the guarantees of Art. 8 of the Convention for the Protection of Human Rights and Fundamental Freedoms regardless of the reasons for which they live in the sanitary security zone, the air emissions from the plant are excessive, the program for improving the environmental situation in the city of Cherepovets has been abolished by the Government of the Russian Federation, and information on the environmental situation is not published anywhere. In the course of consideration of this case, the ECHR referred to the case of Fadeyeva v. Russia. In this case, the court came to similar conclusions, having stated that the respondent Government had not taken any steps to protect the applicants from environmental pollution: failed to resettle them in a safe area and to provide compensation for the possibility of independent resettlement. Moreover, the authorities did not implement effective programs to reduce emissions within a reasonable time. The ECHR held that Art. 8 of the Convention for the Protection of Human Rights and Fundamental Freedoms had been violated and awarded the applicants compensation for non-pecuniary damage in the Judgement of October 26, 2006.

7. Citizens have the right to assist state authorities and local government bodies in the settlement of environmental protection issues.

This authority can be implemented through public environmental control organized by citizens and reporting of revealed offenses to the competent authorities. The procedure for public environmental control is specified in Art. 68 of the Federal Law "On Environmental Protection". According to this article, public environmental control can be conducted both by citizens and by public environmental organizations. Its results are subject to obligatory consideration by public authorities. Any citizen can become a public environmental inspector, register environmental offenses, and inform state environmental supervision bodies.

Public control is closely related to public environmental monitoring of the state of the environment, which is not regulated by law yet, but its development would help create an additional informational resource for state environmental monitoring.

The above list of environmental rights of citizens is not exhaustive; it is supplemented by other laws and bylaws.

The right of citizens to participate in adopting environmentally significant decisions can be mentioned as an example. This right is expressly stated in the Aarhus Convention. Since Russia does not ratify this Convention, it is not mentioned directly in the Federal Law "On Environmental Protection". As follows from par. 7, Art. 6 of the Aarhus Convention, the procedures for public participation shall allow the public to submit, in writing or, as appropriate, at a public hearing or inquiry with the applicant, any comments, information, analyses or opinions that it considers relevant to the proposed activity. Therefore, this does not mean that the public may, at its discretion, prohibit some construction or other types of environmentally hazardous activities. This means exactly discussion of such decisions and projects of hazardous activities.

In addition to decision-making on specific types of activities (for example, construction), the public can also participate in settlement of issues concerning plans, programs, and policies relating to the environment (Art. 7), as well as preparation of executive regulations and/or generally applicable legally binding normative instruments (Art. 8 of the Aarhus Convention).

It should be noted that all these forms of participation in adopting environmentally significant decisions can also be observed in Russia. For example, many decisions on specific types of activities require EIA (Environmental Impact Assessment), which involves the publics participation. Similarly, the public can recommend its representative for the expert commission conducting the state environmental expert review. The Urban Development Code provides for public debates and public hearings, for example, discussing documentation for territorial planning (Art. 28) and urban development zoning (Art. 31) with citizens. Discussion of documents for territorial planning is important because, for example, general layouts of urban districts (or settlements) stipulate disposal sites for solid household waste on a compulsory basis (Art. 23 of the Urban Development Code of the Russian Federation), and residents have recently been far from indifferent to this issue.

In urban development zoning, the territory of an urban district is divided into territorial zones. Urban development regulations are established for each of them. The regulations determine parameters and types of permitted use of land plots and immovable property within a specific territorial zone. In addition to residential, industrial, agricultural, and other territorial zones, urban districts can include recreational zones and zones of specially protected areas.

Consequently, citizens may care about the parameters and types of permitted use established for production zones, including environmentally hazardous industrial facilities and sites of their expected location in the future. The location and parameters of disposal sites for solid household waste must be established within special purpose territorial zones. In recreational purpose territorial zones, urban development regulations set the possibilities (as well particular restrictions and prohibitions) for urban forests, beaches, parks, ponds, sites for leisure and tourism, *etc*. Natural monuments, national parks, and other specially protected natural areas can be located within the boundaries of territorial zones of specially protected natural areas. The location and possible ways of using all these areas can be of great interest to the public, and it can express its considerations.

There is also a range of possibilities for the public to participate in discussing regulations. For example, the Environmental Council was established under the Volgograd Regional Duma. It consists of several leading scholars from Volgograd higher education institutions and discusses draft environmental laws adopted by the Volgograd Regional Duma afterward. Moreover, to create a forest green belt, public environmental organizations can file the corresponding application with the Public Chamber of the constituent entity of the Russian Federation. In this case, the Public Chamber holds public hearings and, if there is a positive decision, submits the outcome document to the legislative authority of the corresponding constituent entity of the Russian Federation. Development and adoption of the 2009 Civil Legislation Development Concept are interesting if we consider the perspectives of such forms of public participation in adopting environmentally significant decisions. Both representatives of the scientific community and practicing lawyers took part in its discussion. As a result, several federal laws that considerably changed the content of the Civil Code of the Russian Federation were adopted. In the case of the formation of a similar environmental legislation development concept, there is experience and procedures for its discussion with further adoption of the necessary laws.

Therefore, the right of citizens to a favorable environment is the possibility for citizens of Russia and other persons staying in the Russian Federation on legal grounds to live in Russia in terms of the state of the biosphere, which ensures the maximum level of their physical and mental health as well as to use the national system of means that eliminate the threats to the biosphere of the country caused by human activity.

ENVIRONMENTAL DUTIES OF CITIZENS AND LEGAL ENTITIES

Environmental duties of citizens and legal entities are the type and measure of the necessary conduct established by the state to ensure a favorable environmental quality. There is a liability for their non-fulfillment. Therefore, in contrast to rights of citizens, which are exercised freely and at ones own discretion, duties, as a form of regulation of social relations provided for by the Constitution of the Russian Federation and environmental legislation, are based on the principle of power, which implies state coercion if necessary. Environmental duties are closely related to legal rights – they are paired, interrelated categories. There can be no situation when citizens have some right but state authorities or legal entities, users of natural resources, have no corresponding duty. Environmental duties of citizens and public environmental associations are stipulated by Article 58 of the Constitution of the Russian Federation as well as Articles 11-12 of the Federal Law “On Environmental Protection”.

According to Article 58 of the Constitution, everyone has the duty to preserve nature and the environment and treat natural resources with care. Article 11 of the Federal Law “On Environmental Protection” reproduces these duties almost word for word. It specifies that citizens have the duty to preserve nature and the environment; treat nature and natural resources with care; comply with other legislative requirements. The duties of public and other non-commercial associations are summarized even more shortly in Article 12 – “to comply with the requirements in the field of environmental protection”. However, this list is not exhaustive; it is supplemented with other articles both of the Law on

Environmental Protection and other environmental legal acts.

We should note that the Constitution of the Russian Federation distinguishes not only between human and civil rights (for example, not providing foreigners with electoral rights) but also duties. For example, according to Article 59 of the Constitution, the duty to defend the Homeland is imposed only on citizens. The Constitution uses the term "everyone" concerning the duty to treat nature and the environment with care, expanding this duty on Russian, foreign citizens, and stateless persons staying in the territory of Russia.

There are several classifications of environmental duties:

1. Environmental duties of citizens and legal entities, and as for the latter, we should mention significant differences between the duties of economic entities and public associations.

2. It is necessary to distinguish environmental duties in various fields of interaction between man and nature (construction, waste disposal, transport, agriculture, water use, forest use, *etc.*).

3. Environmental duties can be of a general or special nature. For example, Article 77 of the Law on Environmental Protection related to the general duty of citizens that causes harm to the environment, resulting in its pollution, depletion, damage, or another harmful impact. According to Article 13 of the Land Code, the owners, possessors, users, and lessees of land plots have a special duty, arising out of the rights to the land plots, to protect the land from various types of harmful impact as well as to treat the land as a natural object with care. Therefore, to become a subject with the duty, it is necessary to own a land plot.

Special duties also include the requirement of paragraph 1 of Article 73 of the Law on Environmental Protection, according to which the managers of organizations and officers responsible for making decisions during economic and other activities that have (can have) a negative impact on the environment must complete the training in the field of environmental protection and environmental safety. This duty does not apply to ordinary citizens.

GUARANTEES OF ENVIRONMENTAL RIGHTS OF CITIZENS

Guarantees of environmental rights of citizens should be understood as a set of Russian conditions for the exercise of environmental rights and means of their protection in case of encroachment on them by the state or third parties. Traditionally, legal science distinguishes between general social and special guarantees of civil rights. The system of general social guarantees consists of economic, political, spiritual, and moral guarantees. Analysis of the system of general social guarantees of the civil right to a favorable environment should be started with political guarantees.

Political guarantees of the civil rights to a favorable environment should be understood as the international and domestic policy of the state in the field of environmental protection, activities of political parties, public and other non-commercial environmental associations, and their support by the state. Environmental problems still occupy much less space on the Russian political "agenda" than in European countries (for example, the Green Party in Germany or Sweden has been repeatedly elected to the parliament).

Economic guarantees of the civil right to a favorable environment mean the availability of the economic incentives and sanctions in the country, which make it possible to ensure the compliance of economic entities with environmental requirements and regulations, in particular, to introduce best available technologies at environmentally hazardous production facilities, which will minimize the negative impact on the environment. For example, the economic guarantee that provides conditions for the exercise of environmental rights of citizens is the measures provided for in Article 17 of the Federal Law "On Environmental Protection" and intended for the support of economic and (or) other activities carried out by legal entities and individual entrepreneurs to protect the environment. Consequently, receiving this support (for example, tax incentives), users of natural resources reduce the negative impact on the environment, thereby providing conditions for exercising environmental rights.

Spiritual guarantees of the right to a favorable environment mean the humanitarian, ethical and aesthetic views on nature in society according to which nature is understood as an important intangible value that serves as an essential condition for the existence of life, both of humans and other animal and plants life forms. Articles 71, 73, 74 of the Law on Environmental Protection are dedicated to the settlement of the problem of raising the environmental legal culture of Russians. They proclaim universality, integrity, and continuity of environmental education and establish the role of the state in this process. For example, the Ministry of Education and Science of the Russian Federation has included the compulsory discipline of environmental law in the current state educational standard for higher education institutions that offer jurisprudence programs to students.

The issue of spiritual guarantees (development of environmental legal culture) is much more important for Russia than it may seem at first glance. For example, suppose the population of the country considers it possible to throw waste into the ravine closest to their village. In that case, even perfect legislation on production and consumption waste management will not work. It is possible to introduce separate waste collection as in European countries tomorrow, but is there any confidence that citizens of Russia will sort it out indeed? Another not less important aspect of environmental legal culture is that "radical environmentalists" (especially in European countries), proceeding from the seemingly correct values of nature protection, often attack laboratories in order to "free" test animals, to rid them of the threat of "bad experimenters". However, in addition to the threat of infecting other animals and humans (which can happen if test animals infected with diseases are released), it is also a wrongful act that leads to liability.

The civil right to a favorable environment is secured with the help of not only general social guarantees but also special (legal) guarantees, which include the system of means of personal legal protection. Legal guarantees of the civil right to a favorable environment are a system of state legal conditions and means of its exercise, which include not only laws and bylaws but also activities of various state institutions as well as state authorities, which are obliged to ensure exercise and protection of environmental human and civil rights. The interconnected system of legal guarantees of environmental rights of citizens is headed by constitutional guarantees, which are the basis for guarantees in various branches of law. These include guarantees in environmental law, criminal law, civil law, administrative law and some other guarantees. The division of competence between the Russian Federation and its constituent entities is an important constitutional guarantee of the right to a favorable environment. Due to it, natural resource management, environmental protection, and environmental safety, as well as legislation on environmental protection, are under the joint jurisdiction of the Russian Federation and its constituent entities. The institution of the Commissioner for Human Rights is a particular constitutional guarantee. Along with the Constitution, the Commissioners rights and duties are enshrined in the Federal Constitutional Law "On the Commissioner for Human Rights in the Russian Federation" of February 26, 1997.

The Commissioner has the right to assist citizens by filing claims in court to protect their constitutional right to a favorable environment violated by resolutions or actions (omissions) of state authorities, local government bodies or officials, as well as to participate in the proceedings in person or through a representative in the manner established by law. Annual reports of the Commissioner for Human Rights refer to environmental problems that emerge in the relevant year and the measures taken in response to them.

The important judicial guarantee of this right involves not only the availability of the system of Russian courts considering environmental cases but also the right to resort to interstate authorities protecting rights and freedoms if all national legal remedies have been exhausted. As we have already mentioned above, the ECHR constantly issues judgments in such cases. Decisions on the protection of citizens environmental rights are also adopted in several constituent entities that have constitutional courts of constituent entities of the Russian Federation (the Republic of Tatarstan, Karelia) or statutory courts (Sverdlovsk Region).

Along with constitutional rules and the possibility of judicial protection of their rights, citizens can protect their right to a favorable environmental quality with the help of legal means related to specific branches of law.

Environmental legal guarantees enshrined in the Law on Environmental Protection are of the greatest importance in this regard. They include such environmental legal guarantees as standardization of the quality of the environment, state environmental supervision, environmental monitoring, *etc*.

These guarantees are regulated not only at the federal level but also in laws of constituent entities of the Russian Federation. For example, it is known that the creation of specially protected natural areas promotes improvement of the condition of the environment. This is why a number of constituent entities of the Russian Federation have adopted laws on specially protected natural areas, which stipulate the creation of additional categories (compared with those stipulated by the federal law) of specially protected natural areas of regional and local significance.

The available civil legal guarantees regulate the order of compensation for harm caused to the health and property of citizens. For example, Articles 1084-1094 of the Civil Code of the Russian Federation and Articles 77-79 of the Federal Law "On Environmental Protection" establish the duty of full compensation for harm caused by environmental offenses, the procedure for this compensation as well as the peculiarities of compensation for harm caused by a source of increased danger to the environment. The peculiarity of compensation for harm caused by environmental offenses is that also harm caused to the environment and often leading to the irreparable deterioration of its quality is taken into account in addition to economic losses. Harm to the environment is subject to compensation in accordance with the special methods and rates for damage calculation, and in case they are unavailable – according to the actual expenditures on the restoration of the appropriate quality of natural objects.

Administrative legal guarantees are of great importance among other guarantees of specific branches of law. They consist in the practical implementation of the following legally significant actions by state and municipal authorities and their officials: fulfillment of the legal duties to secure the constitutional right of citizens to a favorable environment; creation of appropriate conditions for its exercise; monitoring its exercise; protection of this right; application of sanctions in case of its violation. An example of the functioning of this group of guarantees is assistance from officials to citizens and their associations in obtaining timely, complete, and reliable environmentally significant information and timely response to complaints, applications, and inquiries from citizens.

In terms of social security law, laws are adopted for social support of citizens affected by radiation due to the accident at the Chernobyl NPP, the Mayak plant, nuclear tests at the Semipalatinsk Test Site, as well as several other categories. Special benefits, in particular, social allowances, are stipulated for them.

CONCLUSION

This chapter discusses the environmental rights of a person and a citizen. International documents and Russian domestic legal acts are analyzed. It explains the specific powers of Russian citizens to create public environmental associations, obtain environmental information, *etc*. It explains the conditions for the implementation and means of protecting citizens environmental rights.

QUESTIONS AND TASKS FOR SELF-CONTROL

1. Give a definition of the human right to a favorable environment. What are the main stages of its formation in international law?

2. What is the difference between human and civil rights in the field of environmental protection?

3. What powers regarding the protection of environmental rights are provided to citizens and their associations by Russian legislation?

4. Can you give practical examples of protection by citizens of their environmental rights?

5. What environmental duties of citizens and public environmental associations do you know?

6. What are the main guarantees of environmental human and civil rights?

REFERENCES

Knox, J.H. (2009). Linking Human Rights and Climate Change at the United Nations. *HELR Harvard Environ. Law Rev.*, *33*, 482.

CHAPTER 3

System of Environmental Management Bodies

Abstract: In this chapter, it is pointed out that management in the area of environmental protection lies in the domain of executive authorities of the Russian Federation and its constituent entities as well as local government bodies. These bodies aim at regulating the interaction between nature and society to ensure a favorable environmental quality. Management activity in environmental protection is carried out exclusively by state executive authorities and local government bodies. Legislative and judicial authorities do not perform any management functions. In a similar manner, public environmental associations and other legal entities are not involved in management. Despite the common goals of environmental management, every level of public environmental management (the Russian Federation, constituent entities of the Russian Federation, local government bodies) has its own level of competence. Management bodies in environmental protection can be classified according to several criteria. The main criterion is the scope of their inherent authoritative powers. According to this criterion, they are divided into general and special competence bodies. Bodies of general competence are distinguished as a special type of public authorities because decision-making in environmental protection is not their special and only function; it is performed along with the fulfillment of other management tasks. The President of the Russian Federation, the Government of the Russian Federation, executive authorities of constituent entities of the Russian Federation, and local government bodies are endowed with general competence.

Bodies of special competence are state authorities that are specially authorized by the Government of the Russian Federation or the President of the Russian Federation to perform the corresponding environmental functions (the Ministry of Natural Resources and Environment, the Ministry of Internal Affairs, *etc*.). According to the nature of their special competence, environmental management bodies are divided into two types: interbranch and branch. Interbranch bodies perform a set of nature protection tasks concerning all (or the majority) of natural objects or types of activities; branch bodies protect the environment in certain life areas (transport, industry, power sector, defense). It is pointed out that the Federal Law “On Environmental Protection” itself does not distribute the powers among specific bodies of general or special competence. The law lists the powers of federal, regional, and local nature protection significance, and these powers are distributed inside each level of authority by other laws and bylaws.

Attention is paid to environmental management functions, *i.e*., the main areas of activities of state executive authorities and local government bodies to ensure a favorable environmental quality and protect environmental human and civil rights (standardization, licensing, expert review, EIA). The state economic regulation of

Aleksey Anisimov and Anatoliy Ryzhenkov

environmental protection is not less important, and it includes the establishment of the system of payments for environmental pollution, tax benefits, and other incentive payments, including measures for the support of environmental entrepreneurship.

Keywords: Authority, Classification, Constituent entities of the Russian Federation, Economic regulation, EIA, Environmental supervision, Expert review, Functions, General competence, Government, Law, Licensing, Local government bodies, Management, Ministry, Object, Powers, President, Special competence, Standardization, Record.

CONCEPT OF ENVIRONMENTAL MANAGEMENT BODIES

Management in environmental protection is understood as activities of executive authorities of the Russian Federation and its constituent entities and local government bodies. They aim to regulate social relations in the interaction between nature and society to ensure a favorable environmental quality. Management activity in environmental protection is carried out exclusively by state executive authorities and local government bodies. Legislative and judicial authorities do not perform any management functions. In a similar manner, public environmental associations and other legal entities are not involved in management. Despite the common goals of environmental management, every level of public environmental management (the Russian Federation, constituent entities of the Russian Federation, local government bodies) is endowed with its own level of competence.

In addition, when we refer to the division of competence between the federal and regional levels, it is necessary to take into account the formation of a subregional management level as a result of the creation of federal districts (nature protection activities of constituent entities of the Russian Federation that are part of the federal districts are coordinated at this level) as well as protection of water bodies according to the "basin principle". The latter means planning and nature protection management activities about the basins of large rivers, for example, the Volga River. Special structural subdivisions performing this coordination are created for this purpose in the structure of the corresponding management bodies (Rosvodresursy, Roshydromet). There have been repeated attempts to give a special legal status to the resort region of the Caucasian Mineral Waters (a special draft federal law is even prepared), however, so far, there is no single body for the management of this territory, and the natural healing resources of this region are located within the boundaries of several constituent entities of the Russian Federation. Accordingly, every constituent entity of the Russian Federation manages its own natural resources.

Management bodies in environmental protection can be classified according to several criteria. The main criterion is the scope of their inherent authoritative powers. According to this criterion, they are divided into general and special competence bodies.

Bodies of general competence are distinguished as a special type of public authorities because decision-making in environmental protection is not their special and only function; it is performed along with the fulfillment of other management tasks. The President of the Russian Federation, the Government of the Russian Federation, executive authorities of constituent entities of the Russian Federation and local government bodies are endowed with general competence.

Bodies of special competence are state authorities that are specially authorized by the Government of the Russian Federation or the President of the Russian Federation to perform the corresponding environmental functions.

According to the nature of their special competence, environmental management bodies are divided into two types: interbranch and branch. Interbranch bodies perform a set of nature protection tasks about all (or the majority) natural objects or types of activities; branch bodies protect the environment in certain life areas (transport, industry, power sector, defense). We should mention the following important circumstance: the Federal Law "On Environmental Protection" itself does not distribute the powers among specific general or special competence bodies. The law lists the powers of federal, regional, and local nature protection significance and these powers are distributed inside each level of authority by other laws and bylaws. For example, let us consider the federal level of environmental management. These powers are distributed among federal executive authorities according to the Decree of the President of the Russian Federation No. 21 of January 21, 2020 "On the Structure of Federal Executive Authorities," as well as the Decree of the Government on each of these authorities. Accordingly, at the level of constituent entities of the Russian Federation, the governors independently determine the structure of their administrations, names of their constituent bodies (committees, departments), and distribute the powers among them. We can observe a similar approach also at the level of local government bodies.

POWERS OF BODIES OF GENERAL COMPETENCE

The President of the Russian Federation, the Government of the Russian Federation, executive authorities of constituent entities of the Russian Federation, local government bodies are endowed with general competence. The below powers of the President of the Russian Federation are of interest to us. First, the

President of the Russian Federation determines the main areas of foreign and domestic policy of the state, including environmental policy. In ordcr to implement it, the President of the Russian Federation approves the structure of federal executive authorities, which include state authorities settling environmental protection issues, as well as determines the competence of some of these authorities and appoints their heads.

Second, the President of the Russian Federation determines the state strategy of the Russian Federation in the area of environmental protection, acts as the subject of legislative initiatives on environmental issues, signs international documents on environmental protection issues (for example, the President of the Russian Federation signed the 2015 Paris Climate Agreement aimed at reducing greenhouse gas emissions that lead to climate change).

Third, the President of the Russian Federation has the right to suspend executive authorities acts that are contrary to the Constitution and federal laws. For example, Decree of the President of the Russian Federation No. 851 of May 15, 2000, suspended Resolution of the Head of Administration of Smolensk Region No. 271 of June 26, 1998 "On Collection of Payments for Pollution of the Natural Environment from Foreign Legal Entities and Citizens Using Vehicles on Roads of Smolensk Region".

The task to implement measures ensuring a favorable environmental quality is also included in the competence of the Government of the Russian Federation. It ensures a single state policy in the field of environmental protection by means of three groups of activities:

1. The Government, with its decrees, approves provisions on federal executive authorities, which determine the specific list of powers of the corresponding executive authority (for example, the Ministry of Natural Resources and Environment of the Russian Federation);

2. The Government adopts decrees specifying rules of federal laws. For example, Decree of the Government of the Russian Federation No. 903 of August 28, 2015, approved the criteria for determination of objects subject to federal state environmental supervision;

3. The Government approves plans and programs to implement strategic areas of environmental protection determined by the President of the Russian Federation. For example, the Government of the Russian Federation developed several program documents in the area of waste management and the protection of rare endangered plants and animals.

Such powers are also inherent in executive authorities of constituent entities of the Russian Federation, which perform legal regulation of environmental protection taking into account the regions specific socio-economic, natural, climatic, environmental, historical, and other peculiarities.

Constituent entities of the Russian Federation exercise their environmental powers through the system of committees, directorates, departments, and other structural subdivisions established by them independently. The names of these bodies and the regional environmental powers distributed among them can vary significantly in different constituent entities of the Russian Federation. For example, in Volgograd Region, most regional powers in environmental protection are exercised by the Committee on Natural Resources, Forestry and Environment of Volgograd Region, the provision on which was approved by the Resolution of the Administration of Volgograd Region of December 19, 2016. This Committee exercises both its natural protection powers and the powers of federal authorities delegated to it according to the established procedure. The own powers of this body include maintenance of the Red Data Book of Volgograd Region, regional environmental supervision, maintenance of the regional waste inventory, creation, and change of the category and regime of protection of specially protected natural areas of regional significance, as well as a range of other powers. Protection of water bodies in federal ownership within the regional boundaries can be attributed to the federal powers delegated to the Committee.

The purpose of environmental activities of local government bodies is to provide additional guarantees of the human and civil right to a favorable environment based on specific local conditions (historical, geographical, natural, climatic, *etc.*). The creation of specially protected natural areas of local significance or allocation of funds of the local budget for the needs of nature protection (for example, greening) can serve as these guarantees.

Environmental issues in urban districts, municipal districts, and settlements can be handled either by a special environmental service, which is part of the local administration or by subdivisions of the local executive authority that manage other sectors of the municipal economy but optionally consider environmental protection issues as well. The selection of a particular model depends on three factors:

1. Whether a municipality is urban or rural. In urban municipalities with a developed industry, the condition of the environment often leads to the creation of individual environmental protection committees in the structure of the local administration. Issues related to the regulation of agricultural production are more relevant to rural municipalities. Environmental issues (for example, in

terms of pollution of agricultural land with pesticides and agrochemicals) can be settled within the framework of agriculture management, and no individual environmental services are established.

2. The environmental situation can vary significantly even in municipalities attributed to the same territories (two urban or two rural ones). This is why we find fundamental differences in the priority of environmental issues, for example, for local government bodies of the city of Cherepovets, which once was recognized as an environmental emergency zone by the state environmental expert review, and the activities of local government bodies of most other urban districts and settlements.

3. Even if the condition of the environment of urban (rural) municipalities is the same, they are different in their economic situation and the possibility to finance nature protection activities.

For example, the urban district of Volgograd has a moderately polluted environment (more favorable for life than in the cities of Cherepovets or Karabash) and, at the same time, financial problems. This is why there is no individual nature protection authority established in Volgograd. Most of the environmental powers belonging to the urban district are exercised by the Department of City Services of the Administration of Volgograd, the provision approved by the Resolution of the Volgograd City Duma of March 22, 2017. Federal legislation on local government and environmental protection refers to the issues of urban districts of local significance: organization of activities for environmental protection within the boundaries of urban districts; participation in the organization of activities for accumulation (including sorting), collection, transportation, processing, utilization, neutralization, the burial of solid household waste; approval of rules of urban district area improvement; organization of use, protection, conservation, reproduction and control over the condition of urban forests, forests of specially protected natural areas of local significance; establishment of rules for the use of common water bodies for personal and domestic needs and provision of the population with the information about restrictions of the use of these water bodies, *etc*. The Provision on the Department of City Services reproduces the rules of federal laws and specifies some of them in detail. For example, the Provision on the Department clearly describes the function of consideration of urban planning documentation regarding its compliance with environmental requirements, mentions the function of participation in the environmental monitoring, coordination, and control over activities for the greening of Volgograd, participation in the examination of the urban district territory to find unauthorized dumps, *etc*. In addition to the urban district, the Federal Law "On the General Principles of Local Government

Organization" also distinguishes other types of municipalities (settlements, municipal districts, and other ones). Accordingly, the range of their natural protection issues of local significance can be different.

POWERS OF BODIES OF SPECIAL COMPETENCE

As already mentioned above, bodies of special competence can be of two types (interbranch and branch), and they can be subordinate to both the Government of the Russian Federation and the President of the Russian Federation. For example, the President of the Russian Federation is in charge of the activities of the Ministry of Internal Affairs and the Ministry of Civil Defense, Emergencies and Disaster Relief, and the Government of the Russian Federation – of the Ministry of Natural Resources and Environment. The current list of federal executive authorities is defined in Decree of the President of the Russian Federation No. 21 of January 21, 2020, "On the Structure of Federal Executive Authorities". According to this Decree, the structure of federal executive authorities consists of two interbranch bodies of special competence and six branch bodies. Most powers in environmental management belong to the interbranch body of special competence – the Ministry of Natural Resources and Environment (Minprirody) of the Russian Federation.

This Ministry includes five services (agencies) that directly perform the environmental management functions assigned to the Ministry of Natural Resources and Environment.

1. The Federal Service for Hydrometeorology and Environmental Monitoring (Roshydromet). It monitors (*i.e.*, applies an observation system for) the condition and the pollution of the environment and also exercises state supervision over the work concerning the active impact on meteorological and other geophysical processes. This body is entrusted with the obligations of the Russian Federation under international agreements of the Russian Federation, including the Convention of the World Meteorological Organization, the United Nations Framework Convention on Climate Change, and the Protocol on Environmental Protection to the Antarctic Treaty signed in Madrid on October 4, 1991.

2. The Federal Service for Supervision of Natural Resources (Rosprirodnadzor). It performs control and supervision functions in the field of natural resource management and environmental protection, issues permits for emissions and discharges of harmful substances into the environment (excluding radioactive substances), carries out the state environmental expert review, protects fauna,

approves the attribution of waste to a particular hazard class, maintains the register of facilities that have a negative impact on the environment, issucs complex environmental permits. Moreover, this body fulfills Russias international obligations arising out of the Convention on International Trade in Endangered Species of Wild Fauna and Flora of March 3, 1973, and it is also a specially authorized body for state regulation in the field of the protection of Lake Baikal.

3. The Federal Agency for Water Resources (Rosvodresursy). It takes measures to prevent the negative impact of water on other natural objects and human health as well as to protect water reservoirs.

4. The Federal Agency for Forestry (Rosleskhoz). It organizes the use and protection of forests, attributes forests to the category of protection forests, establishes designated areas of forests, coordinates forest fire fighting activities, *etc*.

5. The Federal Agency for Subsoil Use (Rosnedra) organizes the rational use and protection of subsoil, particularly issues licenses for subsoil use, arranges the state geological study of subsoil, and maintains the unified system of geological information.

Therefore, the main function of the Ministry of Natural Resources and Environment of the Russian Federation consists in the coordination of the activities of its agencies (services) and approval of various rules and procedures for users of natural resources and public authorities (for example, establishment of the order of maintenance of the Red Data Book, rules for development of technological regulations, forms of environmental impact declarations, rates and methods for estimation of harm to the environment).

The Federal Service for the Oversight of Consumer Protection and Welfare (Rospotrebnadzor) is the second interbranch environmental management body. Nature protection tasks of this body include development and approval of state sanitary and epidemiological rules and hygiene regulations; federal state sanitary and epidemiological supervision over compliance with sanitary legislation; provision of state authorities, local government bodies, and the population with the information about the sanitary and epidemiological situation and the measures taken to ensure sanitary and epidemiological well-being of the population, *etc*.

Along with interbranch bodies of special competence, branch environmental management bodies have also been pointed out here. They are different from interbranch bodies because they perform one particular function in environmental management. Six types of these bodies are distinguished.

1. The Ministry of Internal Affairs of the Russian Federation (MVD of Russia) takes measures to prevent and suppress various types of offenses, including environmental ones. In particular, authorities of internal affairs (police) consider cases of administrative offenses stipulated by Article 8.22 of the Code of Administrative Offenses of the Russian Federation (releasing motor vehicles exceeding the regulatory limits for the content of pollutants in emissions or the regulatory noise level for operation), Article 8.23 of the Code of Administrative Offenses of the Russian Federation (operating motor vehicles exceeding the regulatory limits for the content of pollutants in emissions or the regulatory noise level), paragraph 2 of Article 11.17 (throwing garbage or other objects on railroad tracks and platforms or overboard sea or inland waterway transport ships) and also some other articles. Moreover, the Ministry of Internal Affairs sets up security perimeters in case of elimination of the consequences of natural and man-made emergencies, participates in ensuring public order, assists nature protection authorities in their fight against poaching.

2. The Ministry of Civil Defense, Emergencies, and Disaster Relief of the Russian Federation (EMERCOM of Russia) carries out work on prevention and elimination of natural and man-made emergencies, fire safety, and safety of people at water bodies.

3. The function of the Ministry of Defense of Russia consists of ensuring protection and restoration of the environment in the course of daily activities and combat training of troops and reducing the impact of environmentally unfavorable factors on the personnel and facilities of the military social infrastructure. Within its competence, the Ministry of Defense provides management in the area of use, protection, conservation, and reproduction of forests located within the boundaries of military forestries, performs federal state supervision functions in the area of industrial safety at hazardous production facilities of the Ministry of Defense of the Russian Federation, ensures the safety (protection) of nuclear materials, nuclear installations and nuclear material storage points at nuclear facilities that are under the jurisdiction of the Ministry of Defense of the Russian Federation, carries out federal state supervision in the area of nuclear and radiation safety during development, manufacture, testing, operation, storage and disposal of nuclear weapons and nuclear power plants for military purposes.

4. The Federal Service for the Supervision of Environment, Technology and Nuclear Management (Rostekhnadzor) functions in the field of supervision of technology and nuclear management, control and supervision in the field of safe work related to the use of subsoil, industrial safety, the safety of the use of nuclear energy (excluding nuclear weapons and nuclear power plants for military purposes), radioactive waste management, licensing of activities in the field of nuclear energy, the safety of hydraulic structures, the safety of production, storage and use of industrial explosives. Moreover, this body is endowed with the fulfillment of international obligations of the Russian Federation arising out of the Convention on Nuclear Safety and the Joint Convention on the Safety of Spent Fuel Management and on the Safety of Radioactive Waste Management.

5. The Ministry of Agriculture of the Russian Federation (Minselkhoz) implements the state policy in land reclamation, improvement of soil fertility, sustainable development of rural areas, safe handling of pesticides and agrochemicals, and well as conservation of aquatic biological resources and their habitat. Therefore, the powers of this authority relate to only one area of economic activities – agriculture.

6. The Federal Security Service (FSB). Powers of this authority include combating ecological smuggling, environmental terrorism, and the circulation of toxic substances.

Moreover, this authority participates in activities related to the control over compliance with federal legislation on internal sea waters, the territorial sea, the exclusive economic zone and the continental shelf of the Russian Federation, and the use and protection of animals and their habitat.

SCOPE OF THE BASIC FUNCTIONS OF ENVIRONMENTAL MANAGEMENT BODIES

Environmental management functions are the main areas of activities of state executive authorities and local government bodies to ensure a favorable environmental quality and protect citizens environmental rights. Many management functions are performed by several federal authorities rather than one of them, and often together with constituent entities of the Russian Federation. For example, several federal authorities and state authorities of constituent entities of the Russian Federation implement state environmental supervision. Some environmental powers are exercised only at the federal level.

It is hardly possible to compile an exhaustive list of all environmental functions of management bodies, given that they are enshrined in dozens of federal, regional, and municipal legal acts, which often duplicate each other. Further, we will consider only the six most significant functions of environmental management.

Establishment of Environmental Regulations

At the very beginning, it is necessary to answer why the legislator has introduced a system of environmental regulations. In our view, the reason for the emergence of environmental regulations is that according to Article 42 of the Constitution of the Russian Federation, everyone has the right to a favorable environment, one of the quality indicators of which is purity (non-pollution) of each of its components. For this right to be exercised, environmental legislation limits the extent of the negative impact of economic and other activities on the environment by establishing environmental regulations where the consequences of these activities can lead to negative changes in the quality of the environment determined by physical, chemical, biological and other indicators. The objective need to introduce regulations is because human production (in contrast to natural one) is based on waste-related technology. As already noted in Chapter 1 of the textbook, the concept of circular economy aims to find ways to reduce the waste of human activity. The institution of regulations itself plays the main role in the achievement of this purpose.

However, the purpose of regulations is not to combat economic entities that have a negative impact on the environment. If it were so, all plants would be closed, and the quality of the environment would be as high as possible after that. Regulations must be considered within the framework of the concept of sustainable development; therefore, the purpose of this institution is to find the balance of economic, environmental, and social interests of citizens, businesses, and the state. The peculiarity of environmental regulations manifests itself in the fact that they, being essentially technical norms, become legally significant upon their approval by competent state authorities. The institution of regulations occupies a special place in the mechanism of environmental law since it contains the criteria of the lawfulness of behavior of the subjects of environmental legal relations, specifying attributes of the sets of elements of environmental offenses included in blanket legal rules. The condition of such institutions as the human and civil right to a favorable environment, environmental supervision, liability for environmental offenses depends on the environmental quality indicators. In case of violation of the established regulations, specially authorized bodies may apply to the court for suspension or restriction of activities of economic entities, impose penalties, and (if there are grounds, therefore) submit materials to the competent authorities to bring the guilty party to criminal liability.

The classification of environmental regulations includes regulations regarding environmental quality and regulations regarding the permissible impact on thc environment. Each of these two groups, in its turn, has its subgroups. The fundamental difference between them is that the quality regulations set the maximum amount of harmful substances that can affect human health, air, water, *etc*. The compliance of the number of harmful substances with the environmental quality regulations implies safety of the environment for the citizens health. In contrast to the quality regulations, the regulations regarding the permissible impact on the environment contain the requirements for the sources of the harmful impact, restricting their activities to certain limits rather than for the condition of the environment. Both groups of environmental regulations are interdependent because the total amount of harmful substances that economic entities can release as a result of emissions, discharges and waste disposal must not affect the environmental quality that is safe for the life and health of citizens.

The environmental quality regulations are regulations that are established in accordance with physical, chemical, biological, and other indicators for environmental condition assessment and the compliance with which ensures a favorable environment. This group of environmental regulations is one of the criteria for the determination of a favorable environmental quality, it is used in the protection of environmental rights of citizens in court. Russia developed this group of regulations one of the first in the world, having established the maximum permissible concentrations (MPCs) of hundreds of harmful substances in the atmosphere, soil, water, *etc*. This group of environmental regulations is introduced for the purpose of environmental condition assessment to preserve natural ecological systems, the genetic fund of plants, animals and other organisms. However, until now, when determining the MPC values, specially authorized bodies rely mainly upon the environment-dependent indicators of human health protection, taking little into account the peculiarities of protecting various species of flora and fauna.

The system of environmental quality regulations includes the following regulations:

1. Regulations established in accordance with chemical indicators of the condition of the environment. There are maximum one-time and average daily MPCs for each pollutant. If the MPC is exceeded according to the monitoring data, the corresponding measurements make it possible to determine the extent, for example, 5 MPCs.

2. Regulations of the maximum permissible levels of impact, including harmful physical impact (noise, heat, vibration, *etc*.) as well as radiation exposure.

3. Regulations established in accordance with biological indicators of the condition of the environment, including species and groups of plants, animals and other organisms used as environmental quality indicators, as well as MPCs of microorganisms. Other environmental quality regulations can be established.

To ensure the appropriate quality of the environment, the legislator provides for a system of permissible impact regulations.

The regulations regarding the permissible impact on the environment are established in accordance with indicators of the impact of economic and other activities on the environment and ensure compliance with the environmental quality regulations. Regulations of this type establish the requirements for the sources of the harmful impact, restricting their activities to certain limits, rather than for the quality of the environment. Particular limits (parameters) of emissions, discharges, or other types of harmful impact are established for each source of the harmful impact (for example, each pipe at the enterprise).

Specially authorized bodies (Rosprirodnadzor) calculate the total pollution index from all man-made facilities, which in aggregate must not cause an excess of MPC values. Seven subgroups can be distinguished in this group of environmental regulations: regulations of permissible emissions and discharges; technological regulations; technical regulations; regulations of production and consumption waste generation; regulations of permissible physical impact (levels of exposure to heat, noise, vibration, electromagnetic fields, and other physical impacts); regulations of permissible withdrawal of components of the natural environment; regulations of permissible anthropogenic load on the environment.

Radioactive and highly toxic substances are of the greatest danger among all these types of negative impacts on the environment. The values of regulations of permissible emissions and discharges of radioactive and highly toxic substances are calculated by legal entities and individual entrepreneurs carrying out economic activities at facilities of category I, and this calculation is included in the complex environmental permit (Art. 31.1 of the Federal Law "On Environmental Protection"). Complex environmental permits are documents issued by authorized federal executive authorities to legal entities or individual entrepreneurs carrying out economic and (or) other activities at facilities that have a negative impact on the environment. Complex environmental permits contain obligatory requirements in the field of environmental protection. Complex environmental permits are issued by Rosprirodnadzor for seven years on the basis of positive findings of the state environmental expert review regarding the materials substantiating the permit. The values of regulations of permissible emissions and discharges are also calculated by legal entities (individual entrepreneurs) carrying out economic activities at facilities of category II. For facilities of category II, calculating the values of regulations of permissible emissions and discharges, excluding radioactive substances, is an appendix to the Environmental Impact Declaration.

What is to be done if economic entities cannot ensure compliance with environmental regulations? In these cases, under Article 23.1 of the Federal Law "On Environmental Protection", temporarily permitted emissions and discharges are established, which is one of the most convincing proofs that the institution of regulations is focused on achieving the objectives of the transition to sustainable development, in this regard legal entities are given the possibility to continue their activities. Temporarily permitted emissions and discharges are established by permits for temporary emissions or discharges or complex environmental permits. For the period of gradual achievement of the values of regulations of permissible emissions and discharges, technological regulations, economic entities are obliged to develop a program for the improvement of environmental efficiency (for facilities of category I) or an action plan for environmental protection (for facilities of categories II and III). Economic entities annually submit reports on implementing the action plans for environmental protection and programs for the improvement of environmental efficiency to the federal executive authorities authorized by the Government of the Russian Federation or executive authorities of the corresponding constituent entities of the Russian Federation.

The system of environmental regulations under consideration will be in force till the development and adoption of technical regulations provided for by the Federal Law "On Technical Regulation". Environmental regulations will be part of the content of the general technical regulations in relation to processes (methods) of production, operation, and disposal of products regarding environmental and sanitary safety. The main significance of technical regulations will consist in the fact that they will serve as uniform and permanent (stable) safety criteria for the objects of technical regulation, on the one hand, forcing producers to output products that comply with the specified safety requirements, on the other hand, indicating for consumers what kind of products they must be.

First technical regulations have already been adopted. Resolution of the Customs Union Commission No. 877 of December 9, 2011 (revised on June 21, 2019) "On Approval of the Customs Union Technical Regulation Wheeled Vehicles Safety" can be mentioned as an example.

Licensing of Environmentally Hazardous Activities

The implementation of the state authorization policy is one of the most proven methods of state regulation of the economy. Varieties of the authorization policy include expert reviews, a record of economic entities and licensing of their activities. The implementation of this policy is one of the forms of manifestation of the imperative method of legal regulation of relations, including those in the field of interaction between nature and society.

A license is a special permit that gives legal entities or individual entrepreneurs the right to carry out activities of a particular type (performance of works, provision of services, *etc.*) and is confirmed by a document issued by a licensing authority.

Accordingly, licensing is the activity of a specially authorized executive authority in granting, reissuing licenses, extending their validity period, maintaining the register, exercising license control, *etc*. Federal Law No. 99-FZ of May 4, 2011, "On Licensing of Certain Types of Activities," regulates the procedure for the issue of licenses. This law establishes an exhaustive list of licensed types of activities and determines the licensing procedure. The law also establishes several types of licensed activities that are not within its scope and are regulated by other federal laws. These types of activities include the use of nuclear energy.

According to this law, there are two criteria to attribute a particular type of activity to the licensed ones: the risk of damage to private and public interests; inadequacy of other methods of impact. Consequently, licensing is a compromise making it possible to guarantee the rights and legitimate interests of citizens, society, and the state in terms of the formation of a market economy.

Environmental licensing is the function of state environmental management consisting of the establishment by federal executive authorities of conditions and procedures for obtaining permits for a range of activities that negatively impact the environment.

As mentioned above, environmental law regulates social relations in three areas of interaction between nature and society: establishes environmental requirements for certain types of activities (in the industry, power sector, defense, agriculture, *etc.*); determines the peculiarities of the protection of certain types of natural objects (forests, water, subsoil, *etc.*); determines the procedure for the protection of areas with a special environmental legal regime. Based on the preceding, all types of activities that fall within the scope of environmental licensing are the specification of the first group of requirements – the requirements for certain types of activities. The most environmentally significant types of activities subject to compulsory environmental licensing are as follows:

1. Operation of production facilities with the explosion, fire, and chemical hazards of hazard classes I, II, and III. In this case, licenses are issued by Rostekhnadzor. The said types of facilities are varieties of hazardous production facilities with the operation procedure that is regulated by Federal Law No. 116-FZ of July 21, 1997, “On the Industrial Safety of Hazardous Production Facilities”.

2. Activities for storage and destruction of chemical weapons. Destruction of chemical weapons is the irreversible transformation of toxic chemicals, ammunition, devices, and equipment to render them in a condition not suitable for use as chemical weapons. Destruction of chemical weapons is performed in accordance with the Convention on the Prohibition of the Development, Production, Stockpiling, and Use of Chemical Weapons and on their Destruction of January 13, 1993 and Federal Law No. 76-FZ of May 2, 1997 “On the Destruction of Chemical Weapons”. Licenses of this type are issued by the Ministry of Industry and Trade of the Russian Federation.

3. Activities for collection, transportation, processing, utilization, neutralization, placement of waste of hazard classes I-IV (activities for collection, use, neutralization, placement of waste of hazard class V are not subject to licensing). These licenses are issued by Rosprirodnadzor. To obtain this license, the applicant must have waste placement facilities (land plots, buildings, structures, equipment, special vehicles, permanent staff, *etc.*). For example, special requirements for vehicles (garbage trucks) include their satellite navigation equipment – in order to minimize the risks of unloading the collected waste outside the places equipped for its placement (special landfills). Moreover, the project documentation for the facilities where it is planned to place waste must be approved due to the state environmental expert review.

4. Activities in the field of hydrometeorology and related fields and works for active impact on hydrometeorological and geophysical processes and phenomena. Activities in the field of hydrometeorology and related fields are understood as determination of meteorological, climatological, hydrological, and other characteristics of the environment; determination of the level of pollution (including radioactive) of the air, soil, water bodies, and near-Earth space; preparation and provision of information to consumers regarding the state of the environment and its pollution (including radioactive); formation and maintenance of data banks in the field of hydrometeorology and related areas. These licenses are issued by Roshydromet. In its turn, works for active impact on hydrometeorological processes and phenomena are understood as activities for the protection of agricultural plants from hail, regulation of precipitation,

fog dispersal, carried out to regulate these processes and phenomena, as well as to reduce the possible harm caused by them to the population and the economy.

In addition to the Federal Law "On Licensing of Certain Types of Activities", licenses for environmentally hazardous types of activities are also issued in accordance with Federal Law No. 170-FZ of November 21, 1995 "On the Use of Nuclear Energy". In accordance with this law, the following types of activities in the field of use of nuclear energy are subject to licensing: placement, construction, operation, and decommissioning of nuclear installations, radiation sources, storage points for nuclear material, and radioactive substances, radioactive waste storage facilities.

Legal Regulation of Environmental Impact Assessment (EIA) and State Environmental Expert Reviews

Environmental Impact Assessment (EIA) is a procedure carried out before economic entities start activities potentially hazardous to the environment by identifying their possible adverse effects and assessing them, taking into account public opinion, as well as developing measures to reduce and prevent the negative impact on the environment.

EIA is carried out about any planned economic and other activities and only those the substantiation documentation of which is subject to environmental expert reviews in compliance with the Federal Law "On Environmental Expert Reviews" of November 23, 1995. The EIA materials include a set of documentation prepared during the environmental impact assessment of planned (projected) economic activities, and they are developed to ensure environmental safety and protection of the environment. The EIA materials ensure the identification of the character, intensiveness, and extent of the possible impact of planned (projected) economic and other activities on the environment, analysis and record of this impact, assessment of environmental and related social and economic consequences of the implementation of these activities and the development of measures for the prevention and (or) reduction of these consequences with consideration of the public opinion. The EIA materials are prepared by the customer (an individual or a legal entity) planning economic activities, the environmental consequences subject to preliminary assessment stipulated by the Federal Law "On Environmental Expert Reviews". The preparation of the EIA materials by the customer (executor) must involve the use of complete, reliable, and relevant source information, means and methods of estimation, calculation, assessment, the necessary consideration of alternative ways to implement the planned (projected) economic and other activities, including a way to cancel the activities, as well as public participation in the organization of the environmental impact assessment. The main procedural issues of EIA are set forth in Order of the Ministry of Natural Resources and Environment of the Russian Federation No. 999 of December 1, 2020 "On the Approval of Requirements for Environmental Impact Assessment Materials".

Lets consider the correlation between EIA and environmental expert reviews briefly. EIA determines the possible impact and the search for alternatives, while expert reviews are the establishment of the compliance of documents and (or) documentation with environmental requirements.

Therefore, EIA is prior to the state environmental expert review. Environmental expert reviews are the establishment of the compliance of documents and (or) documentation substantiating the economic and other activities planned in connection with the implementation of the object of the environmental expert review with the environmental requirements established by technical regulations and legislation in the field of environmental protection for the purpose of the prevention of the negative impact of these activities on the environment. The following characteristic features of environmental expert reviews should be highlighted: they have a preventive nature (with special goals and objectives arising from this), they are characterized by a special set of subjects, procedure form, and the binding nature of their results.

There are several classifications of the types of environmental expert reviews.

According to the subject criterion, there are the state environmental expert reviews and public environmental expert reviews, and the state environmental expert reviews are conducted by executive authorities of both the Russian Federation and its constituent entities. According to the criterion of consideration time and procedures, there are primary and secondary environmental expert reviews. The secondary environmental expert review is organized voluntarily or on the basis of the court decision. Environmental expert reviews can have positive or negative results. Due to the implementation of the reform of urban development activities, the scope of environmental expert reviews has sharply reduced (as compared to the original idea of the 1990s).

This is why it is now possible to distinguish three forms of expert activities related to verifying compliance with environmental requirements in the case of planned environmentally hazardous economic activities.

1. According to paragraph 6 of Article 49 of the Urban Development Code of the Russian Federation, expert reviews other than the state expert review of the project documentation are not allowed. An exception to this rule is the state

environmental expert review of the project documentation for facilities that are supposed to be constructed or reconstructed in the exclusive economic zone of the Russian Federation, on the continental shelf of the Russian Federation, in internal sea waters, in the territorial sea of the Russian Federation, on lands of specially protected natural areas, in the Baikal natural territory, *etc.*

Consequently, only the state expert review of the project documentation is conducted concerning all other facilities, and environmental safety issues are considered within its framework. The said the state institution conducts expert review under the jurisdiction of the Ministry of Construction, Housing and Utilities of the Russian Federation (it is called Federal Autonomous Institution "Main Directorate of State Expert Review").

Their environmental expert reviews are not conducted.

This measure is quite reasonable due to the need to reduce administrative barriers in construction, although this issue still raises serious discussions in legal science. The Constitutional Court of the Russian Federation expresses its position on this reform in its Ruling No. 1421-O-O of September 30, 2010 "On Refusal to Accept the Complaint of Citizens Natalia Anatolievna Kulakova and Natalia Aleksandrovna Lisitsyna regarding the Violation of Their Constitutional Rights by Article 11 of Federal Law On Environmental Expert Reviews". The court states that amendments to Articles 11 and 12 of the Law on Environmental Expert Reviews did not lead, contrary to the assertion of the applicants, to the abolition of the requirement to conduct an environmental expert review during the preparation of project documentation for construction. The form of this review has changed –instead of the state environmental expert review, state sanitary and epidemiological expert review, and several other expert reviews, the unified state expert review of the project documentation and the results of engineering surveys is now conducted under the Urban Development Code and the Provision on the Organization of the State Expert Review of Project Documentation and Results of Engineering Surveys (approved by Decree of the Government of the Russian Federation No. 145 of March 5, 2007).

1. The state environmental expert review of the project and other documentation beyond the scope of Article 49 of the Urban Development Code of the Russian Federation is conducted according to the procedure established by the Federal Law "On Environmental Expert Reviews". For example, in 2018, the Federal Service for Supervision of Natural Resources (Rosprirodnadzor) and its territorial bodies conducted 1,330 state environmental expert reviews; in particular, 1,155 of them had a positive result and 175 – a negative one (Report, 2019).

2. The Federal Law "On the Industrial Safety of Hazardous Production Facilities" (Article 13) stipulates industrial safety expert reviews, for example, in case of conservation and liquidation of hazardous production facilities, the introduction of new technical devices in these facilities as well as in a number of other similar cases.

However, further, we will limit ourselves to the consideration of environmental expert reviews. The subjects of state environmental expert reviews are specially authorized federal environmental expert review authorities (Rosprirodnadzor) or state authorities of constituent entities of the Russian Federation (for example, in Volgograd Region, it is the Committee on Natural Resources, Forestry, and Environment of Volgograd Region) as well as customers ordering the objects of environmental expert reviews. Customers include legal entities and individuals that order and pay to the specially authorized authorities for the organization of works to verify the compliance of the supposed economic and other activities with environmental requirements. In addition, in case of deviation from the project approved by the state environmental expert review, the customer is obliged to pass the expert review again.

The objects of environmental expert reviews are materials and documents presented by customers for the state or public environmental expert reviews. Their list is included in Articles 11 and 12 of the Law on Environmental Expert Reviews. The objects of environmental expert reviews are divided between federal and regional executive authorities in the field of environmental expert reviews below.

The objects of state environmental expert reviews of the federal level are as follows: drafts of federal target programs providing for the construction and operation of facilities used for economic activities and having an impact on the environment, regarding the location of these facilities with consideration of the regime of protection of natural objects; drafts of production sharing agreements (used in the field of subsoil use); substantiation materials for licenses in the field of nuclear energy use; drafts of technical documentation for new equipment and technologies the use of which can have an impact on the environment as well as technical documentation for new substances that can enter the natural environment (for example, when nanotechnology is introduced); materials of comprehensive environmental investigations of areas substantiating the assignment of the legal status of ecological disaster zones to these areas; project documentation for capital facilities in specially protected natural areas; project documentation for capital facilities belonging to waste neutralization facilities and (or) waste placement facilities; project documentation for capital facilities belonging to facilities of category I. This list is not exhaustive; in addition, it should be noted that there is no mention of materials of comprehensive environmental investigations of areas for attribution of the status of specially protected natural areas to them.

Executive authorities of constituent entities of the Russian Federation conduct environmental expert reviews of regional drafts of regulatory technical and instructional methodological documents in the field of environmental protection; drafts of regional target programs providing for the construction and operation of facilities used for economic activities and having an impact on the environment; project documentation for facilities that are supposed to be constructed or reconstructed within the boundaries of specially protected natural areas of regional and local significance.

The analysis of provisions of the Law on Environmental Expert Reviews makes it possible to distinguish three stages of the state environmental expert review: the research stage, including its elements – EIA and environmental feasibility; obtainment of the official permit for the project implementation from the state; control over the execution of the conclusion report.

The first stage of the state environmental expert review begins with the presentation of the relevant object (objects) to the experts. To be accepted for the state environmental expert review, documents and materials must contain data on environmental impact assessment of the planned economic and other activities and their environmental feasibility. At the same stage, expert commissions (experts) examine the presented object, verify its compliance with the established environmental and other special norms, rules, and regulations. The duration of the state environmental expert review must not exceed two months and may be extended for one month upon the customers application.

At the second stage, the presented objects receive an expert assessment by acceptance of the conclusion report of the state environmental expert review. This conclusion report must contain substantiated findings on the admissibility (inadmissibility) of the environmental impact of the economic and other activities that are subject to the state environmental expert review and on the possibility of implementation of the object of the expert review. A positive conclusion report confirms the customers compliance with environmental requirements in preparing the examined documentation and gives the right to fund this object from any source. In case of a negative conclusion report, implementing the object of the environmental expert review is prohibited.

At the third stage, the execution of the conclusion report is controlled.

We should note the inconsistency (collision) of the wordings of the Federal Law "On Environmental Expert Reviews" with the provisions of two other federal laws as a problem of the state environmental expert review that has not been resolved. First, with Article 20 of the Federal Law "On Fauna". According to this Article, fertilizers, pesticides and plant growth biostimulants as well as materials justifying the volumes (limits, quotas) of fauna withdrawal and the work for its acclimatization and hybridization are subject to the mandatory state environmental expert review. Meanwhile, the analysis of Articles 11 and 12 of the Federal Law "On Environmental Expert Reviews" makes it possible to conclude that its objects can include "project documentation" or "materials" but not "fertilizers" or "pesticides". In this case, we observe that two laws do not "fit" with each other at the conceptual level; this is why it is impossible to conduct an expert review of fertilizers and similar objects.

Another interesting collision consists in the fact that according to Article 16 of the Federal Law "On Burial and the Funeral Business" of January 12, 1996, the creation of new burial places, reconstruction of existing burial places are possible if there is a positive conclusion report of the environmental and sanitary hygienic expert review. However, the Federal Law "On Environmental Expert Reviews" does not mention burial places (cemeteries) as their objects. This is why the Law on Environmental Expert Reviews requires expansion of the list of their objects – by excluding them from other laws.

In conclusion of this issue, it should be noted that state environmental expert reviews must be distinguished from public environmental expert reviews. Suppose the former is a function of public administration. In that case, the latter is conducted by public environmental organizations at their expense and do not have any independent legal significance (their conclusion reports can become legally binding only if a state authority approves them of the Russian Federation or a constituent entity of the Russian Federation conducting environmental expert reviews). The objects of public environmental expert reviews are the same of state ones, excluding the objects that are state or other secrets protected by law. Public environmental expert reviews are conducted before or at the same time with state environmental expert reviews. Their results must be considered by the expert commissions conducting the state environmental expert reviews.

State Environmental Supervision

State environmental supervision is the activities of federal and regional executive authorities aimed at preventing, identifying, and suppressing cases of non-fulfillment of environmental legislation requirements by conducting inspections of activities of citizens and legal entities as well as by taking measures to eliminate the consequences of the detected offenses. Types of state environmental supervision can be classified according to several criteria.

Federal environmental supervision and state environmental supervision, which is performed by constituent entities of the Russian Federation, should be distinguished in terms of the subjects performing state environmental supervision.

The subjects of federal and regional environmental supervision are differentiated in Article 65 of the Law on Environmental Protection.

Rosprirodnadzor and its territorial subdivisions exercise most federal environmental supervision powers, though many important functions are also performed by Rostekhnadzor and some other federal executive authorities. As for the subjects of regional environmental supervision, for example, all functions in the field of regional environmental supervision belonging to Volgograd Region as a constituent entity of the Russian Federation are performed by the Committee on Natural Resources, Forestry and Environment of Volgograd Region.

The forms of state environmental supervision are divided into preventive and current supervision. The objective of preventive environmental supervision is to exclude economic activities that can have a harmful impact on nature in the future. It is performed at the stage of planning these activities, implementing the project, and commissioning facilities in various ways.

The main of them is the state environmental expert review, environmental licensing, and coordination of the planned activities with nature protection authorities.

A typical example of this coordination is the coordination of activities for territorial planning, urban development zoning, area planning, and some other types of activities with the Federal Fishery Agency provided for by Article 50 of Federal Law No. 166-FZ of December 20, 2004 “On Fishing and Conservation of Aquatic Biological Resources”. The special Decree of the Government of the Russian Federation established the procedure for this coordination in 2013.

Specially authorized federal authorities perform current state environmental supervision at the stage of operation of enterprises and other environmentally significant facilities. The subject of supervision is the following classification criterion for activities of state environmental supervision authorities. For example, the subject of federal environmental supervision is water bodies (including the territory of their protective water zones and coastal protection belts) located in the territory of two or more constituent entities of the Russian Federation, located on the defense and security land, specially protected water bodies and some other water bodies. Moreover, federal supervision is carried out in relation to production facilities (buildings, premises, structures, linear facilities, territories including water, land and forest areas, equipment, devices, things, materials, vehicles, and other objects that are owned and (or) used by citizens and organizations and subject to mandatory requirements) located within the boundaries of specially protected natural areas of federal significance, in the central ecological zone of the Baikal Natural Area, within the boundaries of wetlands of international importance, especially valuable wetlands, *etc*. We should point out supervision over production facilities used to support space activities, ensure defense and security of the state, production facilities in which nuclear installations are operated or which are storage points for nuclear materials, radioactive substances, and radioactive waste, sea ports including those within the boundaries of which coal transshipment, crushing and sorting activities are carried out, pipeline transport facilities intended for transportation of gas, oil and gas condensate, railroad transport infrastructure facilities, production facilities of categories I and II, *etc*.

State environmental supervision as a function of environmental quality management has a range of peculiarities. The first peculiarity consists of the fact that it applies to any types of economic or other activities, all natural objects and their state, and activities of any users of natural resources irrespective of the subordinacy and forms of ownership. There are no closed areas for it.

Its second peculiarity is the content of administrative enforcement measures applied by state inspectors (or by the court upon their notice) against violators of environmental legislation. They include administrative sanctions (warnings, penalties, administrative suspension of activities) and measures of administrative restraint (issue of orders to rectify violations). For example, a state inspector may issue an order on remediation of land polluted by an economic entity.

Along with decisions made in the course and as a result of control (supervision) activities set by Federal Law No. 248-FZ of July 31, 2020 “On State Control (Supervision) and Municipal Control in the Russian Federation”, officials of authorities performing state environmental control (supervision), being state inspectors in the field of environmental protection, also have the right to submit materials related to violations of legislation in the field of environmental protection to the authorized bodies for the settlement of issues regarding initiating criminal cases as well as to file claims for the compensation of harm caused to the environment and its components as a result of violations of the mandatory requirements, within the established competence and according to the established procedure.

Considering environmental supervision as a function of environmental management, we should mention that local government bodies participate in it in an incomplete manner. For instance, they carry out municipal forest and land control, as well as control in the field of the use and protection of specially protected natural areas of local significance.

Having provided state environmental supervision authorities with a range of serious powers to check activities of economic entities punish them in case of offenses, the legislator tried to ensure a balance of private and public interests and for these purposes, established a number of guarantees of rights of entrepreneurs during control and supervisory checks.

This issue is regulated by Decree of the Government of the Russian Federation No. 1096 of June 30, 2021, "On Federal State Environmental Control (Supervision)". As follows from this legal act, state environmental control involves using the risk assessment and management system. During state environmental control, the control authority attributes control objects to one of the following categories of harm (damage) risk: extremely high risk, high risk, significant risk, medium risk, moderate risk and low risk. The control authority can perform the following types of scheduled control (supervision) activities: visit for inspection purposes, patrol examination, documentary check and on-site inspection. Depending on the attributed risk category, the frequency of one of scheduled control (supervision) activities is as follows: once a year for the category of extremely high risk, once in 2 years for the category of high risk, once in 3 years for the category of significant risk, once in 4 years for the category of medium risk and once in 5 years for the category of moderate risk. The control authority can carry out the following preventive activities: provision of information, generalization of law enforcement practice, the announcement of a caution, preventive visit and counseling. State environmental control includes scheduled control (supervision) activities, unscheduled control (supervision) activities, and control (supervision) activities based on the inspection program. Scheduled control (supervision) activities are carried out on the basis of the plan of scheduled control (supervision) activities for the subsequent calendar year, agreed upon with the prosecutors offices (which is one of the guarantees of the rights of entrepreneurs).

Along with state environmental supervision, which is a function of state environmental management, it is necessary to distinguish two other types of environmental control that are not types of state management functions. They are industrial and public environmental control.

Industrial environmental control is carried out to ensure the implementation of measures for environmental protection, rational use and restoration of natural resources in the course of economic and other activities, as well as to comply with the requirements in the field of environmental protection established by legislation in the field of environmental protection. Legal entities and individual entrepreneurs carrying out economic and (or) other activities at facilities of categories I, II, and III develop and approve the industrial environmental control program, carry out industrial environmental control in accordance with the established requirements, document information, and store data obtained as a result of industrial environmental control. They are obliged to provide federal executive authorities authorized by the Government of the Russian Federation or executive authorities of the corresponding constituent entities of the Russian Federation with reports on the organization and results of industrial environmental control.

The most stringent requirements for industrial environmental control are stipulated for facilities of category I (the most environmentally hazardous facilities), for example, creating a system of automatic control over emissions and discharges of pollutants.

Public environmental control is carried out to exercise everyones right to a favorable environment and prevent violation of legislation in the field of environmental protection. Control of this type is carried out by public associations and other non-commercial organizations as well as citizens. The results of public environmental control submitted to state authorities of the Russian Federation and constituent entities of the Russian Federation, local government bodies are subject to mandatory consideration according to the procedure established by legislation.

Public environmental control, like state supervision, is carried out in preventive and current forms. Preventive control can manifest itself in the participation of citizens, public and other non-commercial associations in public debates in the course of EIA, referendums on environmental issues, participation in public environmental expert reviews, and appointment of their representatives for participation in the state environmental expert review. Citizens and their associations carry out current environmental control, requiring state authorities, local government bodies, economic entities to provide information on the state of the environment and measures for its protection, notifying the competent authorities of environmental offenses known to them, filing claims to courts for reversal of decisions on construction, reconstruction or operation of facilities with economic and other activities that harm the environment, for limitation, suspension and termination of economic and the activities that have a negative impact on the environment, *etc*.

State Registration of Facilities that have a Negative Impact on the Environment

State registration of facilities that have a negative impact on the environment is performed to obtain reliable information about these facilities, determine the areas of application of best available technologies, application of program-objective methods in planning, and state environmental supervision.

State registration of facilities that negatively impact the environment consists of maintaining the state register of the Russian Federation and constituent entities of the Russian Federation. Each facility included in the register receives its own unique non-repeating number, which is to be kept until the corresponding facility is liquidated. Information on the levels, volume or mass of emissions and discharges of pollutants, disposal of production, and consumption waste contained in the state register is publicly available, except for information attributed to data that are state or commercial secrets. State registration of facilities that have a negative impact on the environment is performed on the basis of applications filed by legal entities or individual entrepreneurs no later than within six months from the date of commencement of operation of the said facilities.

All facilities that harm the environment and are subject to environmental supervision must be registered. Accordingly, if a facility is subject to federal environmental supervision, it is registered by Rosprirodnadzor (its territorial bodies), and in case of regional environmental supervision – by authorities of the constituent entity of the Russian Federation. Facilities that harm the environment are capital facilities and (or) other facilities as well as their totality united by a single purpose and (or) inextricably linked physically or technologically and located within one or several land plots. Facilities that hurt the environment are divided into categories I, II, III and IV of the negative impact on the environment. Facilities that hurt the environment rather than activities of legal entities or legal entities themselves are subject to state registration. Accordingly, if a facility does not comply with the Criteria for attribution of facilities that have a negative impact on the environment to facilities of categories I, II, III, IV approved by Decree of the Government of the Russian Federation No. 1029 of September 28, 2015, this facility is not a facility that hurts the environment and it is not subject to state registration.

Any default or delay in fulfillment of the duty to apply for state registration of the mentioned facilities that hurt the environment entails penalties under Article 8.46 of the Code of Administrative Offenses of the Russian Federation.

State Environmental Monitoring

State environmental monitoring is a system of observation of the state of the environment implemented by federal and regional executive authorities by ensuring the functioning of observation networks, creating information resources, and forming the state data fund. According to the same rules, environmental monitoring is carried out in a single system (according to the same rules) only by state authorities. From the definition above, it follows that the function of environmental monitoring is not assigned to local government bodies, although the relevant municipal authorities take part in this work in some cities with an environmentally unfavorable situation. What is the purpose of state environmental monitoring?

It is possible to distinguish four public legal objectives: observation of the state of the environment and activities of environmentally hazardous facilities for collection of reliable environmental information; storage, processing, and analysis of this information; provision of authorities, citizens, and legal entities with environmental information; adoption by public authorities of adequate management decisions based on the identification, assessment, and forecasting of changes in the state of the environment.

A typical example of the latter can be the consideration of environmental information in the development of territorial planning and urban development zoning documents (for example, so that local government bodies would not plan residential areas in zones of emissions of industrial facilities. In the cases of Fadeyeva and Ledyayeva heard by the European Court of Human Rights, residential buildings are built exactly in the emission zones). Another example is the provision of environmental information to state environmental supervision autshorities, which can check the compliance of economic entities with the requirements of environmental legislation and bring them to liability (in case violations are detected) based on this information. The third example is the adjustment of the limits for the extraction of aquatic bioresources based on environmental monitoring data on the state of fish stocks.

It should be noted that one of the objectives of state environmental monitoring under law is not only the obtainment and assessment of information but also the determination of the connection between the impact of natural or anthropogenic factors on the environment and changes in the state of the environment, that is, the identification of causal relationships between pollution and its consequences. The Federal Service organizes state monitoring for Hydrometeorology and Environmental Monitoring with the participation of other authorized federal executive authorities, executive authorities of constituent entities of the Russian

Federation and State Atomic Energy Corporation Rosatom.

State monitoring is carried out using stationary and mobile points to observe the state of the environment.

The single system of state monitoring includes three subsystems according to three main areas of environmental protection:

1. Monitoring of pollution of certain natural objects (monitoring of the air, land, fauna, forests, subsoil, water bodies, hunting, and aquatic biological resources are specially distinguished).

2. Monitoring the effects of certain types of environmentally hazardous human activities (monitoring the radiation situation).

3. Territorial monitoring is distinguished separately for internal sea waters and the territorial sea of the Russian Federation; the exclusive economic zone of the Russian Federation; the continental shelf of the Russian Federation; the unique ecological system of Lake Baikal.

In addition, it should be noted that monitoring of specially protected natural areas (reserves, national parks, *etc.*) is not distinguished as a special type.

Therefore, as a result of observations, Roshydromet makes forecasts of the following hazardous phenomena and factors: hazardous natural phenomena leading to natural disasters; unfavorable natural conditions for certain areas of economic activities (for example, for the development of agriculture or marine navigation); chemical, radioactive and thermal pollution, physical, chemical, and biological (for surface water bodies) processes; changes in the components of the natural environment also leading to climate change in the future. As for accessibility, the environmental information obtained in the course of monitoring (from a legal point of view) can be of two types: information of general purpose about the actual and estimated state of the environment (provided free of charge to an unlimited range of persons) and specialized information (provided for a fee at the request of consumers). In conclusion, it should be noted that the territorial principle is used to distinguish global, national, regional, and local monitoring. Global environmental monitoring emerged in 1972 after the resolutions of the United Nations Conference on the Human Environment held in Stockholm.

Several related types of monitoring should be distinguished at the national level. For example, environmental monitoring should not be equated with social and hygienic monitoring. The latter is carried out to assess and identify the changes and forecast the state of the health of the population and the habitat, establish and eliminate the harmful impact of the habitat factors on people; it is regulated by sanitary legislation (Art. 45 of the Federal Law of March 30, 1999 "On Sanitary and Epidemiological Well-Being of the Population"). In order to enhance the system of state environmental monitoring in the future, it is planned to take measures to improve information exchange between authorities of the federal, as well as federal and regional, levels, to use more widely the monitoring results in making forecasts of the countrys socio-economic development and to improve the collection of information and forecasts of global climate change.

State Economic Regulation in the Area of Environmental Protection

The experience of most countries shows that the use of economic incentives for environmental protection is more effective than the application of only administrative sanctions with economic entities. This circumstance was realized in the late 80s of the 20th century, and since then, Russia has unevenly but gradually expanded the list of economic measures of state stimulation in the field of environmental protection. The doctrine and legislation distinguish three main economic levers of state influence on the behavior of economic entities polluting the environment: economic sanctions (*i.e.*, collection of payments from them for the negative impact on the environment), economic incentives (tax benefits, in case of compliance with the requirements of environmental legislation) and economic guarantees (state stimulation of environmental insurance, auditing, tourism, *etc*., supporting those forms of business activities that contribute to the preservation of the environment).

The use of natural resources and the negative impact on the environment are paid in Russia; they are regulated by economic, budgetary, tax, and other legislation. Tax legislation distinguishes between taxes and fees. The difference between them is that fees (in contrast to taxes) allow payers to require some response from the authority (for example, issue of a license). At the moment, environmental payments have the form of fees, and the environmental tax has not been introduced yet, though this need has been discussed for many years by the scientific expert community. The main types of negative impact on the environment subject to payment are as follows: emissions of pollutants by stationary sources into the air; discharges of pollutants into water bodies; storage and burial of production and consumption waste. The subjects making this payment are legal entities and individual entrepreneurs carrying out economic and other activities that have a negative impact on the environment. Economic entities carrying out their activities exclusively at facilities of category IV are exempted from these payments. Moreover, in calculating the payments for entities carrying out activities at facilities of category III, all the volume of emissions and pollutants is recognized as produced within the values of regulations of permissible emissions and discharges.

The amount of payments for negative impact on nature is calculated by the subjects of the payment by themselves on the basis of data received from the industrial environmental control; their exact amount depends on the volume of emissions (discharges, waste), their hazard class as well as the payment rate established by the Government of the Russian Federation with consideration of the special coefficients (0,1,25,100). The purpose of the latter is to encourage economic entities to comply with prescriptions of environmental legislation.

For example, coefficient 0 is applied if emissions (discharges) of pollutants are within the values of technological regulations after introducing the best available technology in the enterprise. On the contrary, coefficient 100 is used if the volume of emissions exceeds the volume established for facilities of category I. Such coefficients are also set for the third type of negative impact, which is waste disposal.

Environmental payments (fees) are stipulated not only by the Federal Law "On Environmental Protection" but also by the Federal Law "On Production and Consumption Waste", which mentions the utilization fee (charged for each wheeled vehicle imported or manufactured in Russia) and the environmental fee (charged from producers (importers) of some types of goods or packing of goods).

The payments collected for negative impact on the environment go into the budgets of constituent entities of the Russian Federation (40 percent) and local government bodies (60 percent); Russian legislation does not stipulate a targeted nature of these payments. This means that going into the budget; these funds can be spent for any needs, not necessarily environmental ones.

An important incentive for the compliance with the prescriptions of environmental legislation is the possibility for legal entities (individual entrepreneurs) to deduct their actual expenses on activities reducing emissions (discharges) of harmful substances (for example, the use and utilization of associated petroleum gas) from the number of payments for negative impact on nature. This possibility is enshrined in the Federal Law "On Environmental Protection".

Although the state declares its support for nature protection entrepreneurial activities in general, environmental legislation (Article 17 of the Federal Law "On Environmental Protection") contains a list of the most priority types of activities that can be supported with the use of funds of the state budget. In particular, this involves investment activities aimed at introducing the best available technology (*i.e.*, the technology created based on modern scientific and technical achievements and included in a special list), assistance in the use of renewable energy facilities, development of new methods of environmental pollution control, *etc*.

At the moment, environmental and tax legislation do not correspond fully with each other regarding the mechanism of creating an effective system of incentives and benefits for environmentally safe activity. Nevertheless, Article 67 of the Tax Code stipulates the possibility of providing investment loans when economic entities organize activities in research or development for environmental protection. Moreover, Article 254 of the Tax Code stipulates reducing the taxable base for corporate income tax in case of expenses on the maintenance and operation of key assets and property intended for nature protection purposes (for example, related to the operation of treatment facilities).

In recent years, state support of environmental entrepreneurship has become particularly important for environmental protection. Some experts estimate the total volume of the environmental goods and services market in the range from 600 billion to 2 trillion US dollars. This markets largest part is companies from the United States, Japan, and Germany. The relevant Russian market is still very insignificant (Urazova, 2007).

Two types of environmental entrepreneurial activity should be distinguished. The first type includes environmental works (construction of environmentally friendly houses, for example, in eco-settlements) and provision of environmental services (environmental insurance, auditing, *etc*.). The second type includes research and development aimed at creating a new generation of wind turbines or other sources of energy, environmentally friendly building materials, *etc*.

The development of the environmental services sector is the most promising in Russia. Contracts for solid household waste management, environmental insurance, auditing, ecotourism, and the sale of carbon units can be attributed to these services. Further, we will consider a number of peculiarities of the said types of environmental contracts.

1. Contracts for the provision of solid household waste management services. The owners of solid household waste and regional operators are obliged to enter into these contracts. In accordance with these contracts, regional operators must accept solid household waste and implement its transportation, utilization, neutralization and burial in compliance with the legislative requirements. The owners (producers) of waste must pay for these services according to specially approved rates.

2. Environmental auditing contracts. These contracts involve the assessment of compliance of legal entities with environmental requirements and regulations as well as the preparation of recommendations to improve their work. There is no mandatory environmental auditing in Russia, and voluntary auditing is not very common yet. However, it can be used if necessary to receive investment from foreign banks or certify Russian products for international markets.

3. Ecotourism contracts. These contracts are a variety of civil law contracts for the compensated provision of services. The main rules of the provision of tourism services are formulated in Federal Law No. 132-FZ of November 24, 1996 "On the Fundamentals of Tourism Activities in the Russian Federation". Ecotourism can be implemented within the boundaries of specially protected natural areas (for example, in national parks) or outside their boundaries, in the places where picturesque untouched areas of wildlife are preserved. Suppose ecotourism is organized within the boundaries of national parks or other specially protected natural areas. In that case, additional obligations are imposed on their organizers to preserve these areas with the regime of special protection.

   Ecotourism is not only one of the most rapidly developing sectors of environmental entrepreneurship but also a means of Russias achievement of the goals and objectives of sustainable development. For example, ecotourism facilitates the settlement of a number of countrys economic objectives, promoting the growth of Russias revenue. In general, tourism, including ecotourism, directly or indirectly affects the development of 32 industries of the economy, including the construction of infrastructure facilities, and it is not a capital-intensive type of activity (it does not require the construction of casinos, restaurants, *etc.*) (Bekisheva, 2011).

   Its social functions related to the growth of employment of the local population, increase in its income, growth of the volume of production of organic agricultural products with the subsequent production of healthy food and improvement of the conditions for the recreation for citizens are not less significant (Grif & K., 2002).

   However, the contribution of ecotourism to nature protection is even more important. The fact is that ecotourism development leads to the increased attention of local communities to nature protection in their territory – unauthorized dumps are eliminated (and new ones are not generated), toxic substances are not discharged into rivers and other water bodies, *etc.* Being involved in ecotourism projects, the local population understands that violation of environmental requirements and pollution of the locality can lead to the absence of ecotourists, resulting in a considerable reduction of the income of the local population.

Despite all its advantages, ecotourism development also has a range of risks. Mass visits of ecotourists to ecologically vulnerable natural objects can lead to the deterioration of their quality. These cases have already been registered in Kamchatka (deterioration of the condition of the thermal springs), in the caves of Arkhangelsk Region and on Valaam Island (Korostelev, 2008). In addition, the threat from eco-tourists to the fragile ecosystems of the Russian Arctic is to be studied. A separate issue is an interaction between tour operators and the local population, which is not always successful, and the low level of the environmental culture of some tourists breaking branches of trees, leaving inscriptions on rocks or trying to feed candies to wild animals.

4. Environmental insurance contracts have two varieties – voluntary and compulsory insurance. In both cases, environmental insurance contracts are a variety of more general civil insurance contracts, in particular, their variety related to the insurance of civil liability of persons carrying out activities that are hazardous to citizens and the environment. There is still no compulsory environmental insurance in Russia; however, insurance is applied in a number of areas of activities related to nature protection, for example, the insurance of civil liability for harm resulting from accidents at hydraulic structures or hazardous production facilities. Voluntary environmental insurance is almost absent in modern Russia, mainly due to the lack of an appropriate legal framework.

5. Contracts for the sale of carbon units were first introduced by Article 10 of Federal Law No. 296-FZ of July 2, 2021 "On the Limitation of Greenhouse Gas Emissions" and stipulate "circulation of carbon units", *i.e.*, the sale of quotas for greenhouse gas emissions, which should be recorded in the special register. These contracts are not commonly used in Russia yet.

CONCLUSION

The chapter examines the system of environmental protection management bodies that has been developed in Russia. The powers of bodies of general competence and bodies of special competence are explained. The authors analyze the powers of special competence bodies, including the establishment of environmental standards, environmental licensing, control, expertise, and a number of others.

QUESTIONS AND TASKS FOR SELF-CONTROL

1. Define environmental management in the Russian Federation.

2. Describe the functions of the President of the Russian Federation and the Government of the Russian Federation in the field of environmental protection.

3. What environmental powers belong to state authorities of constituent entities of the Russian Federation?

4. What are the environmental powers of local government bodies?

5. What federal authorities perform state management functions in environmental protection?

6. What are the goals, objectives, and types of environmental regulations?

7. What types of environmentally hazardous activities are subject to environmental licensing?

8. What state authorities exercise state environmental supervision? What are its objects and procedure?

9. Explain the need for EIA and the state environmental expert review.

10. What are the purposes of state registration of facilities that have a negative impact on the environment?

11. Describe the main goals and objectives of environmental monitoring.

12. Define economic regulation in the area of environmental protection. What main methods of economic regulation do you know?

REFERENCES

Bekisheva, S.D. (2011). Development of Environmental Entrepreneurship as an Area of Environmental Policy of the Republic of Kazakhstan. *Environ. Law, 5*, 27-32.

Ecotourism on the way to Russia. Principles, recommendations, Russian and foreign experience. Tula: Grif & K.

Report, S. (2019). *On the State and Protection of the Environment in the Russian Federation in 2018.*

Urazova, L.P. (2007). *Management of Environmental Entrepreneurship Development (Candidate thesis, Saint Petersburg Academy of Management and Economics).*

Korostelev, E.M. (2008). *Ecotourism practical course. Study guide.* Saint Petersburg: St. Petersburg State University Publishing House.

CHAPTER 4

Legal Liability for Environmental Offenses

Abstract: The authors suppose that legal liability for environmental offenses is understood as a legal relationship between the state represented by specially authorized authorities and the party that has committed an environmental offense (an individual, an official or a legal entity) and is obliged to undergo state coercion measures in the forms of particular forfeitures (of a person, property or organizational nature) for the violation of rules of environmental legislation.

An environmental offense is a ground and the time of the commencement of legal relations of legal liability; it is a guilty wrongful act entailing legal liability and prohibited by environmental legal rules of the Russian Federation and constituent entities of the Russian Federation; it infringes on the constitutional right of everyone to a favorable environment and also causes harm to the natural environment (its objects and components) or poses a real threat of this harm. An environmental offense (like any other offense) includes four elements: the object, the objective aspect, the subject and the subjective aspect. For the classification of an offense as environmental, the object of the encroachment at the time of its commitment must be in the system of ecological relationships with the environment. Liability for environmental offenses performs a range of functions: stimulating (compliance with rules of environmental legislation),preventive (making it possible to prevent new offenses), compensatory (aimed at compensating for harm to the environment, the life, health and property of people) and punitive (punishment of offenders). The authors raise a question about the number of types of legal liability for environmental offenses.

The Federal Law “On Environmental Protection” itself mentions four types of liability in Article 75: property, disciplinary, administrative, and criminal liability. Having analyzed the scientific doctrine and practice, the authors state that environmental offenses entail civil legal, administrative and criminal liability. Criminal and civil legal liability are regulated only by federal acts. Suppose a person is brought to administrative or criminal liability; in that case, he or she may also have to compensate for the harm caused to the environment. However, it is impossible to bring anyone to both administrative and criminal liability. Particular attention is paid to the issues of compensation for environmental harm, which is taken as negative changes in the quality of the environment that are caused by economic or other human activities involving the destruction of ecological relationships, pollution, and destruction of certain natural components and can result in harm to the life, health or property of citizens (property of legal entities).

Aleksey Anisimov and Anatoliy Ryzhenkov

Keywords: Accumulated harm, Action limitation, Causal relationships, Consequences, Environmental harm, Harm to human health, Industrial safety, Methods, Non-pecuniary damage, Nuclear energy, Object, Objective aspect, Payments, Rates, Responsibility, Set of offense elements, Source of increased danger, Subject, Subjective aspect, Sufferings.

CONCEPT AND TYPES OF LEGAL LIABILITY FOR ENVIRONMENTAL OFFENSES

Legal liability for environmental offenses is understood as a legal relationship between the state represented by specially authorized authorities and the party that has committed an environmental offense (an individual, an official or a legal entity) and is obliged to undergo state coercion measures in the forms of particular forfeitures (of a person, property or organizational nature) for the violation of rules of environmental legislation.

An environmental offense is a ground and the time of the commencement of legal relations of legal liability; it is a guilty wrongful act entailing legal liability and prohibited by environmental legal rules of the Russian Federation and constituent entities of the Russian Federation, it infringes on the constitutional right of everyone to a favorable environment and also causes harm to the natural environment (its objects and components) or poses a real threat of this harm.

There are three exceptions to this definition: first, harm caused by a source of increased danger must be compensated regardless of the fault of the harm-doer; second, harm caused to the environment by a party in a state of extreme necessity will not be considered an offense; third, Article 41 of the Criminal Code of the Russian Federation mentions substantiated risk among the circumstances that exclude criminality of an act. However, the risk will not be recognized as substantiated if it is known to be associated with a threat to the lives of many people, including the threat of environmental disaster, *etc*.

An environmental offense (like any other offense) includes four elements: the object, the objective aspect, the subject and the subjective aspect. For the classification of an offense as environmental, the object of the encroachment at the time of its commitment must be in the system of environmental relations with the environment. This is the difference of environmental offenses from, for example, violation of the right of ownership of natural resources, where the object of encroachment is the authorities of the owner related to the use of the natural resource that is in the ownership. Consequently, if a citizen kills an animal in a zoo, this will not be characterized as "illegal hunting" (Art. 258 of the Criminal Code of the Russian Federation) since the object of civil (property) rather than environmental legal relations is destroyed.

It is necessary to take into account that the negative impact on the subjects of environmental offenses can be both direct and indirect. For example, Article 8.6 of the Code of Administrative Offenses of the Russian Federation attributes land to the subjects of administrative environmental offenses, and Article 8.35 of the Code of Administrative Offenses of the Russian Federation – fauna, *etc*. At the same time, certain sets of elements of offenses do not imply the necessary direct impact on components of the natural environment as a condition of harm caused to environmental relations. For example, Article 8.1 of the Code of Administrative Offenses of the Russian Federation establishes liability for non-compliance with environmental requirements in urban development activities and the operation of enterprises, structures, or other facilities.

Liability for environmental offenses performs a range of functions: stimulating (compliance with rules of environmental legislation), preventive (making it possible to prevent new offenses), compensatory (aimed at compensating for harm to the environment, the life, health, and property of people) and punitive (punishment of offenders).

A separate question is how many types of legal liability are there for environmental offenses?

The Federal Law "On Environmental Protection" itself mentions four types of liability in Article 75: property, disciplinary, administrative, and criminal liability. The term "property liability" is not optimal since a more precise concept, civil legal liability, is used both in the theory of law and in the Federal Law "On Environmental Protection" itself and in other laws. Distinguishing disciplinary liability for environmental offenses is not convincing since employees can be brought to this legal liability for violation of rules of labor law, consequently, for improper performance of the assigned labor duties at the employee's fault. These labor rules and regulations are included in federal laws and by-laws, regulatory legal acts of constituent entities of the Russian Federation, internal labor regulations of organizations, *etc*. In case of their violation, employees are subject to disciplinary action (Art. 192 of the Labor Code of the Russian Federation): reprimand, admonition, dismissal.

Therefore, environmental offenses entail civil legal, administrative and criminal liability. Criminal and civil legal liability are regulated only by federal acts. Suppose a person is brought to administrative or criminal liability. In that case, he or she may also have to compensate for harm caused to the environment or citizens life, health, and property. However, it is impossible to bring anyone to both administrative and criminal liability.

ADMINISTRATIVE LIABILITY FOR ENVIRONMENTAL OFFENSES

An administrative environmental offense is a guilty wrongful action (or omission) of citizens, officials, or legal entities infringing on the constitutional right of every person to a favorable environment, causing harm to the environment (posing a real threat of its infliction), which entails administrative liability.

The current Code of Administrative Offenses of the Russian Federation pays special attention to environmental protection issues, mentioning this among the objectives of legislation on administrative offenses (Art. 1.2 of the Code of Administrative Offenses of the Russian Federation).

Constituent entities of the Russian Federation have the right to adopt their own laws on administrative offenses that are not in conflict with the Code of Administrative Offenses of the Russian Federation and regulate liability for violation of environmental rules introduced by-laws of constituent entities of the Russian Federation (rather than by federal laws). These laws must establish special authorities (inspectorates, committees, chambers, *etc.*) authorized to consider cases on administrative offenses under the legislation of constituent entities of the Russian Federation. The Russian Federation's laws of constituent entities can provide for two varieties of administrative punishment: warnings and penalties.

An example of this lawmaking of constituent entities of the Russian Federation is the Code of Volgograd Region No. 1693-OD of June 11, 2008 “On Administrative Liability”, which provides for administrative liability for damage and (or) destruction of green spaces in common territories of settlements (Art. 6.1); destruction of rare and endangered species of animals or plants (Art. 6.2); violation of the established regime of land use (Art. 7.2); passage and parking of vehicles in green areas (Art. 8.10), *etc*.

All elements of environmental offenses that can lead to administrative liability are classified into four groups. The first group includes sets of elements establishing liability for violation of general environmental legal requirements covering all environmental law institutions. They include violation of legislation on environmental expert reviews (Art. 8.4 of the Code of Administrative Offenses of the Russian Federation), withholding or distortion of environmental information (Art. 8.5 of the Code of Administrative Offenses of the Russian Federation), *etc*.

The second group includes sets of elements establishing liability for violation of rules of protection of certain natural objects. They include damage of land (Art. 8.6 of the Code of Administrative Offenses of the Russian Federation), violation of air protection rules (Art. 8.21 of the Code of Administrative Offenses of the

Russian Federation), violation of water bodies protection rules (Art. 8.13 of the Code of Administrative Offenses of the Russian Federation), violation of rules of sanitary safety in forests (Art. 8.31 of the Code of Administrative Offenses of the Russian Federation), *etc.*

The third group includes sets of elements establishing liability for violation of the legal regime of areas with a special environmental legal regime. A typical example is the violation of rules of protection and use of natural resources in specially protected natural areas (Art. 8.39 of the Code of Administrative Offenses of the Russian Federation). In addition, it should be taken into account that the Code of Administrative Offenses of the Russian Federation (in contrast to the Criminal Code of the Russian Federation) does not contain rules establishing liability for minor environmental offenses in ecological disaster zones.

The fourth group includes sets of elements establishing liability for violation of requirements in the area of environmental protection in economic or other activities (in the industry, transport, *etc.*). They are non-compliance with requirements in the area of environmental protection in production and consumption waste management (Art. 8.2 of the Code of Administrative Offenses of the Russian Federation), violation of rules for handling pesticides and agrochemicals (Art. 8.3 of the Code of Administrative Offenses of the Russian Federation), releasing motor vehicles exceeding the regulatory limits for the content of pollutants in emissions or the regulatory noise level for operation (Art. 8.22 of the Code of Administrative Offenses of the Russian Federation), *etc.*

Considering all these sets of elements of administrative offenses makes it possible to draw the following conclusions. First, the Code of Administrative Offenses of the Russian Federation does not stipulate a state authority that would consider all cases on administrative offenses in environmental protection. Although most of these powers are assigned to Rosprirodnadzor authorities, this public authority is not the only one. Second, along with penalties, offenders may be subject to such administrative punishment as "administrative suspension of activity". This type of punishment implies temporary suspension of activity (for a period of up to 90 days) of legal entities and individual entrepreneurs as well as operation of units, facilities, buildings or structures in case of a threat to the life or health of people, a radiation accident or man-made disaster, significant harm to the condition or quality of the environment (Art. 3.12 of the Code of Administrative Offenses of the Russian Federation). A typical example of the application of this sanction can be Article 8.2 of the Code of Administrative Offenses of the Russian Federation providing for this type of punishment for non-compliance with requirements in the area of environmental protection in waste management.

It should be noted that the courts extremely rarely apply this type of punishment, especially concerning large enterprises, since the suspension of their activities leads to a range of unfavorable social and economic consequences (reduction of tax payments to the budget, unemployment, growth of social payments to citizens, *etc*.). On the one hand, this trend can be considered to implement the concept of sustainable development in practice. On the other hand, many say that environmental legislation is inefficient. Both points of view are right in their own way.

Special attention should be paid to the problem of distinguishing administrative and criminal liability in the field of environmental protection.

The frameworks of the sets of elements of criminal and administrative environmental offenses have much in common, and there are no clear criteria for distinguishing them from each other in the sets of elements of administrative offenses.

They are available in the rules of criminal law, for example, a range of the sets of elements include such a characterizing attribute as harm inflicted to the health or death of a person as a result of pollution of the atmosphere (for example, Article 251 of the Criminal Code). Other sets of elements refer to "grave consequences" (Art. 246 of the Criminal Code), "significant harm" (par. 1, Art. 250 of the Criminal Code); "substantial" and "large" damage (Arts. 255 and 256 of the Criminal Code). The note to Article 260 of the Criminal Code, establishing criminal liability for illegal cutting of forest plantations, describes the scope of the concepts of substantial and large harm: "substantial" means the damage caused to forest plantations or trees, shrubs, and lianas not attributed to forest plantations, calculated according to the rates approved by the Government of the Russian Federation, exceeding five thousand rubles, large – 50 thousand rubles, especially large – 150 thousand rubles. Any specific content of many other evaluative criteria is not described in the Criminal Code of the Russian Federation. Their interpretation is given in Resolution of the Plenum of the Supreme Court of the Russian Federation No. 21 of October 18, 2012 "On Application by Courts of Legislation on Liability for Violations in the Area of Environmental Protection and Natural Resource Management".

For example, the Plenum of the Supreme Court of the Russian Federation explains that "other grave consequences" with respect to Article 246 of the Criminal Code of the Russian Federation (violation of environmental protection rules during works) should be understood, in particular, as the deterioration of the quality of the environment and its components, the elimination of which requires a long time and large financial expenses (for example, mass diseases or death of fauna, including fish and other aquatic biological resources; destruction of conditions for its habitation and reproduction (loss of feeding and breeding grounds, wintering holes, disruption of migration routes, destruction of food resources); destruction of flora leading to a significant reduction of its biomass; land degradation). Mass death (diseases) is understood as an excess of the average level of death (diseases) of animals by three or more times.

Concerning paragraph 1 of Article 247 of the Criminal Code of the Russian Federation (violation of rules for the circulation of environmentally hazardous substances and waste), significant harm to the health of people is expressed in serious or moderate harm to the health of at least one person, and significant harm to the environment – in its pollution, poisoning or contamination, changes in the radioactive background to the values that are dangerous to human health or life, *etc*. Liability for illegal hunting stipulated by subparagraph "a" of paragraph 1 of Article 258 of the Criminal Code of the Russian Federation arises only in case of large damage. The damage caused by illegal hunting is large not only under the number and the cost of captured, damaged and destroyed animals but also with consideration of other circumstances of the act, in terms of the environmental value, significance for a specific habitat, the size of the population of these animals.

Consequently, in addition to the increased degree of social danger, such attributes of the elements as specific features of the subject, the place, the method of an offense, its subject, the amount of damage, the form of fault, and so forth, can be the ground for characterizing the offense as a crime.

It can be concluded that the elements of administrative and criminal offenses relate to each other as general and special rules. The former contains abstract wordings; the latter specify them. This is why administrative rules will apply only to the extent not covered by the attributes of the set of elements of an environmental crime of a similar structure that contains a list of additional attributes and conditions of the act subject to criminal punishment.

CRIMINAL LIABILITY FOR ENVIRONMENTAL CRIMES

Environmental crimes, which have become transnational, have been considered the most dangerous in recent years. Russian statistics of recent years show a steady trend towards increasing the number of environmental crimes, and their latency reaches 95-99 percent. However, although environmental criminality comprises less than 1 percent of the total number of registered crimes in the official statistics, many researchers believe that its real share corresponds to 15-23 percent. Notably, there is not only a stable trend towards the growth of environmental criminality but also good organization and professionalism of its forms, which leads to the most serious consequences (Kletneva, 2007).

Organized criminal groups are created for this criminal business. About 70-80 percent of the committed crimes are transnational. Wrongful acts and the growth of environmental criminality aggravate the environmental crisis. In addition, the high latency of environmental crimes leads to such a negative consequence as the lack of the population's perception of poaching, illegal logging, and other acts as criminal, which, in its turn, stimulates the growth in the number and professionalization of these crimes. The legislator's understanding of this trend caused the inclusion of a special chapter dedicated to environmental crimes in the Criminal Code of the Russian Federation. This chapter consists of both rules that are time-proved and were outlined in the Criminal Code of the RSFSR (for example, pollution of water reservoirs and the air) and fundamentally new elements (environmental protection during works; violation of rules for circulation of environmentally hazardous substances and waste; land damage, *etc*.).

Environmental crimes are guilty, socially dangerous acts or omissions stipulated by the criminal law, encroaching on the constitutional right of everyone to a favorable environment and causing harm to natural objects and systems (or containing its real threat).

Environmental crimes should be classified in the same way as administrative offenses, according to the direct object of encroachment criteria. However, in contrast to administrative offenses, Chapter 26 of the Criminal Code of the Russian Federation, dedicated to environmental crimes, does not set forth the general sets of elements dedicated, for example, to non-provision of environmental information. There will be three classification groups rather than four (as in the Code of Administrative Offenses of the Russian Federation). The first group includes sets of elements of crimes against certain natural objects. They include water pollution (Art. 250 of the Criminal Code), pollution of the atmosphere (Art. 251 of the Criminal Code), land damage (Art. 254 of the Criminal Code), illegal hunting (Art. 258 of the Criminal Code), *etc*.

The second group includes sets of elements establishing liability for violation of requirements in the area of environmental protection that must be observed in economic or other activities. These are a violation of environmental protection rules during works (Art. 246 of the Criminal Code of the Russian Federation), violation of rules for the circulation of environmentally hazardous substances and waste (Art. 247 of the Criminal Code of the Russian Federation), *etc*. The third group includes sets of elements establishing liability for violation of the regime of specially protected natural areas and natural objects (Art. 262 of the Criminal Code of the Russian Federation).

Most revealed environmental crimes include four sets of elements: illegal capture of aquatic biological resources (Art. 256 of the Criminal Code of the Russian Federation), illegal hunting (Art. 258 of the Criminal Code of the Russian Federation), illegal cutting of forest plantations (Art. 260 of the Criminal Code of the Russian Federation) and destruction or damage of forest plantations (Art. 261 of the Criminal Code of the Russian Federation). Those responsible for pollution of water reservoirs and air are brought to criminal liability in single cases, among other things, because it is hard to prove. Criminal sanctions in the form of imprisonment are rarely applied against violators by courts.

As for the personality of a "typical" environmental criminal involved in poaching or illegal logging, this is a non-disabled man aged 30-50 years, with a secondary (secondary specialized) education, who does not have a permanent source of income (unemployed), does not have convictions, have mercenary motives and is prone to environmental nihilism (Lavyghina, 2012).

They quite often act in organized criminal groups, including representatives of law enforcement agencies. They are characterized by the almost complete absence of women among them (logging or hunting require physical strength) and alcohol or drug intoxication. They are usually people with formed non-legal values that deliberately chose the path of crime. In addition, it should be noted that these people have anthropocentric consciousness, which manifests itself in a firm position on the central role of humans, the dominance of their needs, the main function of the natural environment as a source of benefits for the satisfaction of the preferential needs of people.

An objective reason that makes them commit environmental crimes is unemployment and the low level of income in rural areas (even if there is work). Raising the efficiency of the fight against environmental crimes cannot be considered in isolation from the country's general economic and social situation. This problem can be resolved only in the context of the country's social, economic, political, and cultural problems.

It should be taken into account that harm can be caused to the environment as a result of crimes specified in Chapter 26 of the Criminal Code of the Russian Federation.

For example, Article 215 of the Criminal Code provides for criminal liability for violation of safety rules for placement, design, construction, and operation of nuclear power facilities if it could lead to the death of a person or radioactive contamination of the environment. Article 358 of the Criminal Code of the Russian Federation introduces a completely new set of elements of "ecocide" included in the section "Crimes against the Peace and Security of Mankind", which determines its main object. The main difference between ecocide and environmental crimes as such is based on the generic object and the objective possibility of an environmental disaster as the only legally significant and threatening consequence of an act of ecocide (even though environmental legislation does not contain the concept of "environmental disaster").

Environmental terrorism should be distinguished from ecocide. The fundamental difference between them is that ecocide does not involve intimidation of the population or ideological or other concepts; there is no purpose of putting pressure on public authorities. The best-known acts of environmental terrorism are the sarin poison gas attack by Aum Shinrikyo in the Tokyo subway, the mailing of anthrax spores in the United States in 2001(5 people died and 17 were infected), *etc*., as well as more numerous failed attempts (the terrorist attempt to undermine the Baksan Hydroelectric Power Station in the Kabardino-Balkar Republic, Russia, on July 21, 2010; the container with radioactive cesium-137 placed by Chechen terrorists in Izmailovo Park in Moscow in 1995, *etc*.).

Environmental terrorism is one of the varieties of terrorism-related crimes aiming at intimidation of the population and pressure on public authorities using encroachment on the quality of the environment for negative impact on life, health, and property of citizens through destruction (damage) of technological facilities, facilities using nuclear energy (including places of storage of radioactive substances and sources of radioactive radiation) necessary to maintain the life support of the population, as well as through the use of chemical or biological substances hazardous to human life and health. Therefore, its difference from other types of terrorism consists in the object of the impact of terrorists – the state of the environment which is attacked rapidly, and, in its turn, the polluted environment has a negative impact on the life and health of citizens, as well as wild and domestic flora and fauna. In the Criminal Code of the Russian Federation, environmental terrorism is not included in a separate set of elements of a crime; however, paragraph 3 of Article 205 of the Criminal Code of the Russian Federation (the act of terrorism) states a characterizing attribute of this set of elements of a crime, consisting in the encroachment on facilities using nuclear energy or nuclear materials, radioactive substances or sources of radioactive radiation or poisonous, toxic, hazardous chemical or biological substances. This approach corresponds to the established international practice.

At the moment, there is no common international instrument dedicated to environmental terrorism, however, the terms "technological terrorism", "biological terrorism", "chemical," or "nuclear terrorism" are used quite often in dozens of adopted bilateral and multilateral international agreements. What is meant by them? The below varieties of environmental terrorism can be distinguished.

1. **Technological terrorism:** The failed attempt of terrorists to undermine the Baksan Hydroelectric Power Station in the Kabardino-Balkar Republic in 2010 is a typical example of an act of technological terrorism. It would have led to the flooding of the area, a decrease in electricity production in this constituent entity of the Russian Federation, and the death of people in settlements downstream of the river, destruction, or significant damage of their property.

2. **Nuclear terrorism:** According to estimates of Russian experts, three types of threats from acts of nuclear terrorism are the most probable. First, it is the detonation of nuclear weapons. Although a terrorist organization is unlikely to create a powerful nuclear or hydrogen bomb, even a low-yield nuclear device used by terrorists can have extremely negative environmental, economic, social, and political consequences. Second, it is subversion at nuclear power plants (its threat). Even if it does not lead to an explosion of a reactor and radioactive contamination of the area, the psychological effect will be enormous (such; fortunately, unsuccessful attempts were registered in France in 1975 and 1982, in Puerto Rico in 1980, at the Ignalina Nuclear Power Plant in Russia in 1995).

Third, the use of fissile materials for the manufacture of so-called "dirty bombs" that can cause great damage through radiation contamination of a vast territory in a densely populated area. Since it is much easier to create this weapon than the most primitive nuclear device, terrorists are more likely to use it.

3. **Chemical terrorism:** The possibility to commit acts of chemical terrorism is simplified by the widespread of chemical components and technologies in modern industrially developed states, and therefore, they are easily accessible to potential terrorists. They have a low value; the degree and nature of their impact on the environment and human health are not secret, though the weapons created with their use will have an enormous striking effect and cause psychological panic. There can be several forms of a direct manifestation of this type of environmental terrorism: poisoning of water bodies that serve as sources of water supply for cities; contamination of soil with chemicals, which will entail the production of contaminated agricultural products; air pollution in places of concentrated population. A typical example of chemical terrorism is the terrorist sarin poison gas attack by Aum Shinrikyo in the Tokyo subway on March 20, 1995 (12 deaths, thousands of people were intoxicated with the gas).

4. **Biological terrorism:** Bioterrorism is a unique threat. It significantly differs from other types of terrorism because while an explosion or a chemical attack leads to immediate and visible losses, the consequences of the deliberate use of biological weapons will steadily occur after several days or weeks, and the development of a large epidemic in a city is their potential culmination. The use of biological weapons by terrorists is facilitated by the fact that they affect small amounts; it is easy to conceal and use them. Since the infection of people and animals does not manifest itself immediately, this enables terrorists to escape from the crime scene. In addition, there is almost no protection against biological weapons that makes it possible to find a pathogenic microorganism or toxin before its action. Consequently, terrorist attacks with large-scale use of dangerous pathogens (smallpox, plague, anthrax) can lead to enormous human casualties, high economic expenditures required to eliminate the consequences, and destabilize the situation in a particular country or region.

Article 12 of Federal Law No. 492-FZ of December 30, 2020, "On Biological Safety in the Russian Federation" is dedicated to preventing this type of terrorism.

International cooperation in the fight against terrorism, including environmental terrorism, is necessary exactly because of the said circumstances. However, in addition to the political will, which is beyond doubt, several local legal factors are of great importance. They include a different understanding of environmental terrorism in Russia, countries of Western Europe and the United States. In Russia, environmental terrorism is understood as a variety of "classical" terrorism associated with the actuation of explosives and other devices, human losses, and property damage to intimidate the population and pressure public authorities. This term is also observed in other countries. In addition, the United States, Canada, European countries also use the other meaning of the word "ecoterrorism," which is understood as actions of radical environmental organized groups and criminal communities destroying fur and leather articles, releasing experimental and agricultural animals from cages, threatening to "murderers of animals", blowing up cars, *etc*. In Russia, this phenomenon also occurs (although to a lesser extent than in the United States); however, it is not called "terrorism" as it is not aimed at destabilizing activities of the authorities or affecting their decision-making. These radical actions are largely characterized as hooliganism or as deliberate destruction or damage of the property of others.

The methods and the description of the personality of criminals are considerably different in both cases. In contrast to common terrorists, environmental radicals do not try to intimidate society and the state but "fight" against particular, in their view, violators of environmental legislation. At the same time, they do not kill or make anyone disabled, though they cause property damage to many people. Environmental radicals do not try to destroy the environment; rather, they save it despite illegal methods.

Environmental radicals are not religious fanatics but young city dwellers, often students. Violence for them is not a goal in itself but just a means of drawing public attention to environmental problems. They are often opposed to the ideas of anthropocentrism, hold ecocentric views, know the current environmental legislation. Groups of environmental radicals are poorly organized and usually do not have external funding. While there is no sense to enter into negotiations with "classical terrorists", society has to make allies of environmental radicals, find a way to involve them in lawful processes to protect the environment, help them change their methods of environmental protection.

COMPENSATION FOR HARM CAUSED BY ENVIRONMENTAL OFFENSES

Let us single out three sub-issues for the convenience of considering this issue.

4.4.1. General Description of Environmental Harm

Civil law conventionally divides obligations into two groups: contractual and non-contractual. Contractual obligations arise on the basis of a contract concluded by the parties, and non-contractual obligations are fundamentally different from contractual ones in their nature, ways of commencement, and content. They arise not as a voluntary expression of the will of the parties to contracts but as a result of harm caused to the person or property of a citizen, property of a legal entity, and are subject to compensation in full by the person who caused the harm. The general conditions for the commencement of obligations as a result of harm are as follows: the presence of harm; wrongfulness of actions (omissions) of the harm-doer; a causal relationship between wrongful actions (omissions) and harm and, as a rule, the fault of the person who caused the harm (although there are several exceptions to the latter rule).

Regulating the issues of compensation for the consequences of environmental offenses, the legislator uses the terms "harm", "damage," and "loss". For example, Article 42 of the Constitution of the Russian Federation mentions the right to compensation of damage caused by an environmental offense. The Forest Code of the Russian Federation uses the term "harm" but does not use the concepts of "damage" or "loss". The Land Code of the Russian Federation refers to harm, damage, and loss. In their turn, Articles 77-79 of the Federal Law "On Environmental Protection" use the terms "loss" and "harm" but do not use the term "damage". How do all these legal concepts correlate with each other? It appears that harm is a generic concept and can be attributed to property or non-property (including non-pecuniary).

Property harm manifests itself in the form of losses, which are understood by Article 15 of the Civil Code of the Russian Federation as expenses incurred or had to be incurred by the person whose right has been violated to restore the violated right, loss, or damage of the person's property (actual damage) as well as the unreceived income that this person would have received under normal conditions of civil circulation if the right had not been violated (lost profit).

There is no general concept of environmental harm in legislation. Article 1 of the Law on Environmental Protection formulates only the concept of "harm to the environment". It is understood as a negative change of the environment occurring due to its pollution and leading to the degradation of natural ecological systems and depletion of natural resources. Meanwhile, environmental harm can be expressed in the infliction of harm to the environment and the life, health, property of a citizen (property of a legal entity), and in non-pecuniary damage. This is why it can be determined only after the connection of the specified concepts.

Environmental harm is negative changes in the quality of the environment which are caused by economic or other human activities expressed in the destruction of ecological relations, pollution, destruction or depletion of certain natural components and can result in harm to the life, health, or property of citizens (property of legal entities).

Meanwhile, the inevitable deterioration of the health or property of particular persons as a result of an environmental offense does not necessarily have a direct causal link with it. The specific feature of environmental relations is that harmful consequences can manifest themselves after a long time (for example, in the next generation, as it happened after the accident at the Chernobyl Nuclear Power Plant in 1986), only then affecting humans health. In addition, environmental harm is often hard to estimate in money. For example, how to calculate the value of a biological species that has ceased to exist on Earth as a result of illegal hunting or for other reasons? Hence it follows that the monetary evaluation of the harm to the environment and the health of citizens is very conditional. Let us consider some distinguishing features of environmental harm.

1. Environmental harm can manifest itself as property and non-property harm (including non-pecuniary damage). Environmental property harm (environmental losses) manifests itself in the form of environmental pollution, damage, destruction, depletion of natural resources, destruction of ecological systems, which lead to the infliction of pecuniary damage that is to be estimated with the

use of the corresponding rates, methods or by other means. Lost profit is a constituent element of environmental losses; it is non-receipt by a citizen or a legal entity of income that they could have received under normal conditions. For example, an agricultural cooperative could have had a higher crop yield if not for the "acid" rain. Non-pecuniary damage is understood as moral or physical suffering resulting from actions (omissions) encroaching on intangible benefits belonging to a citizen (life, health, *etc.*) or violating a citizen's non-property or property rights.

2. Persons causing harm to the environment are obliged to compensate for it in full according to the current legislation.

The principle of compensation for harm in full is established by Article 1064 of the Civil Code of the Russian Federation, and its content is set forth in Article 1082 of the Civil Code of the Russian Federation. Satisfying claims for compensation for harm, the court obliges the person guilty of harm to compensate for it in kind (to provide a thing of the same kind and quality, repair the damaged thing, *etc.*) or compensate for the caused losses.

3. Peculiarities of the owners' liability of sources of increased danger. A source of increased danger is a particular object of the material world characterized by harmful properties stipulated by law and excluding the possibility of complete human control, thus creating an increased risk to the environment and the population. Consequently, there are two attributes of activities creating an increased risk: harmfulness, *i.e.*, a qualitative characteristic of the use (operation) of a source of increased danger and the impossibility of complete human control over it. It is impossible to formulate an exhaustive list of the sources of increased danger; this is why the legislator does not try to do it. Article 1079 of the Civil Code of the Russian Federation states that increased risk to people is created by vehicles, mechanisms, high-voltage electrical energy, nuclear energy, explosives, strong poisons, construction, and other related activities, *etc*. The civil law framework of the "source of increased danger" includes two varieties: "common" sources of increased danger (*i.e.*, beyond the scope of special rules of environmental law) and hazardous production facilities. Additional parameters and criteria of environmentally hazardous activities of hazardous production facilities are provided for in the Federal Law "On the Industrial Safety of Hazardous Production Facilities". The appendix presents quite specific activities parameters that make it possible to consider production facilities hazardous.

Nuclear energy facilities occupy a special place in the system of hazardous production facilities. About them, civil, environmental, and other legislation provides for additional rules guaranteeing the payment of compensation for the inflicted harm. For example, according to Article 57 of the Federal Law "On the Use of Nuclear Energy", the Government of the Russian Federation ensures payments for compensation for losses and harm that are caused by radiation exposure and are the liability of the operating organizations, to the extent the caused losses and harm exceed the liability limit established for these operating organizations, by providing the necessary amounts up to full compensation for the caused losses and harm.

4. According to Article 1064 of the Civil Code of the Russian Federation, civil liability may arise for lawfully committed acts but only in cases specified in the law. For example, the payment for negative impact on the environment does not exempt subjects of economic and other activities from measures for environmental protection and compensation for harm to the environment. Similarly, economic and other activities carried out by these subjects involve their duty to compensate for harm to the environment, also when there are positive findings of the state environmental expert review for the project of these activities (Act. 77 of the Law of the Russian Federation "On Environmental Protection").

5. Civil legislation distinguishes two types of action limitation periods: general and special. The general action limitation period is three years under Article 196 of the Civil Code of the Russian Federation. Taking into account the significance of the favorable environmental quality for the life and health of citizens, the special action limitation period is established for filing claims for compensation for harm to the environment, twenty years, which is one of the longest in Russia. Based on the provisions of paragraph 4 of Article 208 of the Civil Code of the Russian Federation, the activity limitation does not apply to claims for compensation for harm caused to the life or health of citizens as a result of negative impact on the environment, however, claims made after three years from the emergence of the right to compensation for this harm are satisfied for the past period maximum for three years preceding the claim.

6. Illegally captured animals, their parts, and products made from them are unjust enrichment of the person that captured them (Art. 1102 of the Civil Code of the Russian Federation) with all the consequences that this entails.

7. It should be noted that Article 1065 of the Civil Code of the Russian Federation stipulates the possibility of preventive measures against environmental harm. According to this article, the risk of causing harm in the future can be the basis for a claim for the prohibition of activities that pose this risk. Suppose the caused harm is a consequence of the operation of enterprises, structures or other production activities that continue causing harm or threaten new harm. In that case, the court has the right to oblige the defendant, in addition to compensation

for the harm, to suspend or terminate the corresponding activities. It is noteworthy that along with clarifications on the consideration of disputes on thc limitation, suspension or termination of activities carried out in violation of environmental legislation, Resolution of the Plenum of the Supreme Court No. 49 of November 30, 2017 "On Some Issues of Application of Legislation on Compensation for Harm Caused to the Environment" gives interesting arguments inspired by the concept of sustainable development, which requires finding a balance of environmental, economic and social interests. The Plenum, in particular, states (par. 27) that the court must maintain a balance between the needs of society in preserving a favorable environment and ensuring environmental safety, on the one hand, and the settlement of socio-economic problems, on the other hand. In addition, the court should take into account not only the factors that ensure the normal life of people and organizations (for example, with respect to the activities of city-forming enterprises, combined heat and power plants, treatment facilities) but also the proportionality of the consequences of the termination (suspension, limitation) of the activities to the environmental harm that can occur as a result of both the continuation of these activities and their termination. Moreover, the Plenum especially states that the court can deny a claim for the suspension or termination of the corresponding activities only if their suspension or termination contradicts public interests. The denial of the suspension or termination of these activities does not deprive the affected party of the right to compensation for the harm caused by these activities.

There are often attempts to apply the provisions of Article 1065 of the Civil Code of the Russian Federation about hazardous production facilities, the activities of which are regulated by the Law on Industrial Safety. However, their application encounters several practical difficulties since it is technically hard to prove the potential threat from the operation of these facilities. Hazardous production facilities are closed for free access (because sometimes they produce products that are a state secret). This makes it difficult for the public to collect evidence that these enterprises violate norms and regulations, leading to an environmental accident.

Therefore, there are two closely related manifestations of environmental harm: "primary" harm to the environment (including accumulated harm), and "secondary" harm to the life, health, and property of citizens (including non-pecuniary damage), as well as harm to the property of legal entities.

Compensation for Harm to the Environment

According to Article 1082 of the Civil Code of the Russian Federation, there are two methods to compensate for harm – in kind and monetary terms. Their combination is also possible when one part of the resources is provided in money and the other one – by performing restoration works at the expense or by means of the defendant. Selecting the method of compensation for harm, the court takes into account the facts of the case, for example, whether the harm-doer has or does not have material and technical possibilities necessary for the works to restore the natural environment. Suppose the defendant evades the duties imposed by the court. In that case, the court (commercial court) shall, at the plaintiff's request, decide on the recovery of the damage in monetary form, including the losses caused by the failure to fulfill the court decision. Compensation for environmental harm in monetary form is the most common way to do this. The most convenient form of compensation for harm for the plaintiff is monetary form, and for the defendant –in kind, which is implemented in accordance with the project of restoration works.

Until recently, the defendants' works to restore the damaged quality of the environment were not taken into account by the courts when adopting decisions on the amount of compensation for environmental harm. This issue was considered in Resolution of the Constitutional Court of the Russian Federation No. 12-P of June 2, 2015. The below case was the reason for the claim filed by OOO “Zapolyarneft” with the Constitutional Court of the Russian Federation. An accident at an oil pipeline belonging to Zapolyarneft resulted in harm to the forests. Zapolyarneft spent a particular amount of money to reduce this harm by implementing measures to restore the quality of the damaged land areas. However, the nature protection authority calculating the value of the caused harm did not consider these expenses. As a result, it turned out that, irrespective of whether the harm-doer contributed monetary funds to the reduction of the consequences of the pollution or not, the amount of the collected compensation is the same.

In this Resolution, the Constitutional Court of the Russian Federation states that in the calculation of the amount of harm according to the rates and methods, it is necessary to take into account the reasonable expenses incurred by the harm-doer in the elimination of the consequences of the environmental pollution caused by the harm-doer's activities. These actual expenditures of the harm-doer must be deducted from the accrued amount of compensation for the harm caused to the forests according to the rates and methods of its calculation. This legal position of the Constitutional Court of the Russian Federation led to the supplementation of Article 78 of the Federal Law “On Environmental Protection” of January 10, 2002, with paragraph 2.1, according to which the determination of the amount of harm to the environment involves the consideration of expenditures on the elimination of this harm incurred by the person that caused the corresponding harm.

In monetary terms, compensation for environmental harm is implemented according to the rates, methods, and actual expenditures.

The rates are a way to compensate for harm to the natural environment within the framework of civil liability; it is the recovery of funds from the harm-doer in the amounts that are initially established by by-laws and include the economic value of the damaged components of the natural environment and the amount necessary for their restoration to the previous favorable (natural) condition. Harm is compensated both for territories with a common environmental legal regime and specially protected natural areas according to the rates and methods. In the latter case, the offender pays the rate amount multiplied by the multiplying coefficient. The below rates are applied for harm caused to the environment.

1. Rates for calculating the amount collected for damage caused to forest plantations. A typical example is the Decree of the Government of the Russian Federation No. 1730 of December 29, 2018, “On the Approval of Specific Features of Compensation for Harm Caused to Forests and Natural Objects Located Therein as a Result of Violation of Forest Legislation”. For example, illegal cutting of trees (for instance, unauthorized harvesting of Christmas trees), if such a needle-leaved tree has a truck of at least 12 cm in diameter, the amount of compensation for harm according to the rates will be equal to 50 times the value of the wood of this type of trees. Multiplying coefficients can also be established. For example, suppose a citizen carries out harvesting of food forest resources or collection of medicinal plants which are listed in the Red Data Book of the Russian Federation or a constituent entity of the Russian Federation. In that case, the number of payments according to the rates is to be multiplied by 10.

2. Rates for calculating the amount collected for damage caused to aquatic biological resources. An example, in this case, is the Decree of the Government of the Russian Federation No. 1321 of November 3, 2018, “On the Approval of Rates for the Calculation of the Amount of Harm Caused to Aquatic Biological Resources”. For instance, compensation of harm resulting from the capture of one beluga, regardless of its size and weight, is 206,625 rubles.

At one time, constituent entities of the Russian Federation established rates for calculating the amount of compensation for harm caused, for example, to animals listed in the Red Data Books of the corresponding constituent entities of the Russian Federation. However, in this case, constituent entities of the Russian Federation regulated civil relations attributed to the exclusive federal jurisdiction by Article 71 of the Constitution of the Russian Federation. In this regard, these by-laws are now no longer in force in most constituent entities of the Russian Federation.

The amount of the rate is determined with consideration of the environmental value of the species of plants and aquatic animals and is established for each plant or animal.

The methods for harm calculation are applied in case of harm caused to water, air, fauna, and soil. The methods for estimation of the amount of harm are the ways to compensate for harm to the natural environment with the use of special formulas for calculating harm that reflects natural, climatic, biological, economic, and other indicators and makes it possible both to recover the economic value of the damaged components of the natural environment and to collect the amount necessary to restore them to their previous favorable (natural) condition. An example is Order of the Ministry of Natural Resources and Environment of the Russian Federation No. 238 of July 8, 2010 (revised on July 11, 2018) "On the Approval of the Methods for Calculation of the Amount of Harm Caused to Soil as an Object of Environmental Protection". In addition to soil, these methods are approved concerning water, fauna, and air. Methods of compensation for subsoil harm are still under development.

The payments for harm caused to soil or other components of the natural environment do not exempt the liable party from taking measures to restore the natural environment (for example, land remediation) and from paying fines or compensation for harm to the life, health, and property of citizens. Suppose there are no established rates and methods. In that case, the compensation for harm is based on the actual expenditures on restoring the damaged environment with consideration of all losses incurred.

Therefore, the formula for calculating caused harm is the fundamental difference between the rates and the methods. In the case of the rates, this formula is simple: money is collected in known amounts for a specific variety of trees of a particular age or trunk thickness. In the case of the methods, the amount of harm is calculated according to complex formulas that can include several parameters (five, seven, *etc.*). Therefore, the degree of complexity of harm calculation is very different in these cases.

The above rules have some exceptions and specifications.

1. It should be pointed out that the said rules are general and actually not applied in cases of environmental harm of a global (disastrous) nature. This means that if there is a serious man-made environmental disaster that makes it impossible

for people to live (as it was as a result of the accident at the Chernobyl Nuclear Power Plant), the people are to be resettled, the affected territory must rcccivc the status of an ecological disaster zone and restoration activities must be carried out. It is impossible to compensate for this by means of civil law. However, ecological disaster zones are only mentioned in Article 57 of the Federal Law "On Environmental Protection" of January 10, 2002, there is no special law on them, and this status has not been given to any territory in Russia.

2. The distinguishing feature of the compensation for harm to the environment in case of discharges of pollutants through centralized water disposal systems of settlements and urban districts is that, as a general rule, the harm is compensated by the organizations operating these systems.

3. There are several distinguishing features of compensation for accumulated environmental harm. It is understood as the harm to the environment resulting from past economic and other activities the duties to eliminate that have not been fulfilled fully or in part. Sites of accumulated harm to the environment are identified using inventories and inspection of territories and water areas where economic or other activities were carried out in the past and (or) where ownerless capital facilities and waste disposal facilities are located. The assessment of sites of accumulated harm to the environment involves the determination of the volume or mass of pollutants, waste, and their hazard classes; the size of territories and water areas where objects of accumulated harm to the environment are located, categories and types of permitted land use; the level and extent of negative impact on the environment, including the potential of pollutants to migrate to other components of the natural environment, the possibility of pollution of water bodies, including those that are the sources of drinking and domestic water supply, the possibility of environmental risks; the presence of hazardous substances specified in international agreements at the facilities of accumulated harm to the environment, *etc*.

Accumulated harm to the environment is eliminated at the sites of accumulated harm to the environment included in the state register of sites of accumulated harm to the environment. State authorities of constituent entities of the Russian Federation and local government bodies are entitled to organize the elimination of accumulated harm to the environment. In cases established by the Government of the Russian Federation, the elimination of accumulated harm to the environment is organized by the federal executive authorities that perform state management in environmental protection. The organization of the elimination of accumulated harm to the environment involves necessary inspections, including engineering surveys, development of a project for elimination of accumulated harm to the environment, its coordination and approval, implementation of the elimination of accumulated harm to the environment, check and acceptance of the performed works. The list of the sites of accumulated environmental harm is published on the website of the Ministry of Natural Resources and Environment (Minprirody) of the Russian Federation. It includes over one hundred sites, mainly unauthorized dumps and domestic and industrial waste landfills, located in various constituent entities of the Russian Federation.

Compensation for Harm Caused to the Life, Health, and Property of People by the Negative Impact of the Environment

Property and non-property harm to citizens (secondary harm) follow from harm to the environment (primary harm), this is a distinguishing feature of environmental harm. This harm to the health of citizens is often called "echogenic" with the purpose to highlight this causality (Brinchuk, 2009).

Non-pecuniary damage (moral harm) is one of the best-known varieties of non-property harm. Non-pecuniary damage is understood as moral or physical suffering resulting from actions (omissions) encroaching on intangible benefits belonging to a citizen from birth or under law (life, health, *etc.*) or violating a citizen's non-property or property rights. Non-pecuniary damage can consist in moral feelings resulting from the impossibility to continue active social life, loss of job, temporary limitation or deprivation of any rights, physical pain related to injuries or other damage to health, an illness following moral sufferings, *etc.* These sufferings can occur due to a disability caused by environmental factors, for example, life in an unfavorable environment. There are at least a few examples of compensation for non-pecuniary damage.

For example, in Chelyabinsk, in 1997, the court held to compensate a citizen for non-pecuniary damage caused by the unfavorable impact of the environment exposed to radiation contamination as a result of activities carried out by the Mayak Production Association (Vasilieva and Yakovleva, 1998).

Non-pecuniary damage is subject to compensation in monetary form irrespective of compensation for environmental harm of a property nature aimed at restoring the material position of the affected party. Its compensation aims to mitigate the moral or physical sufferings of the affected party caused by the environmental consequences of offenses. According to paragraph 44 of Resolution of the Plenum of the Supreme Court of the Russian Federation No. 21 of October 18, 2012 "On Application by Courts of Legislation on Liability for Violations in the Area of Environmental Protection and Natural Resource Management", resolving the issue of compensation for non-pecuniary damage, the court should establish how the fact of infliction of harm to the affected party is confirmed, what actions (omissions) caused it, the degree of fault of the harm-doer, what moral or physical sufferings the affected party had, in what amount the affected party estimates their compensation and other circumstances relevant to the consideration of the stated claims. The court estimates the degree of moral or physical sufferings with consideration of the facts of non-pecuniary damage, individual features of the affected party and other specific circumstances indicating the severity of the sufferings. Compensation for non-pecuniary damage caused to the health of citizens by the negative impact of the environment is to be provided irrespective of the fault if this damage is caused by legal entities and citizens carrying out the activities related to the increased risk to the environment (Art. 1100 of the Civil Code of the Russian Federation).

Harm to people's life, health, and property caused by the negative impact of the environment can be compensated in three different ways: by insurance, in judicial proceedings, publicly.

1. Environmental insurance of civil liability for harm to the environment and the life, health, and property of citizens (property of legal entities) involves the payment of insurance premiums used for compensation for harm caused by environmental offenses. Environmental insurance can be compulsory and voluntary, but both types have not been considerably developed in Russia yet.

2. Judicial proceedings involve the initiation of legal action by the affected party claiming compensation for harm to the health or property caused due to violation of environmental legislation. For example, according to Article 1085 of the Civil Code, in case of harm to the health of citizens, compensation is provided for the lost earnings (income) of the affected party that was received or could have been received, as well as additional expenses caused by the harm to the health, including expenses on treatment, additional nutrition, purchase of medicine, prosthetics, nursing care, sanatorium and spa treatment, purchase of special vehicles, training for another profession, if it is established that the affected party needs these types of assistance and care and is not entitled to receive them free of charge. Judicial practice regarding this issue is not considerable due to the distinguishing features of this form of compensation for environmental harm. Suppose citizens affected by the negative impact of the environment claim full compensation for harm to the health or property. In that case, they must prove the presence of the harm and its causal relationship with the wrongful conduct of the harm-doer. The affected persons themselves, members of their families, prosecutors, authorized public authorities, public

organizations representing the interests of the affected persons can file claims with the courts. Several operative facts are to be proved.

a. The fact that the defendant committed an act that violated legislation in environmental protection. For example, violation of environmental legislation often entails administrative punishment. Bringing the party at fault to administrative liability will be the proof of the fact of committing a wrongful environmental act.

b. The fact that the harm to the environment was caused as a result of the environmental offense. In this case, the plaintiff can also refer to the result of the administrative proceedings and the document of a specially authorized state authority on the fact of pollution of the environment at a certain time and in a certain territory.

c. The fact that the harm was caused to the health and property. The affected persons provide the relevant documentary evidence, submitting to the court's health certificates, sick lists, receipts confirming the purchase of medicine, receipts for additional nutrition, *etc*. In addition to compensation for harm to the health and property caused by environmental offenses, citizens have the right to compensation for non-pecuniary damage; its amount must be substantiated.

d. The causal relationship between the negative impact of the environment and the harm itself. This subject is the most difficult to prove. It is necessary to prove the fact that the person was in the place where the harm was caused to the environment. In this case, it is possible to provide a certificate from the workplace, place of residence (local government bodies, territorial authority of the migration service that registers citizens or housing and utilities organization) confirming that the affected person was in the corresponding place at that time and, consequently, was exposed to the harmful impact of the environment. The court has to determine that other factors, including natural ones, do not cause these consequences, and that they do not occur irrespective of the established violation of the law as well as that the wrongful acts are not committed in a state of extreme necessity (for example, to ensure functioning and security of the critical infrastructure).

3. The public (administrative) proceedings imply the duty of the state, even if there is no fault, to provide social assistance to persons who suffered echogenic harm as a result of a man-made accident (disaster). In foreign law, a similar legal framework is called "mass environmental tort" (Kodolova, 2009). These

proceedings also involve the provision of benefits and allowances (compensations) to citizens affected by the unfavorable impact of the environment as a result of accidents. These proceedings were first implemented after the Chernobyl Nuclear Power Plant accident. Such benefits and compensations are provided for by the Federal Law of January 10, 2002 "On Social Guarantees for Citizens Exposed to Radiation as a Result of Nuclear Tests at the Semipalatinsk Test Site", Federal Law No. 175-FZ of November 26, 1998 "On Social Protection of Citizens Exposed to Radiation as a Result of the Accident at the Mayak Production Association in 1957 and Discharges of Waste into the Techa River" and some other laws. For example, Law of the Russian Federation No. 1244-1 of May 15, 1991, "On Social Protection of Citizens Exposed to Radiation as a Result of the Accident at the Chernobyl NPP" provides for compensations and benefits for different categories of affected persons, including participants in the elimination of the consequences of the accident at the Chernobyl Nuclear Power Plant in the exclusion zone, citizens who got or had radiation sickness, other diseases, persons who became disabled as a result of the Chernobyl accident, citizens engaged in the operation of the Chernobyl Nuclear Power Plant and in work in the exclusion zone, citizens evacuated from the exclusion zone and resettled (being resettled) from the evacuation zone, *etc.*

As mentioned in Resolution of the Constitutional Court of the Russian Federation No. 18-P of December 1, 1997 "In the Case Concerning the Review of the Constitutionality of Certain Provisions of Article 1 of Federal Law of November 24, 1995 'On Introduction of Amendments to the Law of the Russian Federation 'On Social Protection of Citizens Exposed to Radiation as a Result of the Accident at the Chernobyl NPP", this man-made accident of the 20th century, was extraordinary in its consequences and led to incalculable environmental and humanitarian losses. It resulted in the considerable violation of the right to a favorable environment enshrined in Article 42 of the Constitution and, as a consequence, also other constitutional rights and interests of citizens related to the protection of the life, health, housing, property, as well as the right to freedom of movement and choice of place of stay and residence, which were infringed so significantly that the caused harm was irreparable. This gives rise to special nature of relations between citizens and the state that consists in the fact that the state assumes the duty to compensate for this harm, which, because of its extent and the number of affected persons, cannot be compensated according to the procedure established by the civil, administrative, criminal and other branch legislation.

CONCLUSION

The chapter formulates the definition of responsibility for environmental offenses. The peculiarities of administrative responsibility for environmental offenses are explained and the grounds for distinguishing criminal and administrative responsibility. The classification of environmental crimes is carried out. The specifics of environmental damage and the procedure for its compensation are explained.

QUESTIONS AND TASKS FOR SELF-CONTROL

1. Define liability for environmental offenses and environmental offenses.

2. Describe the distinguishing features of administrative liability for environmental offenses as well as the grounds for differentiating between criminal and administrative liability.

3. Define environmental crimes. What groups of environmental crimes are provided for by the Criminal Code of the Russian Federation?

4. Define environmental harm. What are its distinguishing features?

5. Describe the procedure for compensation for environmental harm. What are the rates and methods for compensation for environmental harm?

6. Describe the procedure for compensation for harm caused to the life and health of citizens by environmental offenses.

7. Give details of the procedure for compensation for non-pecuniary damage caused by environmental offenses.

8. Explain what should be meant by accumulated environmental harm.

REFERENCES

Brinchuk, M.M. (2009). Environmental Liability as an Independent Type of Legal Liability. *State and Law, 4*, 48.

Kletneva, E.G. (2007). *Environmental Criminality in the Russian Federation: the Concept, Causes, Conditions and Prevention.* Kazan State University.

Kodolova, A. (2009). Mass Environmental Torts in Russian and Foreign Law. *Economy and Law, 6*, 52-58.

Lavyghina, I.V. (2012). Criminological characteristics of the personality of criminals committing environmental crimes in Irkutsk Region. *Criminological Journal of Baikal State University of Economics and Law, 2*, 51-56.

Vasilieva, M.I., Yakovleva, O.A. (1998). Distinguishing Features of Compensation for Non-Pecuniary Damage Caused by Radiation Contamination of the Natural Environment (Based on the Court Case). *State and Law, 3*, 38-39.

CHAPTER 5

Legal Regulation of Environmental Protection in Certain Fields of Human Activity

Abstract: The authors prove that with the purpose to implement the tasks of ensuring the appropriate quality of the environment in Russia, environmental legislation provides for a system of measures, which, along with giving a special legal status to certain specially protected areas or establishing rules and regulations for the protection and rational use of natural objects, also includes special environmental requirements mandatory for observance and execution by all legal entities, individual entrepreneurs and citizens engaged in various types of economic and other activities that have a negative impact on the environment. The list of these types of activities is not exhaustive and includes special rules and requirements for real estate construction, operation of industrial, power and agricultural facilities, transport, *etc.* The requirements are comprehensive and thus different from the duties imposed on users of natural resources and third parties using certain natural resources (forests, water, *etc.*). In particular, rules dedicated to the protection of forests from fires contain sufficiently unique prescriptions that can be used only to protect forests. In a similar manner, the measures for fauna protection through the maintenance of the Red Data Book are clearly localized by this natural object. The comprehensive nature of the requirements for certain types of activities consists in the fact that they are aimed at regulating the activities threatening several natural objects rather than one. Requirements for environmentally safe operation of power facilities are a typical example in this case. Requirements for construction and operation of nuclear power stations are intended to exclude any repetition of the tragedy of the Chernobyl Nuclear Power Plant, when the radiation had a negative impact on not one component of the natural environment (land, forests, water, fauna, air) but all at once, and the environment contaminated with radiation caused harm to the life and health of hundreds of thousands of people. Harm to nature and the health of citizens from tests of nuclear weapons or from more peaceful activities, for example, the use of pesticides in agriculture is equally complex with regard to its consequences. In the latter case, violation of environmental requirements in the field of chemicalization of agriculture results in harm to land, surface and ground water bodies.

Keywords: Activities, Agriculture, Chemical weapons, Defense, Green fund, Human settlements, Industry, Missiles, Ozone layer, Pesticides, Power industry, Protective zones, Requirements, Sanitary protection zones, Technical regulations, Transport, Urban development, Waste, Zones with special conditions of use, Zoning.

Aleksey Anisimov and Anatoliy Ryzhenkov

CONCEPT AND SIGNIFICANCE OF ENVIRONMENTAL REQUIREMENTS FOR VARIOUS TYPES OF ECONOMIC AND OTHER ACTIVITIES

With the purpose to implement the tasks of ensuring the appropriate quality of the environment in the Russian Federation, environmental legislation provides for a system of measures, which, along with giving a special legal status to certain specially protected areas or establishing rules and regulations for the protection and rational use of natural objects, also includes special environmental requirements mandatory for observance and execution by all legal entities, individual entrepreneurs and citizens engaged in various types of economic and other activities that have a negative impact on the environment. The list of these types of activities is not exhaustive and includes special rules and requirements for real estate construction, operation of industrial, power and agricultural facilities, transport, *etc.*

The requirements for certain types of activities are restrictions and prohibitions established for certain types of economic or other activities of people in various areas of the economy (industry, transport, and so forth) intended to ensure a favorable environmental quality.

The requirements are comprehensive and thus different from the duties imposed on users of natural resources and third parties using certain natural resources (forests, water, *etc.*). For example, rules dedicated to the protection of forests from fires contain sufficiently unique prescriptions that can be used only to protect forests. In a similar manner, the measures for fauna protection through the maintenance of the Red Data Book are clearly localized by this natural object. The comprehensive nature of the requirements for certain types of activities consists in the fact that they are aimed at regulating the activities threatening several natural objects rather than one. Requirements for environmentally safe operation of power facilities are a typical example in this case. Requirements for construction and operation of nuclear power stations are intended to exclude any repetition of the tragedy of the Chernobyl Nuclear Power Plant, when the radiation had a negative impact on not one component of the natural environment (land, forests, water, fauna, air) but all at once, and the environment contaminated with radiation caused harm to the life and health of hundred thousands of people. Harm to nature and the health of citizens from tests of nuclear weapons or from more peaceful activities, for example, the use of pesticides in agriculture is equally complex with regard to its consequences. In the latter case, violation of environmental requirements in the field of chemicalization of agriculture results in harm to land, surface and ground water bodies.

In addition, it should be noted that the distinctive features of the protection of certain components of the natural environment (land, water, subsoil, *etc.*) and requirements for certain types of activities can naturally overlap. There are no contradiction, problems or collisions regarding that. For example, land protection involves measures to increase fertility of soil of agricultural lands. In their turn, environmental requirements in agriculture involve regulation of reclamation, use of pesticides, state support measures for agricultural production and so forth, *i.e.*, they overlap to some extent. This is explained by the fact that requirements for certain types of activities (also in agriculture) are of a more complex nature, not denying measures for protection of certain components of the natural environment but, on the contrary, supplementing and strengthening them. Another example can also be given. The Armed Forces of the Russian Federation occupy a huge area of land and forests and are subject to general requirements for the protection of these natural objects. However, taking into account the multifaceted nature of the activities of the Armed Forces and various types of negative impact on the environment that they have, the legislator has developed special environmental requirements for the activities of the Armed Forces of the Russian Federation, which bring various particular restrictions and prohibitions down to the "common denominator".

The complex nature of the impact of certain activities on the environment led to an equally complex set of prohibitions and restrictions, as well as management decisions for their implementation. For example, the special nature of environmental threats from nuclear power plants caused the necessity of licensing and additional expert reviews of their activities; environmental threats from hydroelectric power plants required the establishment of the need to develop the safety declaration for these facilities; the construction and operation of plants producing ozone depleting substances is completely prohibited. With respect to hazardous production facilities, which are regulated by the corresponding law, there is a complex set of requirements for environmental protection in the industry that provides for the requirements for design, construction and operation of these facilities, the need to carry out industrial safety expert reviews, development of the industrial safety declaration, special requirements for employees and compulsory insurance of activities. Taking into account that these industrial facilities include plants producing, for example, toxic and explosive substances, the development of special environmental requirements is preventive and makes it possible to avoid accidents there that would entail harm not only to land or air but to all or most components of the natural environment and, accordingly, to the life, health and property of citizens.

There can be no exhaustive list of environmental requirements for certain types of activities in principle since life does not stand still. For example, now the Federal

Law "On Environmental Protection" does not mention nanotechnology, however, it is already obvious that its mass use in foreign countries has shown their negative impact on the environment, this is why additions to this Law are inevitable.

If we try to classify all environmental requirements for certain types of activities, within the first classification, we can distinguish requirements at the preoperational stage (design and construction of facilities) and the stage of operation of industrial or other facilities that are hazardous for the environment. Within the second classification, related to already constructed facilities, according to the criterion of the nature of protective measures, we can distinguish their two groups: restricting activities of the facilities themselves (or establishing additional conditions for their work) and restricting economic and other activities in the immediate vicinity of industrial, agricultural or other hazardous facilities. The establishment of sanitary protection zones around industrial or agricultural facilities is a typical example of the latter territorial measures of environmental protection.

The third classification of environmental requirements for certain types of activities divides them into general, applied to activities or processes that have no significant negative impact on the environment, special, applied only by virtue of the direct indication of the law for the types of activities that are especially dangerous for the environment (for example, hazardous production facilities) and additional, related to the objectives of the protection of certain types of natural objects in the course of economic and other anthropogenic activities (for example, requirements for agricultural legal entities and farmers to take into account fauna protection interests).

The above requirements, contained in both the Law on Environmental Protection and other federal laws, laws of constituent entities of the Russian Federation and bylaws, are detailed and form the institution of the particular part of environmental law. This institution is not new for environmental legislation since it existed in the 1991 Law on Protection of the Natural Environment. Certain rules containing environmental requirements for various types of activities were transferred to the Law on Environmental Protection without any particular changes (Art. 49); a number of other rules were adjusted (Art. 34); some emerged for the first time (Art. 46). In general, this chapter of the Law underwent the least changes (in contrast, for example, to the chapter on economic regulation of environmental protection).

LEGAL REGULATION OF ENVIRONMENTAL PROTECTION OF SETTLEMENTS

Despite the vast area of Russia, it is densely populated in settlements, which occupy only about 1.2 percent of the total area of the country. The residence of a considerable number of people in a small territory leads to many various conflicts of a political, economic, social, environmental and other nature. The dynamic development of these social relations caused the emergence of a special area of environmental protection in environmental law, which has significant distinctive features.

These problems are settled by introducing general urban development requirements for environmental protection of cities, establishing special environmental legal regimes for certain parts of cities (where specially protected natural areas are located), developing additional measures for the protection of certain natural objects (green spaces, water bodies) or restricting certain types of environmentally hazardous activities.

The priority and content of the said activities in a specific city depends on the state of the environment in its territory, the economic situation and the level of environmental legal culture of the relevant officials.

1. Comprehensive protection of ecological systems of settlements is implemented with the use of urban development and legal means. This area is distinguished because the combined emissions and discharges of urban economic entities into the environment, waste disposal in suburban areas, pollution of urban natural resources lead to a cumulative negative effect. Particular types of harmful impact, separately posing low risk to the environment, combining with other ones, form environmentally hazardous substances. This explains not only the need to protect individual parts of settlements or comply with environmental requirements in the course of economic activities but also the development of a comprehensive strategy for protection of the territory of the entire settlements with consideration of the cumulative anthropogenic impact on urban ecosystems. The most efficient way to avoid these environmental problems is the appropriate urban development of settlements as well as environmentally safe placement of hazardous production facilities. It is necessary to distinguish environmental requirements within planning, construction and operation of certain facilities and within planning and development of the territories of the whole municipalities, especially urban ones. The latter task is carried out due to special legal urban development methods and means.

The availability of the urban planning documentation for the development of the territories is an undoubted step forward to ensure sustainable development of urban and rural settlements of the Russian Federation.

The comprehensive measures of urban development are as follows:

a) **Territorial planning:** According to paragraph 1 of Article 9 of the Urban Development Code of the Russian Federation, territorial planning is aimed at determining the purpose of territories in its documents on the basis of a set of social, economic, environmental and other factors with the purpose to ensure sustainable development of territories, development of the engineering, transport and social infrastructures, to ensure the consideration of interests of citizens and their associations, the Russian Federation, constituent entities of the Russian Federation and municipalities. Territorial planning documents can be of three types: those of the Russian Federation; constituent entities of the Russian Federation; municipalities. Territorial planning schemes are developed at the federal level in the following areas: federal (railroad, air, sea, inland waterway, pipeline) transport, federal highways; defense of the country and national security; power industry; higher education, healthcare. Materials substantiating territorial planning schemes of the Russian Federation in the form of maps reflect capital facilities, other facilities, territories, zones which influenced the determination of the planned location of facilities of federal significance, including: special economic zones, specially protected natural areas of federal, regional, local significance; territories of cultural heritage sites; zones with special conditions of use, *etc.*

The project of the territorial planning scheme of the Russian Federation is subject to approval by the supreme state executive authority of the constituent entity of the Russian Federation in the territory of which, in accordance with the said project, it is planned to locate facilities of federal significance, in terms of the possible influence of the planned facilities of federal significance on the socio-economic development of this constituent entity of the Russian Federation, the possible negative impact of these facilities on the environment in the territory of this constituent entity of the Russian Federation.

In its turn, the supreme state executive authority of the constituent entity of the Russian Federation submits the project of the territorial planning scheme of the Russian Federation and the materials substantiating it to the local government bodies of municipalities where it is planned to locate the facilities of federal significance or the environment of which can be affected by the negative impact of the planned facilities of federal significance. Moreover, the materials substantiating the territorial planning schemes of the constituent entity of the

Russian Federation in text form show the data on generation, utilization, neutralization and placement of solid household waste that are contained in the territorial schemes in the area of waste management, including solid household waste management.

The federal and regional levels of urban development determine the strategy for the development of the corresponding territories (of the Russian Federation in general or the constituent entity of the Russian Federation), while the level of direct consideration of the environmental factor in settlements is determined in the urban planning documentation of the local government bodies, including the general layouts of urban districts and settlements. The locations of various facilities of local significance (electricity, heat, gas and water supply for the population, water disposal; local highways; processing, utilization, neutralization, placement of solid household waste, *etc.*) as well as the boundaries of specially protected natural areas, other territories and zones that influenced the choice of locations for these local facilities are marked on the maps that are part of the general layout.

b) **Documents Urban development zoning:** Urban development zoning documents (Land Use and Development Rules) are another type of urban planning documentation, which reflects environmental factors of the development of settlements. The Land Use and Development Rules are the urban development zoning document which is approved by regulatory legal acts of local government bodies, state authorities of constituent entities of the Russian Federation - the cities of federal significance Moscow, Saint Petersburg and Sevastopol. One of the main purposes of the development of the Land Use and Development Rules is to create conditions for sustainable development of the territories of municipalities, save the environment and cultural heritage sites. They include the map of urban development zoning and urban development regulations. Urban development zoning within the boundaries of municipalities results in residential, public and business, production zones, zones of engineering and transport infrastructures, zones of agricultural use, recreational zones, zones of specially protected areas, special-purpose zones, zones of military facilities and some other zones.

There are established urban development regulations for each of these zones, *i.e.*, they determine the types of permitted use of land plots as well as everything that is under and above their surface and is used in the course of their development and subsequent operation of capital facilities, limiting (minimum and (or) maximum) dimensions of land plots and limiting parameters of permitted construction and reconstruction of capital facilities as well as restrictions of the use of land plots and capital facilities.

For example, in accordance with paragraph 3 of Article 35 of the Urban Development Code of the Russian Federation, in residential zones, the urban development regulations allow the placement of free-standing, built-in or attached social and community facilities, healthcare facilities, facilities of pre-school, primary general and secondary (complete) general education, religious buildings, parking lots, garages, facilities related to the residence of citizens and not having a negative impact on the environment.

Consequently, construction of industrial facilities in the middle of residential areas is strictly prohibited by urban development legislation. Moreover, paragraphs 8, 10 of Article 36 of the Urban Development Code of the Russian Federation states that if land plots and capital facilities located on them do not meet the requirements of the urban development regulations in terms of the types of permitted use, dimensions or other parameters, and thus pose a risk to human life and health and the environment, a ban may be imposed on their use. The need to carry out the above complex procedures is due to the special place of the category of land of settlements in the structure of the land fund of the Russian Federation.

c) Area planning. Area planning documentation is prepared to ensure sustainable development of areas, in particular, to distinguish elements of the planning structure, to establish the boundaries of land plots, to establish the boundaries of zones of the planned location of capital facilities. It is obligatory to prepare area planning documentation to locate capital facilities, for example, in case if it is planned to locate capital facilities that are not linear within the boundaries of specially protected natural areas or within the boundaries of the category of land of the forest fund.

The materials substantiating area planning projects indicate also the places of access to common water bodies and their watersides and contain the list of environmental protection measures as well as the scheme of the boundaries of zones with special conditions of use.

d) Architectural and civil engineering. Architectural and civil engineering, construction, reconstruction and capital repairs of capital facilities must involve the consideration of measures to prevent and eliminate environmental pollution, application of resource-saving, low-waste, non-waste and other technologies that help to prevent and eliminate environmental pollution and protect the environment. Commissioning of these facilities is conducted only after full environmental protection measures, including measures to restore the natural environment, remediate or conserve land, that are stipulated by the project documentation of capital facilities.

2) Special environmental requirements in cities include the following measures.

a) Measures to ensure the population's sanitary and epidemiological well-being. Special sanitary rules are developed for this purpose, they include requirements regarding the quantity and types of environmentally hazardous substances in components of the natural environment for prevention of harm to the health of city population. In addition, sanitary protection zones separating plants from residential areas are established within this group of restrictions and prohibitions.

b) Special measures to protect forests and water in settlements.

These measures are necessary because pollution, for example, of the Volga River in sparsely populated areas will lead to dissolution in water and reduction of the concentration of harmful substances. Although this will kill the fish, there may be no harm to human health. On the other hand, if water is polluted close to the drinking water supply intake as well as if city residents swim on the beaches or use contaminated water to irrigate garden plots, this can cause mass diseases of the city residents. To prevent this environmental harm, it is necessary to develop additional measures to protect water resources in settlements or in their immediate vicinity. In a similar manner, the role of green spaces in maintaining a favorable environmental quality of cities is that they act as filters in purifying city air from soot, dust, gas and smoke emitted into the air by industrial enterprises and motor vehicles, enrich the air with oxygen, serve as a means of noise control, have a positive effect on the climate, protect water supply sources from pollution and serve as a place for organized leisure of city residents.

The green fund of urban and rural settlements is a range of areas with forest and other plantations. Urban forests, green zones, forest and parkland zones can be part of the green fund of settlements. All of them are attributed by the Forest Code of the Russian Federation to the category of protection forests, and their use in economic activities is limited. For example, the use of toxic chemicals, hunting, agriculture, construction and operation of capital facilities (except hydraulic structures), *etc.* are prohibited in urban forests or forests of green zones.

Article 62.2 of the Federal Law "On Environmental Protection" pays particular attention to the procedures for creation of the forest green belt. The following activities are prohibited in the areas included in forest green belts: use of toxic chemicals; placement of production and consumption waste of hazard classes I-III; construction of livestock farms; development of mineral deposits, *etc.*

In order to create forest green belts, non-profit organizations, state authorities or local government bodies submit motivated applications for the creation of forest green belts to the public chamber of the corresponding constituent entity of the

Russian Federation in the territory of which it is planned to create the forest green belts. The public chamber of the corresponding constituent entity of the Russian Federation organizes public hearings within 30 days after the receipt of the application for the creation of the forest green belt. Decisions on the creation of forest green belts and their areas or decisions on the refusal of their creation are adopted by state legislative (representative) authorities of constituent entities of the Russian Federation, and in case the forest green belts are created around cities of federal significance or in the territories of several constituent entities of the Russian Federation – by the Government of the Russian Federation. The territories of the green fund of urban and rural settlements are located, as a rule, within the boundaries of recreational zones (Art. 35 of the Urban Development Code of the Russian Federation).

According to the functional purpose, green spaces forming the green fund of urban and rural settlements are located in territories of three types: common territories (public gardens, boulevards, urban forests, *etc.*); territories of limited use (within residential, industrial and other areas); special-purpose territories (sanitary protection and security zones). Protection of the green fund of urban and rural settlements involves a system of measures ensuring safety and development of the system of green spaces necessary to normalize the environmental situation and to create a favorable environment. The said measures can consist in the imposition of duties on citizens and legal entities and implementation of the green fund protection measures by state authorities and local government bodies (for example, local government bodies of Volgograd planted 5,305 green items in 2018). One of areas of activities aimed at greening urban territories is the transition from the strategy of creating individual (single) green islands to the creation (maintenance and restoration) of large green masses. Urban forests occupy a special place among these green spaces in cities. They differ from other forests, first of all, due to the small area of the occupied territory, which is limited to the boundaries of settlements. Moreover, urban forests are created artificially, although there are examples when natural forests that grew on the land occupied by urban settlements underwent great changes and turned into recreational zones.

Along with the protection of green spaces, protection of water bodies located within their boundaries is an essential objective of the protection of the environment of settlements. This interrelation manifests itself in the fact that growth of urban areas increases the anthropogenic load on aquatic ecosystems, which, in its turn, leads to deterioration of the quality of drinking water and increased mortality of the population.

Like in cases of protection of other natural objects, the task of water protection is solved by imposing duties on the subjects of water relations (citizens and legal entities as well as public legal entities), including requirements for economic and other activities, as well as by giving a special environmental legal status to certain water bodies. The legislator points out the distinctive features of the protection of the surface and ground water of cities and regulates both the general order of water protection and specification of these requirements according to the type of activities or location of the source of pollution.

With the purpose of water protection, the law establishes a range of measures to protect the sources of drinking water supply, prohibitions on pollution and littering of water bodies (in Moscow, there are ships collecting garbage and oil spills on the Moskva River), waste disposal within the boundaries of cities is prohibited in order to protect the surface and ground water of settlements, *etc.* The regulation of the regime of ground water use, including urban rivers flowing in pipes underground (the Tsaritsa River in Volgograd) is a particular issue. Harmful substances are accumulated in these rivers without control, and violation of the regime of use and protection of water in cities can lead to the destruction of buildings, flooding of the territories and asphalt sinkholes, which poses a risk to the life, health and property of city residents.

c) Protection of urban fauna. Urban areas may be inhabited by both natural fauna (birds, hedgehogs, frogs) and domestic animals that have lost their owners. City authorities try to protect the first variety of animals (for example, some of them are included in the Red Data Book of Moscow), though many of them are carriers of diseases (rats, birds). Authorities try to cope with stray animals by establishing animal shelters, using sterilization and vaccination. However, there is still the threat to the health of citizens, both with respect to epidemiological indices and from bites from stray animals, and this problem is still far from being solved.

d) Environmental requirements for the preservation of urban specially protected natural areas.

Both common and completely degraded ecosystems can be located within the boundaries of settlements (or whole settlements can be aggregates of these ecosystems). Individual intact natural areas are also likely to be found in cities. The latter, being located in the middle of economic activities of people are the most vulnerable, being exposed to various factors of anthropogenic activities every day. This causes a special approach to the organization of their protection. The status of specially protected natural areas given to a part of the territory of settlements (as well as its inclusion in large specially protected natural areas) entails a range of various legal consequences. Taking into account the main purpose of land of settlements, to serve as a spatial operational basis for residential, industrial, public, business and other areas, it should be noted that these consequences include a change in the possibilities for development of these territories. If specially protected natural areas are located in settlements, the boundaries of protection zones, where economic and other activities that cause harm to specially protected natural areas, the environment in general or worsen their condition, integrity and safety are prohibited or limited, are established. The data on the location of land plots (their parts) within the boundaries of specially protected natural areas are subject to obligatory inclusion in the document certifying the right to the land plots.

Two options are distinguished according the criteria of the practice of placement of specially protected natural areas and settlements. In the first case, specially protected natural areas are located exclusively within the boundaries of settlements (natural monuments, arboretums and botanical gardens). In the second case, specially protected natural areas can include several villages (national parks, nature parks, reserves). For example, in the territory of national parks, in the settlements located within their borders, particular restrictions can be introduced for development of the territory (in case other objects are supposed to be located in the corresponding functional zone). Bans are imposed on the provision of gardens and vegetable patches, as well as on the construction of roads, pipelines, power lines and other economic and residential facilities not related to the functioning of national parks. Therefore, the creation of specially protected natural areas within the boundaries of urban or rural settlements leads to the establishment in those territories of a particular environmental legal regime combining environmental, land and urban development features. Its general sense consists in the establishment of restrictions on development (urban development legislation), economic use (environmental legislation), acquisition of rights to land and transferability of land plots which are given the status of specially protected natural areas and their protective zones (land legislation).

In addition, it should be pointed out that the creation of any specially protected natural areas in settlements does not lead to the emergence of land plots of the category of land of specially protected natural areas and sites within the boundaries of settlements. This conclusion follows from Article 83 of the Land Code of the Russian Federation, according to which "the boundaries of urban and rural settlements separate land of settlements from land of other categories". This is why the creation of arboretums, natural monuments or specially protected natural areas of other types within the boundaries of settlements will lead to their inclusion in a special territorial zone with the establishment of the corresponding regime of prohibitions and restrictions.

ENVIRONMENTAL REQUIREMENTS IN MILITARY AND DEFENSE ACTIVITIES

The Armed Forces of the Russian Federation are one of the largest users of natural resources. 12.8 million hectares of land, including 5.1 million hectares of forests with military garrisons, training grounds, airfields, warehouses and other military and defense facilities, are assigned to the Ministry of Defense of Russia. According to some data, about 0.8 percent of harmful emissions in the Russian Federation belong to the Armed Forces of the Russian Federation. Military and defense activities can be considered in two aspects: as the source of pollution of the environment and as an object of protection from impact of the polluted environment.

In the first sense, military activities are as follows:

1. activities carried out by defense industrial enterprises during production of military products;
2. everyday activities of the Armed Forces of the Russian Federation in the places of permanent deployment, in the course of training, maneuvering, combat duties, *etc.*

The below types of activities cause the greatest harm to nature.

1. Rocket and space activities. For example, significant areas in Arkhangelsk Region are contaminated with metal structures and residues of toxic components of rocket fuel as a result of numerous launches of rockets from Plesetsk Cosmodrome. The Ministry of Defense of the Russian Federation is to compensate the owners of land plots, land users, land possessors and tenants for direct property damage resulting from falling separating rocket parts, according to the reports of specially established commissions, and executive authorities of constituent entities of the Russian Federation are to allocate land plots to the Ministry of Defense of the Russian Federation for separating rocket parts falling during rocket launches from cosmodromes, launch facilities and bases of intercontinental ballistic missiles of the Ministry of Defense of the Russian Federation.

2. Burial of toxic and highly toxic waste in the seas. In 1945-1947 English, American, and Soviet commanders sank about 400,000 tons of trophy and their own munitions with toxic agents (mustard gas, phosgene and so forth) in the Baltic and North Seas. The operation was carried out without the necessary measures ensuring environmental safety. The allies mistakenly believed that the

chemical munitions would be covered with a thick layer of silt and would be mothballed. These expectations did not come true. The containers have been significantly destroyed by corrosion and there is a great risk of large-scale contamination of the said seas – from about 50 to 100 thousand tons of chemicals can get into the water. The USSR applied burials also later, and the exact location of dozens of emergency compartments of nuclear submarines replaced in the course of their repairs is not known. There is evidence that there are about 17,000 burial sites for radioactive and other hazardous waste in the northern seas. In the 1990s, activities for burial of munitions at sea were officially prohibited by Decree of the Government of the Russian Federation No. 710 of July 23, 1993 "On Measures for Comprehensive Settlement of the Issue of Handling Radioactive Waste and Cessation of Burial of Radioactive Waste at Sea".

3. Destruction of nuclear, chemical and bacteriological weapons. There were seven main storage sites for chemical weapons in the Russian Federation for many years: Shikhany village (Saratov Region), Mardykovsky village (Kirov Region), Leonidovka village (Penza Region), Pochep city (Bryansk Region), Shchuchye city (Kurgan Region), Kizner village and Kambarka city (Udmurtian Republic). The destruction of chemical weapons at these sites, often located in the immediate vicinity of settlements, repeatedly gave rise to public discontent due to the real or supposed negative impact on the health of the citizens. This led to numerous protests under environmental mottos (the situation around the Shikhany site for destruction of chemical weapons in Saratov Region was particularly tense). The adoption of additional safety measures and the participation of foreign observers in the destruction procedures eventually made it possible to neutralize the situation. The destruction of chemical weapons has been already finished and this problem is solved.

4. Tests of new weapons at sites. For example, 124 nuclear blasts, including 19 above-ground blasts, took place at the Semipalatinsk Test Site in 1949-1963. These nuclear tests had an enormous negative impact on the health of citizens and their children living in the immediate vicinity of the test site. Federal Law No. 2-FZ of January 10, 2002 "On Social Guarantees for Citizens Exposed to Radiation as a Result of Nuclear Tests at the Semipalatinsk Test Site" was adopted for the purpose of social protection of the affected persons. Such tests were carried out also in other places. For example, a nuclear bomb with an explosive power of 40 kilotons of TNT equivalent was detonated in the course of combined arms exercises at the Totsk Test Site in Orenburg Region in September 1954. The explosion resulted in the formation of two main contamination zones: the epicenter area with a radius of 20 km and the nearest

radioactive trace at a distance of 210 km (in the northeast direction). As there was no information about the contamination of the area for a long time, the radiation consequences of the explosion had a negative impact on the health of thousands of people, and they have not received compensation. Nuclear weapons were repeatedly tested at the Tsentralny Test Site of the Russian Federation (the Novaya Zemlya islands). There was no special legal act adopted in relation to compensation for harm to the health of that military personnel for a long time.

In 2016, Order of the Minister of Defense of the Russian Federation No. 590 of September 22, 2016 was adopted to restore justice. It instructed to determine the procedure and conditions for issue of certificates to citizens from the special risk units in order to extend to them the social benefits and compensations for persons affected by radiation as a result of the accident at the Chernobyl NPP.

5. Electromagnetic radiation pollution of the environment as a result of the extensive use of radio-technical facilities in the Armed Forces of the Russian Federation. For example, there were excesses of permissible values of electromagnetic fields in Severodvinsk, Monchegorsk and other garrisons.

The above list related to the impact of the Armed Forces of the Russian Federation on the environment and the health of the population is not exhaustive. Scientific literature mentions the negative impact on the environment in connection with oil leaks from military warehouses, the lack of modern cleaning means (or their non-use) in a certain number of boiler houses in troop deployment areas, pollution of air with exhausts from vehicles including armored vehicles, pollution of the water areas of naval bases by whole and sunken ships and vessels to be scrapped, *etc.* One of the problems discussed in environmental legal science is the issue of compensation for harm caused by explosion of old ammunition. In this regard, Article 41 of the Federal Law "On Environmental Protection" reasonably emphasizes: the environmental requirements established by law for civilian capital facilities apply to military and defense facilities, weapons and military equipment to the same extent. There are two exceptions to this rule. The first exception relates to emergencies which may lawfully prevent the Armed Forces of the Russian Federation from fulfilling environmental requirements. The list of these emergencies is determined by the federal law. Another exception is the need to keep state secrets (public environmental expert reviews are not conducted in relation to military facilities for this reason).

To increase the efficiency of nature protection activities, the Minister of Defense of the Russian Federation issued Order No. 530 of September 14, 2015 "On Approval of the Provision on Environmental Security Bodies of the Armed Forces of the Russian Federation". According to paragraph 4 of this Order, environmental safety bodies of the Armed Forces of the Russian Federation include the (environmental safety) service of the Armed Forces Headquarters, environmental safety services of military districts, environmental safety services of fleets, environmental safety services of associations and formations, regional environmental centers of military districts and environmental safety services (officials) of military units. The purpose of environmental safety bodies is to reduce (prevent) the negative impact of military facilities, pieces of armament and military equipment on personnel and social infrastructure facilities, to prevent and eliminate the environmental consequences of natural and man-made emergencies at military facilities during daily activities of the troops. Moreover, the objectives of environmental safety bodies include clean-up (remediation) of the territories of military facilities from contamination during daily activities of the Armed Forces of the Russian Federation, as well as training military and civilian personnel in environmental protection bodies and the formation of their environmental culture.

Having mentioned many environmental problems related to military defense activities, we should also point out the consequences from activities of the Armed Forces of the Russian Federation that are positive for nature. They consist in the fact that there are preserved populations of bustards, marmots and many other rare animals and plants in numerous training grounds, which are close for economic activities and hunting. Such "military reserves" are observed also along the state border of the Russian Federation, where there is no free access.

ENVIRONMENTAL REQUIREMENTS FOR THE ESTABLISHMENT OF ZONES WITH SPECIAL CONDITIONS OF USE

The category of "zones with special conditions of use" first emerged in Article 1 of the Urban Development Code of the Russian Federation and started being widely used in urban development legislation. It was subsequently specified in Article 105 of the Land Code of the Russian Federation stipulating 28 types of various "special zones". Part of them is not related to environmental protection (for example, zones of protected military facilities), part is related indirectly (for example, flooded and waterlogged zones) and, finally, the third part of zones with special conditions of use is directly aimed at resolving environmental issues. Within the boundaries of zones with special conditions of use, restrictions and prohibitions are established for placement and (or) use of immovable property located on these land plots and for the activities that are incompatible with the purposes of the establishment of zones with special conditions of use. In addition, as a general rule, the land plots included in the zones with special conditions of use are not withdrawn from their owners.

According to the purpose of their establishment, all environmentally significant "spccial zoncs" can be divided into three groups:

a. Zones intended for protection of sites from anthropogenic pollution or harmful physical impact from outside. These sites include, for example, specially protected natural areas.
b. Zones established for protection of population and territories from negative impact of hazardous industrial facilities (for example, sanitary protection zones).
c. Zones established simultaneously for two purposes: protection of facilities from external impact and protection of the environment from negative impact of the facilities themselves (for example, transport protective zones).

Let us consider the legal regime of five most important zones.

1) Sanitary protection zones. Sanitary protection zones are established in relation to the capital facilities that operate, are reconstructed or to be constructed and are the sources of chemical, physical and biological impact on the human environment if their impact exceeds the sanitary and epidemiological requirements. These can be various industrial facilities (especially hazardous industrial facilities), agricultural facilities (livestock farms), nuclear power facilities and many other facilities. Sanitary protection zones create a barrier between environmentally hazardous production facilities and residential areas as well as other social facilities, restricting the possibility of the use of this territory and mitigating the consequences of negative impact of production facilities on the environment. This ensures safety of the population during the operation of the facilities under normal conditions.

The Federal Service for the Oversight of Consumer Protection and Welfare (Rospotrebnadzor) or its territorial bodies make decisions on the establishment, change or termination of the existence of sanitary protection zones. Within the boundaries of sanitary protection zones, it is not allowed to use land plots to locate residential buildings, educational and medical facilities, open-air sports facilities, organizations for recreation of children and their health improvement, recreational zones, as well as to do the gardening, locate facilities for production and storage of medicines, food industry facilities, wholesale warehouses for alimentary raw materials and food products, waterworks complexes for preparation and storage of drinking water, use of land plots for production, storage and processing of agricultural products intended for further use as food products.

Sanitary protection zones and the restrictions on the use of land plots located within their boundaries are considered to be established from the day of record of the data about these zones in the Unified State Register of Immovable Property. The issues related to creation of sanitary protection zones are regulated by the Sanitary Rules (bylaws, in particular, decrees of the Chief Sanitary Doctor of the Russian Federation – the Head of Rospotrebnadzor). According to them, all industrial enterprises, their separate buildings and structures, on the basis of the capacity, conditions of the implementation of the technological process, the nature and the extent of the harmful impact, are divided into five classes, for which the corresponding dimensions of sanitary protection zones are established: 1000, 500, 300, 100 and 50 meters. The criterion for determination of the dimensions of sanitary protection zones is non-exceedance the MPCs for pollutants for air of settlements as well as the MPLs for impact on air on their external borders and beyond them.

Measures for greening of the territory of sanitary protection zones are taken to reduce the negative impact. Sanitary protection zones can be located on land of several categories, as a rule, land of settlements and land of special purpose.

2) Protective zones. As already mentioned above, there are two types of protective zones. The first type (protective zones of specially protected natural areas) are to protect valuable natural systems from anthropogenic activities of people. These protective zones are created around reserves, national parks, nature parks and natural monuments on the adjacent land plots and water bodies. Within the boundaries of protective zones, it is prohibited to carry out activities that have a negative (harmful) impact on the ecological state of the corresponding natural systems. The minimum width of the protective zones of state nature reserves or national parks is one kilometer.

Similarly to specially protected natural areas, the status of territories with a special legal regime is given also to protective zones of hydrometeorological facilities.

For reliable information about the condition of the environment and its pollution around stationary observation points, protective zones are created in the form of land plots and parts of water areas limited in the site drawing by a closed line which is separated from the boundaries of these points, as a rule, at a distance of 200 meters in all directions. In protective zones of stationary environmental observation points, there are established restrictions on economic activities which can affect the reliability of information about the condition of the environment (its pollution).

The second type of protective zones resolves two issues – protection of valuable economic objects from external impact and protection of the environment and human health from the impact of these objects themselves. A typical case of this variety of zones is protective zones of the main transport routes created to prevent economic and other activities that can lead to the destruction of highways or railroads (for example, due to excavation works) since this can cause a range of negative environmental consequences. The purposes of the creation of protective zones around power facilities are similar. For example, in protective zones of hydropower facilities, their safe operation requires compulsory approval of mineral exploration and mining, organization of recreation, construction of berths, bridges, refloating, dredging, blasting, *etc.*

3) Water (fish) protective zones. According to Article 65 of the Water Code of the Russian Federation, water protective zones are territories adjacent to the coastline of seas, rivers, streams, channels, lakes and reservoirs in which a special regime of economic and other activities is established in order to prevent pollution, littering, siltation of these water bodies and depletion of their water, as well as to preserve the habitat of aquatic biological resources and other fauna and flora. Within the boundaries of water protective zones, coastal protection belts are established, and in their territories there are additional restrictions of economic and other activities.

The width of the water protective zone of seas, rivers, streams, channels, lakes and reservoirs outside the territories of cities and other settlements are established from the corresponding coastline. The width of the water protective zone of rivers or streams is established from their source for rivers or streams with a length of up to 10 km – 50 m; from 10 to 50 km – 100 m; from 50 km and more – 200 m. Within the boundaries of water protective zones, it is prohibited to locate cemeteries, cattle burial grounds, disposal facilities for production and consumption waste, chemical, explosive, toxic, poisonous and toxic substances, burial sites for radioactive waste; to take aviation measures to control pests; to drive and park vehicles; to construct and reconstruct filling stations, warehouses for fuel and lubricant materials, to locate specialized storage facilities for pesticides and agrochemicals, to apply them, *etc.*

Within the boundaries of water protective zones, it is allowed to design, construct, reconstruct, commission, operate economic and other facilities subject to equipment of these facilities with structures ensuring protection of water bodies from pollution, littering, siltation and water depletion. In order to preserve the conditions for reproduction of aquatic biological resources, the fish protective zones are established, and in their territories there are restrictions of economic and other activities. Fish protective zones are the territories adjacent to the water areas of water bodies of commercial fishing importance. The dimensions of fish protective zones and the list of restrictions of economic and other activities in general corresponds with the parameters of water protective zones.

4) Sanitary security zones of the sources of drinking and domestic water supply. These zones are created on the basis of decisions of executive authorities of constituent entities of the Russian Federation. Sanitary security zones are organized for all water pipelines regardless of departmental affiliation, supplying water from both surface and ground sources. The main purpose of creating and maintaining the regime in sanitary security zones is sanitary protection of the water supply sources and facilities as well as the territories in which they are located from contamination. Sanitary security zones are organized within three belts. For example, the first belt (of the strict regime) includes the territory of water intake, sites of all water supply facilities and water supply canals. Its purpose is to protect the place of water intake and water intake facilities from accidental or deliberate contamination and damage. The second and third belts (of restrictions) include the territory intended to prevent contamination of water of the water supply sources. According to Article 44 of the Water Code of the Russian Federation, it is prohibited to discharge wastewater into water bodies within the boundaries of sanitary security zones of the sources of drinking and domestic water supply.

5) Districts of sanitary (mountain sanitary) security. Districts of mountain sanitary security are a particular variety of protective zones, they are established around therapeutic and recreational areas and resorts, which today are not varieties of specially protected natural areas. According to paragraph 3 of Article 16 of the Federal Law of February 23, 1995 "On Natural Healing Resources, Therapeutic and Recreational Areas and Resorts", districts of sanitary (mountain sanitary) security include up to three zones. In the territory of the first zone, it is prohibited to reside and to carry out all types of economic activities, excluding works related to the studies and the use of natural healing resources for therapeutic and recreational purposes, subject to application of environmentally friendly and rational technologies. In the territory of the second zone, it is prohibited to locate facilities and structures not related directly to the creation and development of the area of health resort treatment and recreation as well as to carry out works polluting the environment and natural healing resources and leading to their depletion. In the territory of the third zone, there are restrictions on location of industrial and agricultural organizations and structures as well as on economic activities accompanied by pollution of the environment and natural healing resources and their depletion.

ENVIRONMENTAL REQUIREMENTS IN PRODUCTION AND CONSUMPTION WASTE MANAGEMENT

The issue of waste disposal has long gone beyond the national framework and become a global, worldwide issue. Its relevance to the Russian Federation is due to the fact that in 2018 in the territory of Russia there were 7,266,000 tons of waste, in general for the period of 2010-2018 the amount of waste increased by 94.5 percent. The main contribution to the total amount of waste is made by waste of hazard classes 4 and 5, *i.e.*, almost non-hazardous or low-hazardous waste (98.2 percent of the total amount of the waste generated in the country). In case of solid household waste, 87 percent is moved to burial sites (landfills), over 2 percent – to waste incineration plants, and a little over 10 percent of waste was transported to waste incineration plants (Report, 2019).

Despite valuable fractions in solid household waste, in the course of their burial at least 9 million tons of waste paper, 2 million tons of polymeric materials and 0.5 million tons of glass are irretrievably lost every year. Today about 15 thousand authorized waste disposal sites occupy a total area of about 4 million hectares in Russia, and this territory increases annually by 300-400 thousand hectares. Waste storage places (landfills and dumps) are sources of the negative impact on the environment, and not only in relation to land and soil but also air, because of decomposition of certain types of waste and fires that are difficult to extinguish, and water resources (especially groundwater), when harmful substances enter them from the surface of the earth. Waste landfills often serve also as a source of “biological pollution” as they contribute to the reproduction of rats, cause unwanted swarms of birds, stray animals, *etc.* Small unauthorized waste dumps, which are numerous and poorly controlled by municipal authorities, also have a material negative impact on the environment.

Two Articles of the Federal Law “On Environmental Protection” and two separate Federal Laws, No. 89-FZ of June 24, 1998 “On Production and Consumption Waste” and No. 190-FZ of July 11, 2011 “On the Management of Radioactive Waste and Amendments to Certain Legislative Acts of the Russian Federation”, are dedicated to waste management issues. Production and consumption waste are substances or subjects which are generated in the course of production, during performance of works, provision of services or in the course of consumption, which are removed, intended to be removed or subject to removal. Accordingly, waste management is activities for waste collection, accumulation, transportation, processing, utilization, neutralization and placement. Waste is not the same with respect to its environmental hazard, this is why the legislator makes its classification, which implies clear legal consequences regarding its management:

1) According to the criterion of origin, production waste and consumption waste are distinguished. The former poses the greater environmental hazard.

2) According to the degree of hazard to the environment and human health, waste is divided into five classes, including: class I – extremely hazardous waste (for example, containing mercury); II – highly hazardous waste (for example, waste battery acid); III – moderately hazardous waste (metallurgical slag, waste machine oil); IV – low-hazardous waste (asbestos waste); V – almost non-hazardous waste.

This classification is greatly significant for determination of the need to obtain a license to carry out activities in the field of waste management. At the moment, licensing is necessary for activities for collection, transportation, processing, utilization, neutralization and placement of waste of hazard classes I-IV. Activities for management of waste of hazard class V is not subject to licensing.

Another difference of waste of hazard classes I-IV and V consists in the fact that waste certificates must be issued for waste of classes I-IV. Most of waste of hazard class V is solid household waste, its management has its own distinctive features. Solid household waste is the waste generated in residential premises in the course of consumption by individuals as well as the goods that have lost their consumer properties in the course of their use by individuals in residential premises for satisfaction of their personal or domestic needs. Solid household waste also include waste generated in the course of activities of legal entities and individual entrepreneurs, their content is similar to the waste generated in residential premises in the course of consumption by individuals. For management of this category of waste, regional operators carrying out the corresponding activities are created in constituent entities of the Russian Federation. The status of regional operator is given for 10 years. In its turn, management of waste of classes I and II is implemented by a special organization – the federal operator. Today, this is the Federal State Unitary Enterprise "Radioactive Waste Management Enterprise "RosRAO". From the above it follows that the legislator stipulates two exceptions to the general rule of waste management (this type of environmental entrepreneurship can be performed by any organization that meets the statutory requirements): for waste of hazard classes I-II and for solid household waste.

The most general requirements in the field of production and consumption waste management are as follows:

1) In design, construction, reconstruction, capital repairs of buildings, structures and other facilities, in the course of operation of which waste is generated, it is necessary to plan places (sites) for accumulation of such waste. It is prohibited to commission buildings and other facilities that are related to waste management

and are not equipped with technical means and technologies for neutralization and safe placement of waste.

2) The place of construction of waste disposal sites is determined on the basis of special (geological, hydrological and other) studies. Special sanitary protection zones are established around waste disposal sites. The place of construction of solid household waste disposal sites is selected according to the Territorial Scheme of Waste Management.

3) In the territories of waste disposal sites and within the limits of their impact on the environment, the owners of the waste disposal sites as well as the persons who possess or use these sites are obliged to monitor the state and pollution of the environment.

4) It is prohibited to bury waste within the borders of settlements, forest and parkland, resort, therapeutic and recreational zones as well as water protective zones, in the catchment areas of ground water bodies which are used for drinking and domestic water supply purposes. It is prohibited to bury it in places of mineral deposits and mining operations if there are a threat of pollution of mineral deposits and a treat to safety of mining operations.

5) Waste disposal sites are recorded in the state register of waste disposal sites.

6) Burial of waste which include useful components to be utilized is prohibited.

7) Territorial schemes of waste management and the federal scheme of solid household waste management are approved to organize and carry out activities for accumulation (including sorting), collection, transportation, processing, utilization, neutralization and placement of waste. The territorial scheme of waste management is developed and approved by authorized executive authorities of constituent entities of the Russian Federation in accordance with territorial planning documents. This scheme must include data on the location of the sources of waste generation in the territories of constituent entities of the Russian Federation (and the sources of its generation are to be marked on the maps of the constituent entities of the Russian Federation); data on the quantity of the waste generated in the territories of constituent entities of the Russian Federation with a breakdown by types and hazard classes of waste; data on the location of places of accumulation of waste in the territories of constituent entities of the Russian Federation, *etc.* The federal scheme of solid household waste management includes information contained in territorial schemes of waste management and related to solid household waste management.

8) Individual entrepreneurs and legal entities carrying out activities in the course of which waste of hazard classes I-V is generated are obliged to attribute the corresponding waste to a specific hazard class. The attribution of waste of hazard classes I-V to a specific hazard class is confirmed by the federal executive authority authorized by the Government of the Russian Federation.

9) In order to ensure protection of the environment and human health and to reduce the amount of waste, the regulations for waste generation and the limits for its disposal are established with respect to legal entities and individual entrepreneurs carrying out economic and other activities leading to waste generation.

10) The construction, reconstruction and technical re-equipment of facilities for the processing, utilization, neutralization and placement of waste of hazard classes I and II are implemented by federal operators for the management of waste of hazard classes I and II according to a specifically approved investment program.

11) It is prohibited to import waste of hazard classes I-IV to the Russian Federation to bury and neutralize it. It is also prohibited to import radioactive waste to the Russian Federation to store, process or bury it, but there are already some exceptions, which should be considered in detail. One of these exceptions is stipulated by paragraph 4 of Article 48 of the Law of the Russian Federation "On Environmental Protection", it is the possibility to allow import of irradiated heat-generating nuclear reactor assemblies to the Russian Federation from foreign countries for temporary technological storage and (or) their processing if in relation to the corresponding project state environmental expert reviews and other state expert reviews stipulated by legislation of the Russian Federation have been conducted, the general reduction of radiation exposure risk and increased environmental safety as a result of the implementation of the corresponding project have been substantiated. However, even if federal laws did not mention the possibility to import hazardous and radioactive waste to the Russian Federation, this activity is not excluded by virtue of the provisions of paragraph 4 of Article 15 of the Constitution, according to which "if an international agreement of the Russian Federation establishes rules other than those stipulated by law, the rules of the international agreement apply". For example, in case of supplies of fuel for nuclear power plants to foreign countries, international agreements quite often stipulated also the duty of the USSR (and then the Russian Federation) to accept back the radioactive waste. Rules of international agreements ratified by the Russian Federation but not the rules of the Federal Law "On Environmental Protection" of January 10, 2002 apply in these cases.

The Federal Law "On Production and Consumption Waste" determines the general waste management rules, which are specified by other regulations. They stipulate the distinctive features of management of radioactive waste, biological waste, medical waste, substances destroying the ozone layer, emissions of harmful substances into the atmosphere and discharges of harmful substances into subsoil and water bodies. For example, with respect to medical waste, these distinctive features are specified in Article 49 of Federal Law No. 323-FZ of November 21, 2011 "On the Fundamentals of Protection of the Health of Citizens in the Russian Federation". This Article divides medical waste according to the degree of its epidemiological, toxicological and radiation hazard as well as its negative impact on the environment into the following classes: "a" epidemiologically safe waste, its composition is similar to solid household waste; "b" epidemiologically hazardous waste; "c" extremely epidemiologically hazardous waste; "d" toxicologically hazardous waste, its composition is similar to industrial waste; "e" radioactive waste. Special SanPiN (Sanitary Rules and Regulations) are dedicated to management of this waste (Decree of the Chief Sanitary Doctor of the Russian Federation No. 163 of December 9, 2010 "On Approval of SanPiN 2.1.7.2790-10 'Sanitary and Epidemiological Requirements for Medical Waste Management'").

To sum up, we should note that the understanding of waste underlying environmental legislation, both useless and harmful substances to be removed and placed in special landfills, is justified only for today's historical moment and level of technological development. In foreign countries, which have well developed mechanisms of separate waste collection, 50-70 percent of waste is useful raw materials for the processing industry. In the countries which approach the transition to circular economy standards (Sweden), the amount of recyclable waste is close to 95-99 percent, and in the understanding of Russia there is almost no waste. In addition, it is impossible to make decisions regarding some types of waste at the national level (concerning space debris or pollution of the ocean), which requires international cooperation.

ENVIRONMENTAL REQUIREMENTS IN TRANSPORT

Five types of transport are distinguished at the moment: road, railroad, air, water and pipeline transport. For the said types of transport there are both general environmental requirements and requirements stipulated only for a specific type of transport. The general environmental requirements are as follows:

a) For road, railroad, air and water transport there are established general environmental requirements for industrial production of means of transportation, standards for their safe use (fuel requirements) as well as (except for water transport) established protective zones for protection of transport systems from external threats.

b) Established special requirements for transportation of hazardous waste, chemical and radioactive substances, *etc.*, which results in the introduction of additional requirements for the operation of means of transportation in order to reduce the possibility of leakage (loss) of hazardous harmful substances.

c) In relation to road, railroad, air and water transport, there are regular checks for compliance with technical regulations for emissions of pollutants into the atmosphere.

Within each type of transport, there are also established specific requirements for environmental safety in the course of its operation.

a) Road transport. The first area of the state environmental policy in the field of road transport is the reduction of harmful impact of transport on the environment by increasing the share of environmentally friendly vehicles and the transition to global environmental standards Euro-6 (Russia shifted to Euro-5 standards on January 1, 2016) in the operation of road transport. The transition of transport to new types of environmentally friendly fuel is regulated by the special Technical Regulation of the Customs Union "On Requirements for Automobile and Aviation Gasoline, Diesel and Marine Fuel, Jet Fuel and Heating Oil" of October 18, 2011. Within this area, Russia shifts to the use of alternative types of fuel, in particular, natural gas, for vehicles.

These measures are due to the limited world reserves of oil, the need to reduce greenhouse gas emissions, the possibility to expand the export of oil and petroleum products due to the resources released in the domestic market after the replacement of liquid motor fuels with gas fuel as well as the significant experience in the production of vehicles with gas engines and gas-cylinder equipment. The most promising plan within this area is the transition to electric vehicles, *i.e.*, vehicles that use electric drives with one or several electric motors instead of internal combustion engines, these electric motors are powered by self-contained power sources. Electric vehicles do not produce noise or emissions of harmful substances into the atmosphere. The difficulty in their development is the lack of a network of charging stations in Russia as well as the unresolved technical problem of the small distance of functioning.

The second area is the development of the mechanism of compensatory financing of the generation of waste in the form of tires and abandoned old vehicles. For these purposes, the Federal Law "On Production and Consumption Waste" (Art. 24.1) stipulates that the recycling fee is paid for each wheeled vehicle imported to

Russia or manufactured in Russia to ensure environmental safety, including protection of human health and the environment from the harmful impact resulting from the operation of vehicles, taking into account their technical characteristics and wear. Accordingly, the environmental fee is paid for "tires and air chambers" (Art. 24.5 of the Law).

The third area is the construction of new transport junctions in cities, which reduces traffic jams and emissions into the atmosphere. We should point out the construction of bypass highways due to which transit transport does not enter settlements.

The fourth area is the establishment of roadsides of highways (25-150 meters) with a limited regime of use.

In addition to road transport, the environment is negatively affected by fuel stations servicing road transport, car washes, service stations, motor depots, garages and other facilities that have a negative impact on the environment as a result of unauthorized waste disposal, wastewater discharges and soil pollution.

b) Railroad transport. Federal Law No. 17-FZ of January 10, 2003 "On Railroad Transport in the Russian Federation" (Art. 22.1) establishes the duty of the infrastructure owners, carriers and organizations, individual entrepreneurs providing auxiliary services during transportation by rail to carry out works to ensure environmental safety in public railroad transport and sanitary and epidemiological well-being of the population. Protective zones are established to ensure safe operation of railroad tracks and other railroad transport facilities and safety of the population, railroad workers and passengers in areas prone to landslides, rockslides, washaways, mudflows and other negative impact and in places of high-speed trains (Art. 9).

A range of environmental requirements in the field of use of railroad transport are provided for in Technical Regulation No. 710 of July 15, 2011 "On the Safety of Railroad Transport Infrastructure". According to this document, design of railroad transport infrastructure facilities must involve the consideration of regulations for permissible anthropogenic load on the environment, measures to prevent and eliminate environmental pollution as well as methods of production and consumption waste disposal, application of resource-saving, low-waste, non-waste and other modern technologies which contribute to environmental protection, restoration of the natural environment and rational use and reproduction of natural resources. Design, construction and commissioning of railroad transport infrastructure facilities must involve the consideration of measures ensuring preservation of the migration routes of wild animals and their permanent habitats, including in breeding and wintering periods. Operation of railroad transport facilities often results in everyday land pollution due to garbage dumping along the relevant highways. Moreover, spilled fuel and oils contaminate soil and are washed away by rain into water reservoirs. Train crashes, when hazardous goods from destroyed freight cars and tanks get into the soil and water bodies, are a particular threat from the operation of railroad transport.

c) Air transport. The main environmental threats from air transport consist in the fact that airports have a negative acoustic impact on the environment (noise), create electromagnetic fields, contaminate the soil with oil and fuel residues and pollute the air. The main environmental restrictions are stipulated by Article 47 of the Air Code of the Russian Federation. According to this Article, there are "airfield environs" with a special legal regime. The main purpose of their establishment is to limit the use of land plots and other immovable property items in the territories adjacent to the airfield to ensure safety of flights. These requirements include the limitation of the number of stories of buildings in the adjacent territories, placement of facilities that can interfere with the operation of ground services and aircraft, prohibition of hazardous production facilities, facilities that contribute to the attraction and mass gathering of birds (prohibition of waste dumps near airfields), *etc.* Special mention should be made of such pollution as airplane de-icing in airports. In 2016, Rosprirodnadzor clarified in a special letter that the drainage systems that remove excessively applied or spilled chemicals to the treatment facilities must be in working order. The treatment facilities must ensure sewage sanitation, preventing contamination of the water bodies and the surface. No leakage to the environment is permitted during storage and pumping of chemicals. Due to the fact that the use of chemicals is widespread, the territorial bodies of Rosprirodnadzor were instructed to check compliance with environmental rules and requirements for handling chemicals during routine inspections.

d) Water transport. The main environmental threat is accidents and leakages (ignition) of oil, with possible contamination of urban drinking water supply systems, the risk of death of aquatic (fish) and semi-aquatic living organisms (including birds). The basic environmental requirements in water (sea and river) transport were adopted in 1973 by the International Maritime Organization (IMO), an agency of the United Nations that developed the International Convention for the Prevention of Pollution from Ships supplemented with the 1978 Protocol. The Convention contains six annexes dedicated to the prevention of sea pollution by oil, control of pollution during transportation of noxious liquid substances, cargo containers and tanks, prevention of pollution of water bodies by sewage and garbage and air pollution. The said provisions of international law were followed in the Inland Water Transport Code of the Russian Federation No. 24-FZ of March 7, 2001 and also reflected in section 6 of Order of the Ministry of

Transport of the Russian Federation No. 463 of October 26, 2017 "On Approval of the General Rules of Navigation and Mooring of Vessels in and on Approaches to Sea Ports of the Russian Federation".

e) Main pipelines. The development of special environmental requirements for pipeline transport facilities is necessary because pipelines belong to hazardous production facilities. Ignition of oil, gas or other products in case of pipeline damage, open fire and thermal impact of this fire, smoke, soil contamination by toxic products (for example, oil) from pipelines or water bodies pose a hazard in case of an accident if the pipelines are under water. The construction of main pipelines itself leads to a range of negative environmental consequences. They include destruction of forests, the fertile layer of soil, pollution of adjacent land by construction debris and other waste and disruption of migration routes of wild animals. Protective zones with a special legal regime are established to reduce the environmental hazard of already built pipelines. In these zones, it is completely prohibited to arrange dumps, emit and discharge caustic, aggressive corrosive substances and fuel and lubricant materials; to carry out recreational activities, make fires and place fire sources; to fence and obstruct protective zones; to locate buildings and structures not related to the pipeline service facilities, *etc.* Some types of activities in protective zones are possible but only subject to notification and consent to these activities of the organization operating the pipeline. For example, in protective zones, the owners of land plots can carry out field works and works related to temporary flooding of irrigated agricultural land upon prior written notice to the owner of the main pipeline or the organization operating the pipeline.

ENVIRONMENTAL REQUIREMENTS IN AGRICULTURE

The harmful impact of agricultural production on nature was underestimated for many years, but since the 1960s agriculture has come to the fore in environmental pollution. This is due to two main reasons. First, construction of livestock farms and complexes with no treatment of the resulting waste. For example, only one pig-breeding complex for 100 thousand animals or a cattle complex for 35 thousand animals can cause pollution equal to environmental pollution produced by a large industrial center with a population of 400-500 thousand residents (Timofeev, 2003).

Second, violation of rules and regulations of the use of mineral fertilizers and pesticides, which together with rainfall and groundwater often entered rivers, lakes and other surface water bodies, thereby causing damage to both water bodies themselves and fish resources and fauna and flora of water bodies. This is why a new main area of the interaction between ecology and economy has emerged in theory and practice of environmental protection – the protection of the environment and the health of citizens in the field of agricultural production. This area is implemented by imposing a range of duties in the field of environmental protection and rational use of natural resources during the economic activities on the subjects of agricultural production (farmers, agricultural cooperatives and other producers of agricultural goods).

The following options of the protection of the environment and the health of citizens from the negative impact of agricultural production can be distinguished within this area: protection of the environment during the operation of agricultural facilities; protection of the environment during land reclamation; protection of the environment in the field of chemicalization of agriculture; protection of nature from the use of GMOs and during the cultivation of organic products.

Environmental protection in agriculture is the activities of state authorities of the Russian Federation and its constituent entities, local government bodies, legal entities and individuals aimed at preserving and restoring soil fertility, using rationally land and other natural resources, preventing the negative impact of agricultural production on the environment, producing organic products and ensuring food security.

1) Environmental requirements for the operation of agricultural facilities. Environmental legislation does not clarify the concept of agricultural facilities. Other federal laws (for example, the Tax Code of the Russian Federation) or bylaws provide no exhaustive list of these facilities either, only mentioning "livestock farms", "reclamation facilities", "internal water pipelines" and a range of other facilities among agricultural facilities.

A more complete list of agricultural facilities is included in the Sanitary Rules – the regulations establishing sanitary and epidemiological requirements (including the criteria of safety and (or) harmlessness of environmental factors for people, hygiene and other regulations) non-compliance with which poses a threat to the life or health of people as well as a threat of the emergence and spread of diseases.

For example, according to the Sanitary Rules 3.1.084-96 (approved by Decree of the State Committee on Sanitary and Epidemiology Surveillance of Russia No. 11 of May 31, 1996), planning, construction, reconstruction and modernization of livestock breeding complexes, poultry farms, meat packing plants and other enterprises for the production, processing and storage of livestock products must involve the provision of the most favorable conditions for the maintenance of animals, production of livestock products and prevention of pollution of the environment by industrial waste and pathogens of infectious diseases of people and animals. Therefore, agricultural facilities can be understood as a system of buildings and structures intended for the cultivation, production and processing of agricultural products, raw materials and foodstuffs, the placement and operation of which may have a negative impact on the environment.

One of the ways to observe environmental requirements during the operation of these facilities is the establishment of sanitary protection zones around them. As in other similar cases (with respect to industrial facilities), the establishment of sanitary protection zones in agriculture is necessary for the creation of a "barrier" between enterprises and residential areas (or other agricultural lands) to ensure the right of citizens to a favorable environment. In most cases, environmental legislation directly prohibits, for example, the commissioning of livestock farms and other production complexes that do not have treatment facilities and sanitary protection zones. The sufficiency of the width of sanitary protection zones is confirmed by calculations of estimated pollution levels, for example, in accordance with the calculation of dispersion in the atmosphere of pollutants contained in the emissions of the facilities as well as by the results of laboratory studies of the air in the areas where similar operating facilities are located. Specific dimensions of sanitary protection zones are determined in accordance with the Sanitary Rules, which distinguish five hazard classes of agricultural facilities. Depending on the hazard class, the dimensions of sanitary protection zones can vary from 50 to 1000 meters.

Along with the establishment of sanitary protection zones, environmental legislation imposes other two duties on the possessors of agricultural facilities:

a) The duty of producers of agricultural goods to comply with the requirements related to improvement of land fertility and soil protection measures. Special Federal Law No. 101-FZ of July 16, 1998 "On State Regulation of Ensuring the Fertility of Agricultural Land" is dedicated to this issue.

b) Mandatory measures taken by citizens and legal entities to protect fauna, the complete list of these measures is included in Article 22 of the Federal Law "On Fauna". The essence of these measures is to prevent the use of technologies and mechanisms causing mass death of animals and change of their habitat during agricultural production. During field works, it is necessary to use the technology, specially equipped agricultural machinery and the procedure that exclude the possibility of animal death. It is prohibited to discharge any wastewater and waste in places of spawning, wintering and mass concentration of aquatic and semi-aquatic animals.

2) Environmental requirements for land reclamation, the use of reclamation systems and hydraulic structures. Land reclamation is the fundamental improvement of land through hydraulic, chemical, anti-erosion, agro-technical

and other reclamation measures. The main purpose of land reclamation consists in increasing the efficiency and sustainability of arable farming, ensuring guaranteed agricultural production based on the preservation and improvement of land fertility as well as in creating the necessary conditions for the involvement of unused and low-yield land into agricultural circulation and the formation of a rational structure of agricultural areas.

A new type of reclamation measures is the creation (development) of reclamation protective forest plantations – forest plantations of natural origin or artificially created on agricultural land or on land for agricultural production in order to prevent soil degradation on pastures, soil erosion and protection from the impact of unfavorable phenomena of natural, anthropogenic and man-made origin through the use of functions of climate regulation, soil protection, erosion prevention, water regulation and other useful functions of forest plantations in order to preserve and improve land fertility. The main environmental requirement for the use of reclaimed land is that construction of facilities on this land and performance of other works not intended for land reclamation must not deteriorate the soil water, air and nutrient regimes and impede the operation of reclamation systems, separately located hydraulic structures and protective forest plantations. Reclamation systems are certified, research and development projects in the field of land reclamation are organized and financed, reclaimed land is registered and monitored in order to ensure compliance with environmental requirements for reclamation.

3) Environmental requirements in the field of chemicalization of agriculture

There are many pests causing damage to agricultural production in the territory of the Russian Federation. In various constituent entities of the Russian Federation, agricultural crops are damaged by about 50 species of polyphagous pests, more than 100 species of specialized pests and more than 70 species of diseases and 300 species of weeds. In this regard, balanced chemicalization of agriculture is the most important area for increasing the yield of agricultural crops, and, at the same time, one of the most urgent problems in the process of ensuring the high quality of agricultural land. The purpose of chemicalization is to increase the yield and the volume of agricultural products.

However, along with the positive impact on the yield, the use of pesticides and agrochemicals has also a negative effect – contamination of soil and food. The environment is contaminated with chemicals both in the course of their production, storage, transportation and use and in case of violation of the rules of utilization and removal of chemical waste. A striking example of the danger of pesticides, for example, is that they are very stable and spread far from where they are used (in particular, in the 1960s, they were found in the liver of penguins in thc Antarctic – clearly far from agricultural areas).

Considering issues of protection of the environment from chemicalization of agriculture, it is necessary to distinguish between two concepts: pesticides and agrochemicals.

Pesticides are substances or mixtures of substances, in particular, those used as plant growth regulators, pheromones, defoliants, desiccants and fumigants, and preparations of chemical or biological origin intended for pest control. Agrochemicals are fertilizers (mineral, organic, organomineral, microbiological) and chemical ameliorants intended for plant nutrition and land (soil) fertility regulation. Peat, animal and crop waste, silt and sewage sludge used for the production of organic and organomineral fertilizers, and mixed mineral fertilizers are not recognized as agrochemicals.

The general environmental requirement for their use is that it is allowed to use only those pesticides and agrochemicals which have passed registration tests, necessary expert reviews and registration.

State registration of pesticides and agrochemicals is carried out on the basis of reports of expert reviews of the results of registration tests of the pesticides and agrochemicals. The state registration of pesticides and agrochemicals is generally valid for ten years but can be reduced up to three years. Registration tests of pesticides and agrochemicals are carried out to develop and substantiate the regulations for the use of pesticides and agrochemicals. The said regulations ensure the efficiency of the use of pesticides and agrochemicals and their safety for human health and the environment. The efficiency of the use and the safety of pesticides and agrochemicals for human health and the environment are approved upon completion of their registration tests. A specially authorized federal authority organizes registration tests and carries out state registration of pesticides and agrochemicals. It is the Ministry of Agriculture of the Russian Federation.

Expert reviews of the results of registration tests of pesticides and agrochemicals are to confirm that the necessary number of registration tests of pesticides and agrochemicals has been carried out to determine their biological efficiency, safety of their use for human health and the environment, which is reflected in the reports of the expert reviews, which include information on restrictions necessary to comply with sanitary and epidemiological requirements as well as requirements in the area of environmental protection. Expert reviews of the results of registration tests of pesticides and agrochemicals consist of the following components:

1) Sanitary and epidemiological expert reviews performed by the federal executive authority implementing federal state sanitary and epidemiological control (supervision);

2) State environmental expert reviews of draft technical documentation for pesticides or agrochemicals performed by the federal executive authority in the field of environmental expert reviews;

3) Expert reviews of regulations for the use of pesticides and agrochemicals organized by the federal executive authority performing functions of state policy development, statutory regulation and provision of state services in the agricultural sector.

Individual entrepreneurs and legal entities engaged in wholesale and retail trade have the right to purchase and sell pesticides and agrochemicals that have passed state registration and are included in the State Catalogue of Pesticides and Agrochemicals allowed for use in the territory of Russia. Storage of pesticides and agrochemicals is allowed in specialized storage facilities and bulk storage of pesticides is prohibited. During storage of pesticides and agrochemicals, it is necessary to observe the requirements excluding harm to the health of people and the environment. Transportation of pesticides and agrochemicals is allowed only in specially equipped vehicles. The procedure for use of pesticides and agrochemicals is determined by federal executive authorities with consideration of the phytosanitary, sanitary and environmental situation, the needs of plants in agrochemicals, land (soil) fertility as well as the rations of animals.

The safety of the use of pesticides and agrochemicals is ensured through the compliance with the established regulations and rules of use that exclude their negative impact on the health of people and the environment. Pesticides and agrochemicals are used only along with the use of special machinery and equipment. The procedure for use of pesticides and agrochemicals is determined by sanitary rules. It is prohibited to use toxic chemical preparations that do not degrade. For all chemicals permitted for use in agriculture, there are the established MPCs at sites of the environment, the procedure for record and storage of pesticides as well as the rules according to which chemical treatment of crops, plantations and other agricultural lands is carried out only upon their preliminary examination, determination of the degree of pest infestation and the population of beneficial insect species.

An additional guarantee of the environmental safety of the use of pesticides and agrochemicals is the creation of the Federal State Information System of Traceability of Pesticides and Agrochemicals for the purposes of record of batches of pesticides and agrochemicals during their circulation (production, storage, transportation, use, sale, neutralization, utilization, destruction and burial) as well as analysis and processing of the entered data and information and control over the reliability of this information.

To ensure the record of the circulation of pesticides and agrochemicals, legal entities and individual entrepreneurs are registered in the Federal State Information System of Traceability of Pesticides and Agrochemicals free of charge and provide it with reliable and complete information.

A particular problem of protection of the environment from chemicalization means is that a number of constituent entities of the Russian Federation have accumulated tens of thousands of tons of prohibited and unfit pesticides and agrochemicals and the problem of their safe storage and utilization is not solved. As a rule, they are stored in warehouses that are in a dilapidated or critical condition and often in the open air. This problem falls under the category of "accumulated environmental harm". The procedure for their identification, record and assessment is specified in Chapter XIV.1 of the Federal Law "On Environmental Protection" and these sites are subject to elimination.

4. Cultivation of agricultural products using GMO technologies. Genetically modified organisms are the organisms the genetic material of which has been altered using genetic engineering techniques. The introduction of GMO technologies in agriculture makes it possible to create a number of frost resistant crops that are less susceptible to pesticides as well as to strengthen plant protection against insect pests.

The use of GMO technologies makes it possible to reduce carbon dioxide emissions into the atmosphere (due to less use of machinery in the treatment of fields with chemical crop protection agents and the spread of zero tillage) and leads to an increase in the yield of agricultural crops. However, in 2016, a special federal law established a ban on the import into the territory of the Russian Federation and the use for planting of seeds of plants the genetic program of which has been modified using genetic engineering techniques and which contain genetically engineered material, as well as a ban on the cultivation and breeding of plants and animals the genetic program of which has been changed using genetic engineering techniques. These bans, however, do not apply to expert reviews and research projects. These bans (as well as the attitude to GMOs in general) are quite controversial in the expert community of Russia and other countries. In my view, bans on GMOs are bans on progress. The invention of GMOs is the greatest technological breakthrough of our time, comparable to the smelting of first metals or the Neolithic Revolution, to the domestication of animals and plants.

What arguments can be given in favor of the discussion rather than the ban?

a) International law, which regulates the implementation of the concept of sustainable development, implies the search for balance and compromise between private and public economic, environmental and social interests. Deviation in any direction pushes both citizens of a specific country and all the world community away from the achievement of this global goal. At the moment, there are no unequivocal data on the harm or usefulness of GMOs, which is acknowledged by both sides of the discussion. In this situation, it is reasonable to arrange a comprehensive legal compromise, for example, with the prohibition of not all GMO products but their part intended for children or pregnant women, rather than to prohibit completely GMOs, which means uselessness of law of the corresponding state as a regulator of social relations. Otherwise, society as a whole loses.

b) There are a number of legal entities – agricultural producers using genetic engineering technologies, their products and technologies have become the subject of court decisions. These products and technologies should be prohibited. There are no legal grounds to prohibit genetic engineering itself though disputes of biologists must be continued. A serious legal argument in favor of GMOs can be the fact that GMO technologies are extremely common in the United States, however, we see very few successful lawsuits in the courts for compensation for harm caused to citizens by GMOs or for prohibition of GMO technologies themselves.

5. Cultivation of organic products. Organic products are the organic agricultural products, raw materials and food the production of which complies with the requirements established by law (Art. 2 of Federal Law No. 280-FZ of August 3, 2018 “On Organic Products and on Amendments to Certain Legislative Acts of the Russian Federation”).

The Law provides for a number of requirements for the production of organic products. They include the separation of the production of organic products from the production of products not attributed to organic products; the ban on the use of agrochemicals, pesticides, antibiotics, stimulants of growth and fattening of animals, hormonal preparations, excluding those permitted for use by the national, interstate and international standards that are in force in Russia in the field of organic production; the ban on the use of hydroponic plant growing; the ban on the use of ionizing radiation, *etc.*

Organic producers can pass voluntary certification and receive the confirmation of the compliance of their products with international standards for organic products. After they receive this certificate, they can mark the packaging of their products with a special sign of organic products. Russia maintains the Unified State Register of Organic Producers to keep record of them.

ENVIRONMENTAL REQUIREMENTS IN THE POWER INDUSTRY

Power enterprises traditionally include hydroelectric power plants, thermal power plants and nuclear power plants. Each of these power enterprises has its own advantages and disadvantages and poses its own risk to the environment. Their common feature is that all of them are attributed by Article 48.1 of the Urban Development Code of the Russian Federation to especially hazardous and technically complex capital facilities. Accordingly, in case of planned construction of these facilities, the project documentation is subject to the expert review in accordance with the requirements of urban development legislation (with consideration of each type of the said power facilities).

The second general requirement for power facilities is set out in Article 62 of the Water Code of the Russian Federation. According to this Article, water users using water bodies for technological needs of the thermal and nuclear power industries are obliged to observe the temperature regime of water bodies. Water bodies are used by hydropower facilities for electricity generation with consideration of the interests of other water users, compliance with the requirements for the use and protection of water bodies, requirements for the conservation of aquatic biological resources and other fauna and flora, requirements for the prevention of the negative impact of water and elimination of its consequences.

The third requirement is that sanitary protection zones are established around all types of power facilities and all of them are located on the land plots attributed to the special subcategory of land in the land fund of Russia – land of the power industry (included in the category of land of the industry and other special purpose – Article 89 of the Land Code of the Russian Federation).

Environmental Requirements for the Operation of Thermal Power Plants

In contrast to nuclear power plants, the environmental hazard of which after the accident at the Chernobyl Nuclear Power Plant raises (often unreasonably) increased concern of citizens, thermal power plants are considered more environmentally acceptable. However, environmental hazard of thermal power plants consists in the reliability of the systems of fuel combustion products cleaning, since production of 1 billion kWh of their energy leads to the emission of 1 million tons of CO_2, besides other harmful emissions. This is why environmental legislation stipulates that design and construction of thermal power plants must involve their equipment with high efficiency means of cleaning emissions and discharges of pollutants, the use of environmentally safe types of fuel and safe disposal of production waste. Safe types of fuel should be understood as natural gas, mass transition of thermal power plants to which is still impeded by some technical and financial problems. It is possible to reduce the pollution of the atmosphere along with increasing power generation only by introducing newest resource saving technologies. Combined cycle plants already used, for example, at the Sochi Thermal Power Plant, comply with these requirements. This area is defined by the Government of the Russian Federation as a strategic objective for the development of the energy complex of the country, and its fulfillment objectively contributes to the implementation of the provisions of the 2015 Paris Climate Agreement. Meanwhile, environmental legislation establishes that the amount of emissions of pollutants into the atmosphere from thermal power plants must not exceed the established MPEs, and the amount of discharges of pollutants into water bodies – the established MPDs (temporarily agreed emissions and discharges). For the purpose of protection of the population from the environmental consequences of the operation of thermal power plants, the sanitary rules stipulate the establishment of sanitary protection zones around thermal power plants, their dimensions in each specific case depend on the capacity (and the environmental hazard) of the relevant thermal power plant.

Environmental requirements for the operation of hydroelectric power plants

In accordance with the available environmental law terminology, hydroelectric power plants are a variety of hydraulic structures. In contrast to thermal power plants or nuclear power plants, electricity generation by hydroelectric power plants does not entail emissions of harmful substances or production of radioactive waste. The construction of hydroelectric power plants makes it possible to resolve a range of important socio-economic issues related to obtaining cheap electricity and saving natural resources (oil, gas). The environmental hazard of this variety of electric power stations consists in the fact that their construction leads to such negative consequences as flooding of considerable territories, destruction of their ecosystems, historical, cultural, and natural monuments, fauna, fish reserves, *etc.* For example, the famous reserve lake Irryk-Kul in Tatarstan, where the rarest animal, the Russian desman, was found, turned out to be under the Kuibyshev Reservoir; the entire city of Mologa – under the Rybinsk Reservoir, *etc.* Moreover, significant environmental harm is caused by erosion and collapse of the banks of all large reservoirs as well as the presence of cattle burial grounds containing causative agents of dangerous diseases under water and on the eroding banks. These dangerous cattle burial grounds are located under the water, for example, of the Kuibyshev Reservoir in Ulyanovsk Region. The sides of the cattle burial grounds with anthrax in the

Republic of Mari El were eroded by the water of the Cheboksary Reservoir (Usmanova, 2000).

These circumstances led to the requirement of environmental legislation regarding the need to take into account the real needs for electricity in the relevant regions as well as the peculiarities of the terrain in case of location, design, construction, reconstruction, commissioning and operation of hydroelectric power plants. The sense of the latter requirement should be understood as a ban of the further construction of hydroelectric power plants on the rivers of the plain part of the territory of Russia since these projects cause especially negative environmental consequences. Construction of hydroelectric power plants in the mountains will be more reasonable since this will not lead to the flooding of vast areas. Moreover, the construction of hydroelectric power plants must involve measures for timely utilization of timber and the fertile soil layer during cleaning and flooding of the reservoir bed. One of the guarantees of the safety of hydraulic structures is the compilation of the Hydraulic Structure Safety Declaration – the document which contains the guarantees of protection of the life, health and other legitimate interests of people, the environment and economic entities and determines hydraulic structure safety measures according to the relevant class (I-IV). Provision of the Declaration is the necessary condition for obtaining a permit for commissioning and operation of hydraulic structures, their reconstruction, capital repairs, restoration, conservation or liquidation. Another not less important guarantee of safety of hydraulic structures and environmental safety is the compulsory insurance of civil liability for harm as well as the establishment of special protective zones around hydroelectric power plants (Art. 62 of the Water Code of the Russian Federation).

Environmental requirements for the operation of nuclear power plants

Legislative establishment of environmental requirements at all stages of the operation of nuclear installations is due to the consideration of the negative consequences of the accident at the Chernobyl Nuclear Power Plant. This man-made accident of the 20th century extraordinary in its consequences led to incalculable environmental and humanitarian losses. This gave rise to a special nature of relations between citizens and the state that consists in the fact that the state assumed the duty to compensate for the harm which, because of its extent and the number of affected persons, could not be compensated according to the procedure established by the civil, administrative, criminal and other branch legislation. However, in the modern world, the nuclear power industry is still an essential factor of the economic life of the world community. The positive environmental factors of the operation of nuclear power plants include the fact that they do not consume oxygen, do not emit harmful substances (CO_2) into the environment, save oil and gas reserves and other non-renewable natural resources. In contrast to hydroelectric power plants, they do not lead to the withdrawal of fertile land from economic use as a result of reservoir construction, they do not affect fauna and fish reserves. At the same time, nuclear power plants pose the following environmental threats.

1) Nuclear power plants pose an increased risk to the population not only because of possible accidents but also due to the need to bury radioactive waste. This is why nuclear installations, including nuclear power plants, are located subject to the availability, with respect to the project and other supporting materials, of the positive findings of the state expert review of the project documentation for the facilities using nuclear energy that is conducted in accordance with the legislation on urban development activities.

2) The establishment of sanitary protection zones for the population protection in the area of nuclear installations and observation zones for radiation monitoring is the guarantee of environmental safety of nuclear power plants. The dimensions and the boundaries of sanitary protection zones are determined in accordance with the rules and regulations in the field of nuclear energy use and they are coordinated with state sanitary and epidemiological supervision authorities. In sanitary protection zones, it is prohibited to locate residential and public buildings, children's institutions as well as therapeutic and recreational institutions, catering facilities, industrial facilities, auxiliary and other structures and facilities not related to the functioning of nuclear installations. In observation zones, there can be restrictions on economic activities, and the losses caused by the establishment of the zones are to be compensated.

3) A range of additional requirements for the operation of nuclear power plants is a distinctive feature of environmental protection in the field of the nuclear power industry. For example, by virtue of Article 26 of the Federal Law “On the Use of Nuclear Energy”, a permit (license) is required to carry out works in the field of nuclear energy use, which does not apply to thermal power plants and hydroelectric power plants. The adoption of decisions on the issue of permits (licenses) for works in the field of nuclear energy use involves expert reviews of the safety (expert reviews of substantiation of the safety) of facilities using nuclear energy and/or types of activities in the field of nuclear energy use. Finally, it is prohibited to organize unauthorized assemblies, rallies, demonstrations and other similar activities in the territory of nuclear installations. Strikes are prohibited if they pose a threat to the normal operation of nuclear power plants.

Environmental consequences from renewable energy sources

Renewable energy sources are the energy sources which are constantly reproduced due to natural processes and include energy of the sun, wind, ground heat, natural movement of water flows, wood fuel and other types of biomass and biogas. In Russia, less than 1 percent of the total volume of electricity is produced from renewable energy sources. At the same time, the resources of oil and gas are not unlimited, and this means the inevitability of the development of this type of energy sources in Russia. The environmental consequences of the use of wind turbines and solar panels have been long discussed in European science and practice. Undoubtedly, these side effects are not comparable with the risks from the operation of nuclear power plants or the consequences of emissions of harmful substances from thermal power plants. Meanwhile, large numbers of wind turbines can affect the climate by worsening the ventilation of the area. Solar panels cause land shading, which leads to changes in soil conditions and death of plants. Heating of the air as the solar radiation passes through it, which leads to changes in the heat balance, humidity and wind direction, is considered an unfavorable environmental consequence of their work. Overheating and combustion of systems using solar energy with all their consequences are possible.

Acoustic impact is the most important factor of the influence of wind power plants on the environment. Noise can affect fauna, including marine fauna, in the area where wind power plants are located. The probability of harm caused to birds by wind turbines is estimated at 10 percent if the migration routes pass through the wind park. Interference produced by wind turbines can affect the quality of television and microwave radio transmissions as well as various navigation systems in the area where wind parks are located. It remains to add that many citizens of foreign countries consider the appearance of windmills unaesthetic.

In foreign countries, the rapid development of renewable energy sources has already led to a new stage in the development of neighbor law dating back to Roman law. However, now this relates not tree branches or roots disturbing neighbors. In the United States, a number of laws prohibit unreasonable restrictions on the installation of solar generators, for example, prohibit neighbors from planting trees that would provide shade to solar panels of other neighbors. A number of municipalities in Colorado have organized "solar zoning" having designated the areas where any construction (tree planting) that would violate the "solar rights" of neighbors is prohibited. In a similar manner, laws of the States stipulate "rights to wind" that create conditions for the use of wind turbines and restrict the possibilities of interfering with it. The lack of a developed infrastructure of renewable energy sources, the vast territory and the weak legal framework have not yet made the issue of "solar rights" or "rights to wind" relevant in Russia, as it happens in European countries and the United States, they have not led to disputes between neighbors about the impossibility to use wind power in case of installation of groups of wind turbines on neighboring plots. However, the gradual development of the system of renewable energy sources in the Russian Federation will eventually lead to this as well.

More comprehensive regulation of these relations requires adoption of a special federal law, similar to the Law of the Republic of Belarus on Renewable Energy Sources No. 204-Z of December 27, 2010.

ENVIRONMENTAL REQUIREMENTS FOR PROTECTION OF THE OZONE LAYER

The ozone layer is an independent object of environmental protection from pollution and other consequences of the negative impact of economic activities. The distinctive feature of the ozone layer is that it is beyond the territory covered by the state sovereignty. The ozone layer is the top layer of the atmosphere with a thickness of 3 mm which is about 30 km above the surface of the Earth. The ecological function of the ozone layer is that it absorbs ultraviolet radiation, harmful to living organisms and coming from space, and also maintains a favorable temperature regime. This leads to the connection between the protection of the ozone layer and climate change. Pollution of the environment by chemicals and other substances causes the destruction of the ozone layer. Some chemicals (freon) widely used in household appliances and production activities are its main reason (according to the hypothesis shared by most scholars). Moreover, according to the expert estimates, one launch of a spacecraft destructs up to 0.3 percent of the ozone in the atmosphere. Tests of nuclear weapons have even a greater impact on the ozone layer·

As a result, at the moment there are ozone holes in Antarctica, and ozone depletion was registered above many large cities (Moscow, Riga, Saint Petersburg, *etc.*). NASA and the US National Oceanic and Atmospheric Administration (NOAA) recently announced that as of 2012 the area of the ozone hole above Antarctica had reached the maximum value, 21.2 million square kilometers. This area is comparable to the size of the territories occupied by the United States, Canada, and Mexico.

The negative consequences of ozone depletion include the reduction of endurance and service life of some materials (for example, rubber), deterioration of immunity and growth of diseases (cancer, respiratory diseases in humans and growth of diseases in animals), loss of aquatic bioresources and plankton, reduction of agricultural crop yields, *etc.*

The current situation stimulates international cooperation in the field of environmental protection, in which the Russian Federation actively participates. The international community first paid attention to the issue of the ozone layer protection in 1977, when UNEP (United Nations Environment Program) convened a meeting on the ozone layer in Washington (USA). It resulted in the adoption of the World Plan of Action on the Ozone Layer and the establishment of the UNEP coordinating center on the ozone layer. However, this document was purely scientific and advisory.

The 1985 Vienna Convention for the Protection of the Ozone Layer and the 1987 Montreal Protocol on Substances that Deplete the Ozone Layer, to which seven amendments were introduced (1990-1999) are of much greater importance for the protection of the ozone layer. These documents established the list of substances negatively affecting the ozone layer, the mechanism of reduction of their emissions, a decision on mutual information of states on the production and use of these substances as well as on the adopted measures was made. The mechanism of control over the fulfillment of duties to protect the ozone layer was developed. These international documents were signed by 196 states, including Russia, most developed countries as well as many developing countries (Cameroon, Zimbabwe, *etc.*). However, a number of countries long refused to sign them (China, India), requiring that more developed countries provide them with substitutes for ozone-depleting substances.

The provisions of the Vienna Convention and the Montreal Protocol caused the adoption of special international instruments at the level of regional intergovernmental associations for their more comprehensive implementation. For example, the Agreement on Movement of Ozone-Depleting Substances and their Products and Recording Ozone-Depleting Substances in Mutual Trade between the Member States of the Eurasian Economic Union was adopted in 2015. The said documents are taken into account also in the national legislation of many countries. For example, the Kyrgyz Republic adopted a special law “On Protection of the Ozone Layer” of December 18, 2006, and the United States – Title VI of the 1990 Clean Air Act, which is actually the national program of the United States for protection of the ozone layer.

In Russia, issues of the protection of the ozone layer are regulated by Article 54 of the Law of the Russian Federation “On Environmental Protection” and a number of bylaws. For the purpose of protection of the ozone layer of the atmosphere from the negative impact of economic and other activities, they stipulate the establishment of a list of ozone depleting substances, the circulation of which is subject to state regulation in the Russian Federation, the allowable volume of production and consumption of these substances in the Russian Federation, the requirements for circulation of ozone depleting substances, bans on design and construction of facilities for economic and other activities that produce ozone depleting substances and products containing them in the Russian Federation. The Government of the Russian Federation establishes the list of ozone depleting substances the circulation of which is subject to state regulation, the allowable volume of production and consumption of these substances in the Russian Federation, the requirements for circulation of ozone depleting substances, the period of bans on design and construction of facilities for economic and other activities that produce specific ozone depleting substances and products containing them in the Russian Federation.

Environmental monitoring is carried out in relation to the condition of the ozone layer, and Rosprirodnadzor implements state environmental supervision over the compliance with the requirements for handling ozone depleting substances. Non-compliance with these requirements entails administrative sanctions (Art. 8.2.1 of the Code of Administrative Offenses of the Russian Federation). Moreover, since July 1, 2014, it has been prohibited to design facilities for economic and other activities that produce ozone depleting substances and products containing them, and since January 1, 2015, it has been prohibited to construct facilities for economic and other activities that produce ozone depleting substances and products containing them (par. 2 of Decree of the Government of the Russian Federation No. 228 of March 24, 2014 "On Measures of State Regulation of Consumption and Circulation of Ozone Depleting Substances").

CONCLUSION

The chapter notes that in order to implement the tasks of ensuring the proper quality of the environment in the Russian Federation, environmental legislation provides for a system of measures, which, in addition to giving a special legal status to certain territories or establishing rules for the protection of natural objects, includes special environmental requirements that are mandatory for all entities engaged in various types of economic and other activities that have a negative impact on the environment. The list of such activities is not exhaustive. The chapter discusses special rules and requirements for the construction of real estate, the operation of industrial, energy and agricultural facilities, transport, *etc.*

QUESTIONS AND TASKS FOR SELF-CONTROL

1. Describe the concept and significance of environmental requirements for various types of economic and other activities.

2. What are the main areas of legal protection of the environment of settlements?

3. Describe the main environmental requirements for military and defense activities.

4. List the main environmental requirements in zones with special conditions of use.

5. What are environmental requirements in production and consumption waste management?

6. Describe the main environmental requirements in transport.

7. Specify environmental requirements in agriculture.

8. Describe environmental requirements in the power industry.

9. List environmental requirements for protection of the ozone layer.

REFERENCES

Report, S. (2019). *On the State and Protection of the Environment in the Russian Federation in 2018.*

Timofeev, L.A. (2003). Legal Issues of Water Supply of the Population in the Russian Federation. *Moscow: Ministry of Natural Resources and Environment of the Russian Federation; NPP "Kadastr".* Saratov: Publishing House of the Saratov State Agrarian University.

Usmanova, L.F. (2000). *Legal Regulation of Natural Resource Management and Environmental Protection in the Agricultural Sector of the Economy.*

CHAPTER 6

Legal Regulation of Protection of Natural Objects

Abstract: All types of natural objects are closely interlinked with each other. Deterioration of the quality of one of them inevitably leads to particular consequences for the condition of the other elements of the ecological system. This is why legislation stipulates a range of measures aimed at protecting both the environment in general and its constituent components. Land protection focuses on the preservation of soil fertility. From the analysis of the Forest Code of the Russian Federation it follows that there are nature protection rules of a general nature covering all types of forests and special rules specifying these general provisions for certain categories of forests. In particular, the general environmental rules consist in the fact that all forests are subject to protection from fires, pollution (including contamination by radioactive substances) and other negative impact as well as protection from harmful organisms. The legal regime of water bodies varies depending on whether they are located on the surface of the earth or they are ground water bodies. The Government of the Russian Federation approved special rules for protection of both surface and ground water bodies. The task of water protection is solved by imposing duties on the subjects of water relations – citizens and legal entities as well as public authorities. For the purpose of water protection, environmental and water laws establish a range of general and special requirements. The protection of fauna habitat is one of the areas of fauna protection activities. Legislation establishes two regimes of the protection of animals. The general regime of the protection is established by the Federal Law "On Fauna" (based on the criterion of the possibility of being an object of hunting and fishing, two categories of animals are distinguished); the special regime is established in relation to animals attributed to specially protected ones, including those listed in the Red Data Book of Russia. Researchers point out two main problems in the area of rational use and protection of subsoil. They are the inefficient use of subsoil resources with the increasing complexity of field exploitation and the growing impact of mining on the environment. Finally, the consistent system of legal rules regulating the protection of air from anthropogenic impact is considered at the end of this Chapter.

Keywords: Air, Authorities, Citizens, Drilling, Duties, Economic entities, Fires, Forests, Health, Land, Mineral resources, Natural resource, Natural object, Pollution, Protection, Soil, Subsoil, Use, Water, Water protective zones.

LEGAL REGULATION OF LAND PROTECTION

All types of natural objects are closely interlinked with each other. Deterioration of the quality of one of them inevitably leads to particular consequences for the

Aleksey Anisimov and Anatoliy Ryzhenkov

condition of the other elements of the ecological system. This is why legislation stipulates a range of measures aimed at protecting both the environment in general and its constituent components. The latter area of the protection is due to the fact that protection of certain types of natural objects has particular features within the general objective of ensuring a favorable environmental quality. Since all natural objects have a close connection with land, the legislator pays more attention directly to land protection measures. The Land Code, as well as the Federal Law "On Environmental Protection", distinguishes two objects of protection – land and soil. This is not accidental. Protection of soil (and its fertility) is of interest mostly in relation to the categories of agricultural land and the forest fund, where land serves as a means of production. With respect to agricultural land, this protection is implemented in accordance with the Federal Law of July 16, 1998 "On State Regulation of Ensuring the Fertility of Agricultural Land", and in relation to land of the forest fund – in accordance with the Forest Code of the Russian Federation. In relation to other categories of land, measures for soil protection are of a derivative nature. Even there, by virtue of paragraph 4 of Article 13 of the Land Code of the Russian Federation, during construction related to soil disturbance and works related to subsoil use, the fertile layer must be removed and used to improve low-yield land.

The requirement in paragraph 2 of Article 6 of the Federal Law "On Circulation of Agricultural Land" of July 24, 2002 is an essential measure to protect the fertile soil layer. According to it, a plot of agricultural land may be forcibly withdrawn from its owner in judicial proceedings if this land plot is used in violation of legislative requirements, which results in significant reduction in soil fertility of the plot of agricultural land or harm to the environment. The criteria of significant reduction in soil fertility of agricultural land are established by Decree of the Government of the Russian Federation No. 612 of July 22, 2011. Moreover, in order to protect agricultural land, the Government of the Russian Federation adopted Decree No. 1482 of September 18, 2020 "On Signs of the Non-Use of Land Plots of Agricultural Lands for the Intended Purpose or their Use in Violation of the Legislation of the Russian Federation".

These signs include the lack of works for cultivation of agricultural crops on arable land (by at least 50 percent of the plot area), the lack of grazing on pastures, haymaking on hayfields and a number of other signs.

However, despite the particular attention paid by the legislator to the protection of the fertile layer, all land is the most important natural object and an integral part of the environment, this is why land protection measures apply to all land categories in the land fund of Russia (there are seven land categories: land of agricultural purpose, land of settlements, land of industrial and other special purposes, specially protected areas and sites, land of the forest fund, water fund and reserve land).

Is the list of land protection measures the same for all categories of land in the land fund of the Russian Federation? It does not seem so. For example, land of settlements does not serve as the basis for ensuring food security of the country, its use does not involve improvement of its fertility, mineral fertilizers, *etc*. This is why many nature protection activities relevant to agricultural land are not necessary for land of settlements, for example, reclamation. The purposes of forest use on land of the forest fund and in cities are also different. Given that urban forests are used primarily for cultural, sport and recreational purposes (for example, in contrast to exploitable or reserve forests), the purposes and methods of forest protection will be different. For example, aerial protection of forests from fires is not applicable to the protection of urban forests.

Measures to protect urban forests from pests and diseases are much less relevant (in terms of their extent and costs). Similar differences in the goals and methods of land protection can be found with respect to any categories of land in the land fund of the Russian Federation. At the same time, we should mention the general similarity of the goals and objectives of land protection of all categories – the prevention of harmful impact during economic activities on the land as an integral part of the environment and the need to take rapid and effective measures if this harmful impact occurs.

Therefore, the list of specific measures to protect land and soil differs significantly depending on the particular land category of land plots. The largest number of land protection measures is provided for agricultural land plots.

Land protection is a set of organizational and economic agronomic, technical, reclamation, economic and legal measures to prevent and eliminate the processes which deteriorate the condition of land and cases of violation of the land use procedure.

Considering the concept of land protection, it is necessary to determine the relationship between the concepts of land protection and land use. The current legislation specifies one lawful option of this relationship, rational use of land. The need for precise clarification of this term follows directly from the current legislation, which associates various legal consequences with the rational or irrational use of land. Protection of land of any category and its rational use reflect two forms of interaction between society and nature: natural resource management and environmental protection.

When we consider rational use of land, we assume compliance with environmental, urban development and other requirements in the course of use of land plots. In this case there is no need to apply land protection measures, consequently, requirements of rational use and protection of land merge in a particular sense. However, if the requirements stipulated by the legislation are not observed in the course of land use, the quality of land and, accordingly, the environment, deteriorates. In this case, land protection measures are aimed at ensuring the compliance of users of natural resources with the land protection rules and regulations.

It appears that land protection will not be related to the issue of rational use of land only in two cases. This will happen, first, in case of establishment of specially protected natural areas (for example, reserves or natural monuments) completely withdrawn from any economic use and preserved in their natural state for future generations of people, and, second, on reserve land.

The common goals of land protection are prevention of degradation, pollution, littering of land and other negative (harmful) impact of economic activities as well as improvement and restoration of land disturbed in the course of economic and other activities.

The implementation of land protection measures implies the imposition of duties on land users and public authorities. The duties of the holders of rights to land plots stipulated by land and environmental legislation can be divided into three groups.

First, these are preventive measures, they will prevent future harm to land plots. They include preservation of the achieved level of land reclamation; protection of agricultural lands from overgrowth of trees, bushes and weeds; protection of land from water and wind erosion, mudflows, waterlogging, swamping, secondary salinization, desiccation, compaction, pollution by radioactive and chemical substances, production and consumption waste, biogenic pollution and other negative (harmful) impact which results in land degradation.

Second, this is the elimination of the consequences of the deterioration of the quality of land that has already occurred, including the elimination of the consequences of pollution, in particular, biogenic pollution, littering of land, and remediation of disturbed land, restoration of soil fertility, timely inclusion of land into circulation.

Third, this is the preservation of soil fertility in the course of its use during works that are potentially hazardous to land.

State authorities and local government bodies, in their turn, are obliged to develop federal, regional and local land protection programs, with consideration of the specific features of economic activities, natural and other conditions, as well as to implement land conservation, *etc.* To make land users more interested in the preservation and restoration of soil, public authorities may establish economic incentives according to the procedure stipulated by financial legislation. If pollution (littering) of land, despite preventive measures, still takes place, the persons whose activities have led to the deterioration of land quality are obliged to ensure its remediation. Land remediation is a set of measures to prevent land degradation and (or) to restore its fertility by bringing land into a condition suitable for its use in accordance with the intended purpose and permitted use, including by eliminating the consequences of soil contamination, restoring the fertile layer of soil and creating protective forest plantations. Remediation is mandatory for disturbed agricultural land and the disturbed land that has been contaminated by chemicals, including radioactive and other substances and microorganisms the content of which does not comply with environmental quality regulations and requirements of legislation in the field of ensuring sanitary and epidemiological well-being of the population.

The establishment of a special environmental legal regime, which has two varieties, on certain land plots or territories is a particular area of land protection. The first variety refers to land that has been exposed to radioactive and chemical contamination and the production of products complying with the requirements established by legislation is not ensured on this land. Radioactive contamination is the contamination of the surface of the Earth, atmosphere, water or food, food raw materials, feed and other items by radioactive substances in quantities that exceed the level established by radiation safety standards and rules of handling radioactive substances. The level of radioactive contamination of soil is determined in accordance with sanitary rules and regulations, radiation safety rules, *etc.*

Radioactive contamination can result in the emergence of a radioactively contaminated area, which is understood as an area of a territory which is hazardous to the health of the population and the environment, subject to rehabilitation after radioactive contamination as a result of anthropogenic activities or placement of decommissioned radiation facilities that are especially hazardous (Art. 1 of Federal Law No. 92-FZ of July 10, 2001 "On Special Environmental Programs for Rehabilitation of Radiation-Contaminated Areas of the Territory").

With respect to these areas, special environmental programs are developed to ensure radiation safety of the population, general reduction of the risk of exposure to radiation and improvement of the environmental conditions in radiation-contaminated areas by carrying out measures to rehabilitate these areas and to utilize or liquidate decommissioned radiation-hazardous facilities.

The specified land is subject to restricted use, its exclusion from the category of agricultural land or land of other purposes and can be transferred to reserve land for conservation. Land conservation is implemented in relation to disturbed land the negative impact on which has led to its degradation, deterioration of the environmental situation and (or) soil disturbance, and as a result it is not allowed to carry out economic activities if the elimination of these consequences by means of land remediation is impossible for 15 years. It is prohibited to produce and sell agricultural products on this land.

The procedure for use of this land, establishment of protective zones, preservation of residential buildings, production facilities, social, cultural and domestic service facilities located on this land, reclamation and other works on this land is determined by the Government of the Russian Federation with consideration of the maximum permissible levels of radiation and chemical impact.

The persons whose activities have resulted in radioactive and chemical contamination of land, leading to the impossibility to use it for the intended purpose or deterioration of its quality, fully compensate for losses, expenses for decontamination of land exposed to radioactive and chemical contamination, expenses for bringing it into a condition suitable for use for the intended purpose or pay to the owners of land plots their cost in case of transfer of these plots to reserve land for conservation.

Another variety of this land protection involves the establishment of a special protection regime for unique soil by maintaining the Red Data Book of Soils of the Russian Federation and the Red Data Book of Soils of constituent entities of the Russian Federation. Soil having features of special value for the Russian Federation or constituent entities of the Russian Federation is subject to inclusion in these Books, with the establishment of a regime of special protection and withdrawal from active economic use. At the same time, both measures specified above are applied in cases where the size of land plots or other circumstances do not lead to giving them the status of specially protected natural areas or ecological disaster zones.

LEGAL REGULATION OF FOREST PROTECTION

Legal legislation is based on the concept of forest as an ecological system or natural resource. Forests are located on the land of the forest fund and the land of other categories (urban forests – on the land of settlements). In the course of urban development zoning, no urban development regulations are established for the forest fund, however, if forests grow within the boundaries of settlements or on the land of other categories (except the land of the forest fund), they can be included in the recreational or other territorial zones and used for recreation, tourism, sports, *etc.* From the analysis of the Forest Code of the Russian Federation it follows that there are nature protection rules of a general nature covering all types of forests and special rules specifying these general provisions for certain categories of forests. The general environmental rules consist in the fact that all forests are subject to protection from fires, pollution (including contamination by radioactive substances) and other negative impact as well as protection from harmful organisms. Two terms must be distinguished – protection and conservation of forests. The differences are in the nature of negative impact. In case of negative physical, chemical, radioactive or other negative impact, the counteraction to it (including elimination of the consequences) is referred to as "protection" in the Forest Code of the Russian Federation.

In case of biological impact on forests (the threat of harm from pests), measures to counter this threat are called "conservation" of forests.

Let us consider the said groups of measures to protect and conserve forests.

1) Protection of forests from fires. There are measures to prevent forest fires (fire safety measures) and measures to extinguish fires that begin despite all the adopted measures. Fire safety measures for forests include prevention of forest fires, monitoring of fire risk in forests and forest fires, development and approval of plans for extinguishing forest fires and other fire safety measures for forests.

a) Prevention of forest fires involves forest fire prevention measures and provision of means for preventing and extinguishing forest fires. Forest fire prevention measures include construction of forest roads designed to protect forests from fires, construction and operation of landing sites for aircraft and helicopters used for aerial protection and conservation of forests, arrangement of glades, firebreaks, installation of fire barrier lines, fire reservoirs, *etc.* Accordingly, the provision of means for preventing and extinguishing forest fires includes acquisition of fire-fighting equipment, maintenance of firefighting machinery and equipment, communications and warning systems, creation of a reserve of firefighting machinery and equipment as well as fuel and lubricant materials.

b) Monitoring of fire risk in forests and forest fires includes observation and control of fire risk in forests and forest fires, organization of the forest fire detection and record system, the system of observation of their development (with the use of ground, aviation or aerospace means), organization of forest patrols, receipt and record of reports about forest fires and notification of the population and fire departments about fire risk in forests and forest fires.

c) Plans for extinguishing forest fires establish the list and composition of forest fire brigades, firefighting machinery and equipment, the list of forces and means of firefighting units and emergency response teams, measures to coordinate works related to extinguishing forest fires, measures to create a reserve of firefighting machinery and equipment.

If, despite all fire prevention measures in forests, fires occur, the Forest Code of the Russian Federation regulate in detail forest fire extinguishing measures. Extinguishing forest fires includes inspection of forest fires with the use of ground, aviation or aerospace means in order to specify the type and the intensity of forest fires, their boundaries, direction of their movement, *etc.*, delivery of people and means of extinguishing forest fires to the place of extinguishing forest fires and back, localization of forest fires; elimination of forest fires, prevention of their renewal.

For example, in 2018, there were 12,125 forest fires on the land of the forest fund. The forest area covered by fires was 7,408,400 hectares. Compared to 2017, the number of forest fires increased by 1,899 cases and the area of the land of the forest fund covered by fires increased 2.3 times (by 4,199,800 hectares). The Far Eastern and Siberian federal districts are most susceptible to forest fires, they account for 90.4 percent of the total number of large forest fires of the country (Report, 2019).

2) Conservation of forests is aimed at identifying pests (plants, animals and pathogenic organisms that can cause harm to forests or forest resources under certain conditions) in forests and preventing their spread, and in case of the emergence of concentrations of pests attributed to quarantine objects – at localizing and liquidating them.

Conservation of forests includes 2 groups of measures: sanitation measures in forests and liquidation of concentrations of pests.

a) Sanitation measures in forests include forest protection zoning (*i.e.*, identification of zones of weak, medium and strong threat of contamination of forests with diseases); state forest pathology monitoring (the system of observation over the sanitary condition of forests); forest pathology surveys (*i.e.*, assessment of the sanitary condition of forests); prevention of the spread of pests (for example, by cutting damaged forest plantations) and a range of other measures.

b) Liquidation of concentrations of pests in forests involves inspection of the territories contaminated by pests; elimination or suppression of pests, including the use of chemicals; cutting of trees in order to preserve the quality of forest plantations, to protect them from trees infected with pests.

State authorities and local government bodies within their powers limit the stay of citizens in forests, entry of vehicles to them and particular types of work in forests in order to ensure fire or sanitary safety in forests.

3) Protection of forests from pollution and other negative impact.

The use of forests, protection of forests from fires, conservation and reproduction of forests must comply with the requirements for protection of the environment from pollution and other negative impact established by the legislation of the Russian Federation, involve measures to protect forests from pollution (including oil and radioactive contamination) and other negative impact, including measures to preserve forest plantations, forest soil, the fauna habitat, other natural objects in forests, as well as remediation (including reforestation and afforestation) of the land on which forests exposed to pollution and other negative impact are located.

If citizens and legal entities using forests do not fulfill measures to protect forests from fires, pollution or other negative impact and pests, this is the grounds for early termination of lease agreements for forest areas, sales agreements for forest plantations and termination of the right of permanent (perpetual) use of a forest area or the right of gratuitous use of a forest area and termination of easements.

The forests that have been cut down, lost or damaged are to be reproduced. Reproduction of forests includes forest seed production, reforestation, forest care, attribution of land intended for reforestation to the land on which forests are located (Art. 61 of the Forest Code).

The second area of protection and conservation of forests is the establishment of a special system of measures for protection and conservation of forests with respect to certain categories of forests. As follows from Article 110 of the Forest Code of the Russian Federation, forests are divided into protection, exploitable and reserve forests. Forests located on land of other categories can be attributed to protection forests. This classification of forests most clearly reflects the nature protection and nature resource aspect of the interaction between nature and society since the legislator not only regulates the use of forests for economic purposes but also provides for special measures to protect forests as part of the environment.

The greatest number of nature protection requirements is stipulated for protection forests. Protection forests include the forests that are natural sites of a special value, and the special legal regime of use, protection, conservation and reproduction of forests is established in their relation. Thc following categories of protection forests are distinguished: forests located in specially protected natural areas; forests located in water protective zones; forests that perform the functions of protection of natural and other objects; valuable forests; urban forests. The Forest Code of the Russian Federation regulates in detail the features of protection in each group and subgroup of forests. For example, Article 111 of the Forest Code of the Russian Federation specifies that clear cutting of forest plantations can be implemented in protection forests only in exceptional cases.

Moreover, we observe additional sets of prohibitions and restrictions in each variety of protection forests. For example, in forests located in water protective zones, it is prohibited to use toxic chemicals; organize agriculture, excluding haymaking and beekeeping; to create and operate forest plantations; to construct and operate capital facilities, excluding linear facilities, hydraulic structures and facilities necessary for geological survey, exploration and mining of oil and natural gas.

Exploitable forests are to be developed for sustainable, maximum efficient production of high-quality timber and other forest resources, products of their processing, ensuring the preservation of the useful functions of forests. All types of the use of forests are allowed in exploitable forests. Reserve forests include forests in which wood harvesting, excluding wood harvesting by citizens for their own needs, is not planned for twenty years. Therefore, exploitable and reserve forests are covered by the general forest protection requirements, and protection forests – by a range of additional requirements, prohibitions and restrictions for their special protection.

Designated areas of forests can be arranged in protection forests, exploitable forests and reserve forests. They are bank protection and soil protection areas of forests located along water bodies and ravine slopes; forest edges bordering treeless spaces; habitats of rare and endangered wild animals; natural heritage sites; areas with relict plants, *etc.*

For preservation of rare and endangered species of trees, shrubs, lianas and other forest plants, they can be included in the Red Data Book of the Russian Federation or the Red Data Books of constituent entities of the Russian Federation, and in their relation in this case it is prohibited to carry out activities the negative impact of which will or can lead to reduction of the number of these plants and (or) deterioration of their habitat. Therefore, protection and conservation of forests are implemented with consideration of their distinctive biological features and include a set of organizational, economic, legal and other measures for rational use of forests located on land of the forest fund and land of other categories, preservation of forests from destruction, damage, pollution and other negative impact.

LEGAL REGULATION OF WATER PROTECTION

Water bodies are the natural or artificial water reservoirs, watercourses or other water bodies permanent or temporary concentration of water in which has characteristic forms and signs of the water regime. Water bodies are used for the purposes of drinking and domestic water supply, discharge of wastewater and (or) drainage water, electricity generation, water and air transport, timber rafting and other purposes stipulated by the Water Code of the Russian Federation. It should be noted that the relations governed by water legislation do not include relations regarding water located in the environment and not concentrated in water bodies as well as relations regarding water withdrawn from water bodies (they are governed by civil, sanitary and other legislation). The legal regime of water bodies varies depending on whether they are located on the surface of the earth or they are ground water bodies. The Government of the Russian Federation approved special rules for protection of both surface and ground water bodies.

For example, the Rules for Protection of Surface Water Bodies (approved by Decree of the Government of the Russian Federation No. 79 of February 5, 2016) attribute the establishment of the boundaries of water protective zones, prevention of pollution, salinization and depletion of water bodies, their cleaning from bottom deposits and a range of other measures to the measures of protection of surface water bodies. Moreover, surface water bodies that are in state or municipal ownership are common water bodies (publicly available water bodies). This means that every citizen must have unimpeded access to these water bodies and may use them free of charge for personal and domestic (but not entrepreneurial) needs. A strip of land along the coastline of a common water body (waterside) is also intended for common use. Its width is 20 m, except for the shoreline of canals, rivers and streams the length of which from source to mouth is not more than 10 km (the width of their shoreline is 5 m). Every citizen has the right to use (without mechanical vehicles) the waterside of common water bodies for moving and staying close to them, including for recreational and sport fishing and mooring of floating structures.

This form of water use is a variety of common natural resource management carried out without special permits from public authorities (in contrast to, for example, mineral exploration and mining based on special agreements concluded with public authorities) and being a form of the exercise of the constitutional right of citizens to a favorable environment.

Water protection is a system of measures aimed at preserving and restoring water bodies. Water is protected from its depletion, pollution and littering. The criteria of water pollution are deterioration of water quality due to changes in physical, chemical, biological and other properties and appearance of substances harmful to people, animals, birds, fish, food and commercial organisms, depending on the type of water use, as well as the increase in water temperature that changes the conditions of normal life activity of aquatic organisms.

In contrast to pollution, which affects the water quality of water reservoirs, littering is understood as the entry of foreign insoluble objects (for example, wood, slag, scrap metal, construction debris, *etc.*) into water reservoirs without changing the water quality. Water depletion is understood as permanent reduction of reserves and deterioration of the quality of surface and ground water which are sustainable and occur under the influence of human activity. It does not refer to seasonal fluctuations in the flow of water in rivers or to natural changes in the water reserve in seas, lakes, groundwater basins and glaciers.

Like in cases of protection of other natural objects, the task of water protection is solved by imposing duties on the subjects of water relations – citizens and legal entities as well as public authorities.

For the purpose of water protection, environmental and water laws establish a range of general and special requirements.

General requirements cover the protection of most water bodies that do not have a special legal regime of nature protection.

1) Requirements for design, construction and operation of economic and other facilities which can have a negative influence on water. Along with environmental requirements set forth in the Federal Law "On Environmental Protection", the Water Code of the Russian Federation stipulates other two additional prohibitions and restrictions. First, water users using water bodies to withdraw water resources are obliged to take measures to prevent fish and other aquatic biological resources from getting into water intake facilities and to carry out activities to prevent pollution of subsoil water and rise of its level (Art. 61 of the Water Code of the Russian Federation). Second, water users using water bodies for technological needs of the thermal and nuclear power industries are obliged to observe the temperature regime of water bodies (Art. 62 of the Water Code of the Russian Federation).

2) Establishment of general (framework) prohibitions of discharge of harmful substances into water reservoirs. There are two types of these prohibitions. First, Article 44 of the Water Code of the Russian Federation prohibits discharge of

wastewater into water bodies containing natural healing resources, specially protected water bodies, the fish protective zones of Lake Baikal as well as into the sources of drinking and domestic water supply. Second, the Water Code of the Russian Federation reproduces a range of rules of the Federal Law "On Environmental Protection" regarding the inadmissibility of discharge of chemicals (pesticides, agrochemicals) exceeding the MPEs and discharge exceeding the maximum permissible physical impact (for example, discharge of wastewater exceeding the level of radiation).

3) Establishment of certain features of protection of swamps, glaciers and other water bodies the ecosystems of which are under the greatest threat. The measures for their protection include the prohibition to take ice from the mountain glaciers (Art. 58 of the Water Code of the Russian Federation), if this entails depletion of water, and establishment of restrictions on drainage of swamps or their parts (Art. 57 of the Water Code of the Russian Federation), *etc.*

4) Establishment of water protective zones and coastal protection belts, which have already been mentioned in the previous chapter. We should remind that in water protective zones it is prohibited to locate cemeteries, cattle burial grounds, disposal facilities for production and consumption waste, to take aviation measures to control pests; to drive and park vehicles (except for special vehicles), to construct and reconstruct filling stations and warehouses for fuel and lubricant materials. Development of water protective zones itself is not prohibited (par. 16, Art. 65 of the Water Code of the Russian Federation), however, construction, reconstruction and operation of economic and other facilities within the boundaries of water protective zones is allowed if they are equipped with structures protecting water bodies from pollution, littering, siltation and depletion of water in accordance with water legislation and legislation on environmental protection.

In a similar manner, storage of agrochemicals is allowed within the boundaries of coastal protection belts in specialized storage facilities commissioned before January 1, 2013 and located in the territories of sea ports, provided that these storage facilities are equipped with structures and systems preventing the pollution of water bodies.

5) Implementation of a range of preventive measures in order to prevent the negative impact of water on certain territories and facilities. For this purpose, there are measures taken to prevent the negative impact of water and eliminate its consequences, engineering protection of territories and facilities from flooding, waterlogging, destruction of the banks of water bodies, swamping and other negative impact of water. For example, ice-cutting (to eliminate ice jams during

the flood period), deepening of river beds, strengthening of banks (dams) are carried out for this purpose. Moreover, it is prohibitcd to locatc new settlements, construct cemeteries and waste disposal sites within the boundaries of flooded zones.

Water legislation stipulates a range of grounds for suspension or restriction of water use. For example, water use can be suspended or restricted in case of a threat of harm to human life or health, a radiation accident or other natural or man-made emergencies, harm to the environment and in other cases stipulated by laws.

Special environmental requirements for water protection:

1) Requirements for special protection of water bodies included in specially protected natural areas. Moreover, special protection requirements are provided for in relation to water bodies where archaeological cultural heritage sites are located as well as water bodies within the boundaries of reserve museums.

2) Environmental requirements for protection of Lake Baikal. These requirements are set in the Federal Law "On Protection of Lake Baikal" of May 1, 1999. Lake Baikal is a unique and the most ancient (25 million years) lake, it is attributed to the World Heritage sites for a reason. Baikal is the deepest lake in the world and the eighth largest lake by water surface area. The maximum depth of Baikal is 1,637 meters. Lake Baikal has a colossal volume of water, 23 thousand cubic kilometers, exceeding the volume of the five Great American Lakes. Lake Baikal contains about 20 percent of the world's surface fresh water reserves, and about 60 cubic kilometers of unique water quality is reproduced in Baikal annually.

The lake is characterized by exceptional biological diversity. It is home to 1340 animal species and 570 plant species. Twelve specially protected natural areas are directly adjacent to the coast of Lake Baikal. In addition, there are 23 specially protected areas and over 400 natural monuments located in the adjacent territory. The decision taken by UNESCO in 1996 to include Baikal in the List of World Natural Heritage sites is unprecedented since the area of this territory is about 90 thousand square kilometers. It is comparable to the area of Portugal and twice as large as Switzerland or Denmark Turbyanov, L.D. (2004).

The Baikal Natural Area was established to protect this unique lake. It includes Lake Baikal, the water protective zone adjacent to Lake Baikal, its catchment area within the territory of the Russian Federation, specially protected natural areas adjacent to Lake Baikal and the area of up to 200 kilometers wide to the west and northwest of Lake Baikal adjacent to it.

The Baikal Natural Area consists of three ecological zones: central ecological zone, buffer ecological zone and ecological zone of atmospheric influence. For each of these zones, there is a particular set of prohibitions on economic and other activities that can have a negative impact on Baikal ecosystems. For example, clear felling of forests and disposal of production and consumption waste of hazard classes I-III are completely prohibited in the central zone.

3) Environmental requirements for protection of wetlands. These requirements follow from the Convention on Wetlands of International Importance Especially as Waterfowl Habitat of February 2, 1971. The sense of this Convention is that wetlands have a particular environmental value since they are home to unique flora and fauna, especially waterfowl. In this regard, state parties to this Convention must assume obligations to compile a list of these wetlands in their territory and mark them on the map. These wetlands can be included in specially protected natural areas though the Convention does not make it obligatory. To fulfill their international obligations, the states must establish a system of monitoring of wetlands, and, in case of adverse changes in their condition, take immediate measures to protect them. The Volga River delta, the wetlands of which are part of the Astrakhansky State Biosphere Reserve, is a such typical wetland.

4) Environmental requirements for protection of ground water. There are three requirements. First, in the catchment areas of ground water bodies which are used or can be used for the purposes of drinking and domestic water supply, it is prohibited to locate disposal facilities for production and consumption waste, cemeteries, cattle burial grounds and other facilities having a negative impact on ground water. Second, if aquifers are opened during subsoil use, it is necessary to take measures to protect ground water bodies. Third, special requirements are established for the burial of waste and wastewater in subsoil, preventing the negative impact of this pollution on the condition and quality of ground water.

To sum up, we should note that the achievement of the water protection goals depends to a large extent on the successful fulfillment of the objectives related to the protection of other natural objects – land, subsoil and forests. For example, forests preserve and maintain the flows of rainwater and snow melt. Like reservoirs, they regulate and make these flows more even throughout the year. Soil washout in forests is much less than in areas devoid of vegetation. This is why excessive deforestation affects water resources and dramatically increases soil erosion.

LEGAL REGULATION OF FAUNA PROTECTION

Fauna is the totality of all species of wild animals permanently or temporarily inhabiting the territory of the Russian Federation in the state of natural freedom as well as relating to natural resources of the continental shelf and the exclusive economic zone of the Russian Federation. Fauna as an object of legal protection is characterized by a number of features, which are enshrined in environmental and fauna legislation. They are as follows:

a) Belonging to wild fauna (this is why domestic animals (cats, dogs, *etc.*), including those which have lost their possessors, are not covered by fauna and environmental legislation);

b) Wild animals being in the state of natural freedom (it is understood as direct natural connection of animals with the environment. Wild animals in zoos and open-air cages as well as some species of animals (for example, reindeer) kept in semi-free conditions are protected as inventory items in accordance with the requirements of civil law);

c) Establishment of territorial boundaries for wild animals (in the territory of Russia they are included in the unified state fauna fund, which is important for determination of migratory animals);

d) Non-consumability of objects (*i.e.*, when a certain animal passes from the territory of the Russian Federation to the territory of another state and in case of loss of certain animals as a result of hunting or fishing fauna does not vanish in general as the object of protection. The term “consumability” refers not to individual objects or species of fauna (which are certainly consumable) but to the fauna fund in general since even if one wild animal having the said features is saved, the fauna fund is saved).

Some studies sometimes mention also another feature – usefulness, which was enshrined in legislation in the 1960s. However, afterwards most scholars and the legislator rejected the division of animals into useful and harmful as it had always been of a conventional nature. Since everything is interconnected in nature, individual species of animals under various circumstances can be both harmful and useful. For example, hares or wild boars in case of their optimal numbers per 1 km of hunting grounds are useful animals, however, if their numbers are exceeded, they are already harmful because they can cause significant harm to forestry and agriculture.

The use of fauna is study and extraction of animals or receipt of benefit from them by other means to meet the material or spiritual needs of people, with or without withdrawal from their habitat. The use of fauna must not lead to the depletion of fauna biodiversity within the borders of the Russian Federation in the long term.

Protection of fauna is the activities aimed at preserving biodiversity and ensuring sustainable existence of fauna as well as creating conditions for sustainable use and reproduction of fauna. The protection of fauna habitat is one of the areas of fauna protection activities. Legislation establishes two regimes of the protection of animals.

The general regime of the protection is established by the Federal Law “On Fauna”. Based on the criterion of the possibility of being an object of hunting and fishing, this Law distinguishes two categories of animals with the general regime of legal protection: animals that are objects of hunting or fishing (their list is included in the decrees of the Government of the Russian Federation) – in relation to these animals humane methods of hunting are stipulated; animals not attributed to objects of hunting or fishing – their extraction or other use, according to Article 43 of the Federal Law “On Fauna”, is allowed only with permits of specially authorized state bodies.

The special regime is established by the Law of the Russian Federation “On Fauna” in relation to animals attributed to specially protected ones, including those listed in the Red Data Book of the Russian Federation and the Red Data Books of constituent entities of the Russian Federation.

The general requirements for fauna protection include the establishment of a number of restrictions in relation to fauna use, in particular, prohibition of particular types of fauna use in certain territories (water areas), restriction of the use of certain fauna in certain territories (water areas), establishment of periods (time) of fauna use and establishment of allowed types of tools and methods of capture of animals and some other requirements.

The creation of specially protected natural areas is a particular fauna protection measure. For example, in accordance with Article 15 of the Federal Law “On Specially Protected Natural Areas”, commercial hunting and fishing, activities involving the disturbance of the flora and fauna habitation conditions, gathering of biological collections and some other activities are prohibited within the boundaries of national parks. Consequently, all species of plants and animals within this type of specially protected natural areas but not only those listed in the Red Data Book of the Russian Federation are to be protected.

The special regime of protection is established for animals recognized as rare and endangered. This means that their number and habitat have sharply reduced and continue reducing as a result of direct extermination, habitat destruction or for other reasons. These biological species will not be able to survive without active participation of people. The special regime of protection is established for their preservation. There are three levels of record and protection of rare and endangered plants and animals implemented by maintaining the Red Data Books. The first level is participation in the maintenance of the International Red Data Book, the second level is the maintenance of the Red Data Book of the Russian Federation and the third one is the maintenance of the Red Data Books of constituent entities of the Russian Federation.

The need to introduce several levels of the Red Data Books is due to the fact that, according to the International Union for Conservation of Nature (IUCN), from 1600 to 1975, 74 species and 86 subspecies of birds (1.23 percent) and 63 species and 44 subspecies (1.43 percent) of mammals vanished from the face of the earth. The loss of 75 percent of mammal species and 86 percent of bird species is associated with human activity. Nine species and subspecies of mammals and birds have vanished from Russia over the last 400 years.1

The Red Data Book of the Russian Federation is the official document containing a set of data on the state, distribution and measures of protection of rare and endangered species (subspecies, populations) of wild animals, plants and fungi inhabiting (growing) in the territory of the Russian Federation, the continental shelf and in the exclusive economic zone of the Russian Federation.

The animals and plants listed in the Red Data Book of the Russian Federation are attributed to one of the rare status categories: category 0 (Probably Vanished), category 1 (Endangered), category 2 (Declining in Number and/or Distribution), category 3 (Rare), category 4 (Undetermined by Status), category 5 (Restorable and Restoring).

By their legal nature, the Red Data Books are a variety of registers of natural resources and sites. The Ministry of Natural Resources and Environment (Minprirody) of the Russian Federation maintains the Red Data Book of the Russian Federation. The Red Data Book of the Russian Federation must be published at least once in 10 years. Animals and plant that are included in it are to be withdrawn everywhere from economic use.

Any activities that lead to the reduction in the population of animals listed in the Red Data Book or deterioration of their habitat are prohibited. Rare and endangered animals are added to (removed from) the Red Data Book of the Russian Federation and the Red Data Books of constituent entities of the Russian Federation on the basis of the state monitoring data and published scientific data (scientific population estimates).

Legal entities and citizens carrying out economic activities in the territories and water areas that are home to these animals bear enhanced responsibility for annihilation of these animals and plants in accordance with Article 259 of the Criminal Code of the Russian Federation "Destruction of Critical Habitats for Organisms Listed in the Red Data Book of the Russian Federation".

1089 rare and endangered species, including 676 species of plants and fungi and 413 species of animals, are registered in the Russian Federation. The population of rare and endangered species decreases due to the degradation of their habitat as a result of large-scale development of the territories (increased forest use, subsoil use, implementation of infrastructure projects) as well as due to global climate change State Report. (2019).

Extraction of animals belonging to the species listed in the Red Data Book of the Russian Federation is allowed in exceptional cases on the basis of administrative licenses in order to preserve these animals, regulate their population, protect public health, eliminate threats to human life, prevent mass diseases of agricultural and other domestic animals, meet traditional needs of small indigenous peoples, *etc.*

The issue under consideration has another important aspect following from the provisions of international agreements governing the import, export and transit transportation of rare and endangered plants and animals. These international documents include the Convention on International Trade in Endangered Species of Wild Fauna and Flora (Washington, March 3, 1973), which contains lists of species of mammals, birds, reptiles, amphibians, fish, invertebrates and plants. These species as well as their parts or derivatives are exported, reexported or imported in accordance with this Convention. Fulfillment of the requirements of the Convention and the subsequent resolutions and decisions of conferences of member states of the Convention has led to the development and change of national legislation governing the trade and use of species of wild animals and plants (their parts, derivatives and any products from them) included in the lists to the Convention.

The introduction of these requirements in paragraph 3 of Article 60 of the Law of the Russian Federation "On Environmental Protection" means the legislative establishment of state regulation of the relevant activities, including the introduction of certain restrictions on civil circulation of samples of wild animals and plants as well as the establishment of liability for violations in the area of their circulation and use.

Now the circulation of wild animals and plants included in the Appendix to the Convention is regulated on the basis of the Federal Law "On Fauna", the Customs Code of the Russian Federation, other federal laws and a range of bylaws.

From these documents, it follows that the export of animal and plant species, their parts or derivatives falling under the Convention from the territory of the Russian Federation is allowed subject to a special permit of the Administrative Body under the Convention in the Russian Federation, and the import of these animal and plant species to the territory of Russia – subject to a permit of the administrative body under the Convention (or another competent authority) of the exporting country, and in cases stipulated by the Convention – a permit of the Administrative Body under the Convention in Russia.

In the Russian Federation, the administrative bodies, according to this Convention, include Rosprirodnadzor, which is under the jurisdiction of the Ministry of Natural Resources and Environment (Minprirody) of the Russian Federation (in relation to endangered species of wild fauna and flora, except for sturgeon fish species) as well as Rosrybolovstvo (in relation to sturgeon fish species).

However, the efficiency of these measures to protect rare and endangered animals and plants is not sufficiently high enough. According to the foreign expert estimates, the turnover of the illegal trade in wild animals reaches 19 billion dollars per year (4th place after the drug traffic, counterfeiting and the slave trade) (accessed September 18, 2021). In addition, the uncontrolled import and sale of exotic animals withdrawn from nature on the Russian market is hazardous because hardly known infections can be transferred to the country.

LEGAL REGULATION OF SUBSOIL PROTECTION

Subsoil is the part of the earth's crust under the soil layer or, in its absence, under the earth's surface and the bottom of water reservoirs, extending to depths accessible for geological study and exploration. Consequently, subsoil has no lower boundary and extends down to the core of the Earth (although people have not actually drilled wells deeper than 15 km). The legal concept of subsoil is not equated with the mineral resources contained in subsoil (subsoil is a concept broader than mineral resources). Similarly, water and water bodies cannot be equated.

Considering the issue of legal protection of subsoil, it is necessary to have a clear idea of the object of this protection. The peculiar features of subsoil make the anthropogenic impact on it possible both directly and as a result of pollution of soil and water bodies. Consequently, it is necessary to distinguish, on the one hand, the legal protection of subsoil from the harmful impact of the environment and, on the other hand, the protection of the environment from the harmful impact of the consequences of all types of mining operations (the latter term does not relate to mountains, it means operations for the extraction of various types of mineral resources). The conventional view of subsoil use as an inexhaustible source of budget replenishment does not correspond to reality in recent years. Intensified mining and long-distance transportation of mineral resources frequently cause harm to the environment, especially during mining operations. Researchers point out two main problems in the area of rational use and protection of subsoil. They are the inefficient use of subsoil resources with the increasing complexity of field exploitation and the growing impact of mining on the environment.

The said problems manifest themselves in neglecting nature protection activities during the liquidation of mines as well as individual facilities at operating mining enterprises. Direct negative consequences of the impact of subsoil use on the environment are as follows: dust and gas pollution of air during drilling operations (in the course of processing of minerals, associated gas flaring and accidental releases); disruption of the water balance during mining (mining operations often lead to lowering of the ground water level and the storage of liquid waste often contributes to flooding of the adjacent areas); pollution and depletion of surface and ground water from mine openings; deterioration of the quality, disturbance and temporary alienation of land (as a result of soil contamination or flooding of the areas adjacent to mines); generation of a significant amount of industrial waste; violation of the temperature regime of geological processes having a negative effect (growth of seismicity); change of the habitat of wild animals and a range of other consequences.

Taking into account that subsoil is part of the environment, the legislator provides for a range of areas for its protection and rational use, among which the following ones should be pointed out.

The first area is the establishment of mandatory environmental requirements for subsoil users carrying out mining operations. These requirements include the protection of mineral deposits from flooding, inundation, fires and other factors reducing the quality of mineral resources and the commercial value of deposits or impeding their development. Moreover, within this area of protection of subsoil (and the environment from the negative impact of mining operations), in Article 23 of the Law of the Russian Federation "On Subsoil", the legislator intentionally enshrined the rule about the need to prevent subsoil pollution in case of underground storage of oil, gas or other substances and materials, burial of waste of hazard classes I-V, discharge of wastewater, placement of associated water,

water used by subsoil users for their own production and technological needs, water generated by subsoil users engaged in exploration and mining as well as the primary processing of potassium and magnesium salts in rock formations. In addition, it is stated that it is necessary to prevent production and consumption waste disposal in catchment areas of ground water bodies and in places of ground water which is used for the purposes of drinking water supply or technical water supply or the reserves of which are made as a sources of drinking water supply. It is obligatory to follow the procedure for conservation and liquidation of mining enterprises and underground structures not related to mining.

Legislation on subsoil stipulates also a number of guarantees to prevent harmful impact on the environment in the course of subsoil use. The main of them is the possibility to bring violators of the above requirements to liability. Moreover, the public interest in the area of subsoil use is enshrined, for example, in Article 8 of the Law of the Russian Federation "On Subsoil". This Article stipulates that subsoil use in the territories of settlements and zones with special conditions of use may be limited or prohibited if this use can pose a threat to the safety of the life and health of the population and environmental protection. Moreover, by virtue of Article 46 of the Law on Environmental Protection, geological survey, exploration and production of hydrocarbons, their processing, transportation, storage and sale must involve measures for oil and petroleum products spill prevention and response as well as measures for the prevention and elimination of other negative impact on the environment. The mandatory availability of oil and petroleum products spill prevention and response plans is one of these measures.

Other guarantees of environmentally lawful behavior of subsoil users involve also the mandatory implementation of the following measures (this list is not exhaustive): EIA for a number of planned types of mining operations; application of the requirements provided for by the Federal Law "On the Industrial Safety of Hazardous Production Facilities" to ensuring the safety of mining operations, *etc.* Economic guarantees of subsoil protection include the state support measures stipulated by Article 17 of the Federal Law "On Environmental Protection" for activities carried out by economic entities for utilization of associated petroleum gas. A number of additional guarantees of environmental protection are contained in legislation on other natural resources. For example, according to Article 13 of the Land Code of the Russian Federation, during construction related to soil disturbance and works related to subsoil use, the fertile soil layer is removed and used to improve low-yield land. In compliance with paragraph 4 of Article 59 of the Water Code of the Russian Federation, if aquifers are opened during subsoil use, it is necessary to take measures to protect ground water bodies.

The second area consists in the creation of specially protected geological areas. Its idea is that rare geological outcrops, mineralogical formations, paleontological objects and other subsoil areas of particular scientific or cultural value can be declared as geological reserves, sanctuaries or natural or cultural monuments according to the established procedure. Any activities impeding the preservation of the said reserves, sanctuaries and monuments are prohibited. Article 33 of the Law "On Subsoil" states that if rare geological and mineralogical formations, meteorites, paleontological, archaeological and other objects of scientific or cultural interest are found during subsoil use, the subsoil users are obliged to suspend works in the relevant area and inform thereof the authorities which issued the license. This means that subsoil users must familiarize themselves with the latest scientific studies and interest in several branches of scientific knowledge. Moreover, it appears that it is very difficult for a non-specialist to distinguish, for example, individual paleontological finds from pieces of stone processed by nature.

One of the most controversial issues of subsoil protection in foreign countries is the discussion of the environmental consequences of using horizontal drilling and hydraulic fracturing ("fracking"). During this process, a pressurized mixture of water, sand and chemicals is introduced into subsoil to break up rock formations and release natural gas (oil). In addition to the risk that this process will lead to ground water contamination, there are also concerns about surface water contamination as well as concerns about air pollution. These activities can have a negative impact also on the environment of the neighboring states, and if our neighbors (China, Kazakhstan) use these oil and gas production technologies, the negative consequences for the environment can occur in Russia as well. In the United States, the intensified use of hydraulic fracturing for oil field development increased the activities for withdrawal of land plots from their owners for public needs (for example, in the State of Texas). In these cases, the land possessors face more pressure due to the construction of pipelines, causing the establishment of easements. At the moment, the problems of fracking are not relevant to Russia (since conventional fields have not yet been exhausted) but this issue will arise sooner or later.

LEGAL REGULATION OF AIR PROTECTION

Air is the most unique natural object. In contrast to land, water, subsoil, forest and fauna, which are natural objects and natural resources an individualized part of which can be subject to the right of private or public ownership (land plots, ponds, felled wood, mined minerals, animals killed during hunting), air is only a natural object to which no private, state or other ownership is established. It cannot be individualized like other natural resources, and the entire regulatory framework is dedicated exclusively to the issues of its protection (the Water Code of the Russian Federation is dedicated not to air as a natural resource but to the organization of transportation by air). However, despite the lack of any mention of the right of state ownership of air in civil and natural resources legislation, state authorities of the Russian Federation and constituent entities of the Russian Federation actually exercise the powers of the owner, issuing permits for the emission of harmful substances into the atmosphere (thereby using its assimilative potential) and charging the corresponding fees from economic entities.

Air is an essential component of the environment, it is a natural mixture of atmospheric gases outside residential, industrial and other premises.

Air can be used both as a space for emissions from industrial enterprises and other facilities and in the process of common natural resource management, *i.e.*, the use of air by people for natural life support. In contrast to all other types of natural objects, air does not fall under the special regime of protection (like the Red Data Book or specially protected natural areas). It is necessary to take measures to protect it because the level of air pollution is rated as high and very high in 46 cities of the Russian Federation (21 percent of cities with regular air monitoring). 13.4 million residents (12 percent of Russian population) live in these cities. In 2018, the share of cities with excessive air pollution was 58 percent of the total number of monitored cities, there were 37 cities where maximum concentrations of harmful substances exceeded 10 MPCs (Report, 2019).

Air protection is a system of measures taken by state authorities of the Russian Federation and constituent entities of the Russian Federation, local government bodies, legal entities and individuals in order to improve the quality of air and prevent its harmful impact on human health and the environment. The Russian Federation has a consistent system of legal rules regulating the protection of air from anthropogenic impact. The main objective of Russian legislation on air protection is to establish the system of duties for users of natural resources and public authorities.

The duties of users of natural resources (legal entities) involve the need to comply with the specified values of harmful impact on air; to plan air protection activities; to obtain permits for emission of harmful substances (pollutants) into the air and permits for harmful physical impact on the air; to conduct an inventory of emissions; to perform industrial control, *etc.* The air protection requirements applied not only at the stage of operation but also at the stages of design, location, construction and reconstruction of facilities for economic and other activities are a variety of this group of duties.

A number of duties are imposed also on state authorities. They are formation and implementation of a unified state policy in the field of air protection; establishment of the procedure for development and approval of hygiene and environmental regulations for air quality, maximum permissible (critical) loads on ecological systems, maximum permissible levels of physical impact on air and other environmental regulations for air protection; formation of a unified regulatory and methodological framework in the field of air protection; organization and funding of state monitoring of air and its implementation; organization of informing the population about atmospheric air pollution and fulfillment of federal target programs for air protection as well as the exercise of other powers in the field of air protection.

All air protection activities can be divided into two groups. The first group includes general requirements for air protection set forth in the Federal Law "On Environmental Protection" and reproduced (in full or in part) in the Federal Law "On Air Protection": requirements for regulation of the negative impact of economic activities on the air, consideration of air protection requirements at the stage of construction or operation of economic facilities, the need to create sanitary protection zones around industrial facilities that have a negative impact on the air, the need to record and conduct an inventory of facilities producing harmful emissions, *etc.*

The second group consists of special requirements for air protection listed in the Federal Law "On Air Protection" and other federal laws and bylaws.

1. In order to fulfill their air protection duties, public authorities can use means of both environmental and urban development legislation. The latter include planning of development of the road network in settlements and beyond them in territorial planning and urban development zoning documents. These documents show the available and planned highways, motor vehicle parks and other items. Budget funds will be allocated for the construction of these transport infrastructure facilities according to the said documents. This will reduce the anthropogenic load on the air in settlements as a result of, for example, the construction of bypass traffic arteries as well as the regulation of non-stop traffic of transport in city streets, which will eliminate (or decrease) traffic jams and reduce the volume of emissions due to the lack of waiting time at traffic lights.

2. It is prohibited to emit into the air the substances the hazard degree of which for the life and health of people and the environment is not established. Moreover, executive authorities of the Russian Federation and state authorities of constituent entities of the Russian Federation can introduce restrictions on the use of petroleum products and other types of fuel the combustion of which leads to air

pollution in the corresponding territory as well as encourage the production and use of environmentally friendly types of fuel and other energy carriers.

3. It is prohibited to design, locate and construct the facilities for economic and other activities the functioning of which can led to adverse changes in the climate and the ozone layer, deterioration of human health, destruction of the gene pool of plants and animals, the occurrence of irreversible consequences for people and the environment.

4. Transport and other vehicles the emissions of which have a negative impact on the air are subject to regular checks for compliance of these emissions with technical regulations regarding emissions. State authorities of constituent entities of the Russian Federation can within their competence introduce restrictions on the entry of transport and other vehicles to settlements and sites for leisure and tourism in specially protected natural areas and regulate movement of transport and other vehicles in the said areas.

5. In urban and other settlements, state authorities of constituent entities of the Russian Federation and local government bodies organize activities to control emissions of pollutants into the air during periods of adverse meteorological conditions. For example, if there is a forecast of adverse meteorological conditions, legal entities, individual entrepreneurs that have sources of emissions of pollutants into the air are obliged to carry out activities to reduce the emissions of pollutants into the air coordinated with executive authorities of constituent entities of the Russian Federation performing regional state environmental supervision.

6. For the territory of a settlement or its part in which facilities that have a negative impact on the environment and other facilities affecting air quality are located, the authorities of constituent entities of the Russian Federation have the right to organize summary calculations of air pollution if the specified values of hygiene regulations for air quality are exceeded in the territory of the settlement or its part in order to reduce or eliminate the emissions of pollutants and also in other cases to prevent this excess.

To reduce the level of air pollution in individual urban settlements and urban districts (including those with intra-urban division), Federal Law No. 195-FZ of July 26, 2019 "On Conducting an Experiment Concerning the Setting of Quotas for Emissions of Pollutants and Amending Certain Legislative Acts of the Russian Federation on Reducing Air Pollution" prescribes that the experiment concerning the setting of quotas for emissions of pollutants (excluding radioactive substances) into the air must be conducted based on the summary calculations of air pollution in the urban districts of Bratsk, Krasnoyarsk, Lipetsk, Magnitogorsk,

Mednogorsk, Nizhny Tagil, Novokuznetsk, Norilsk, Omsk, Chelyabinsk, Cherepovets and Chita.

On the basis of the corresponding decision of the Government of the Russian Federation, other urban settlements and urban districts with high and very high air pollution can be additionally attributed to the territories of the experiment.

The experiment concerning the setting of quotas for emissions is conducted based on the summary calculations from January 1, 2020 to December 31, 2024. For each territory of the experiment, the Government of the Russian Federation, as advised by the principal officer of a constituent entity of the Russian Federation, approves a comprehensive action plan to reduce emissions of pollutants into the air, including target values for reducing emissions. They must be achieved in the course of implementation of the comprehensive plan. The plan includes a list of activities aimed at reducing emissions from their sources at facilities that have a negative impact on the environment, including public utility, transport and social infrastructure facilities, with values for reducing these emissions, a list of other activities aimed at improving air quality, with the period of these activities, the amount and sources of funding, federal executive authorities, state authorities of constituent entities of the Russian Federation, local government bodies, legal entities and individual entrepreneurs responsible for the implementation of the said activities.

In 2021, the list of air protection measures was supplemented by Federal Law No. 296-FZ of July 2, 2021 “On the Limitation of Greenhouse Gas Emissions”. The Law attributes the following measures to those for the limitation of greenhouse gas emissions: state record of greenhouse gas emissions, establishment of the target values for reducing greenhouse gas emissions and support of activities reducing greenhouse gas emissions and increasing the absorption of greenhouse gas emissions in accordance with legislation of the Russian Federation. For the implementation of the provisions of the Law, the Government of the Russian Federation establishes the target value for reducing greenhouse gas emissions for the economy of the Russian Federation, state record of greenhouse gas emissions (in the form of a register) and the register of carbon units are used and the alienation of carbon units (their transfer to another person) is allowed.

CONCLUSION

The chapter notes that all natural objects are closely interrelated with each other. The deterioration of the quality of one of them inevitably entails certain consequences for the state of the other elements of the ecological system. Therefore, the legislation provides for a number of measures aimed at both protecting the environment as a whole and its components. The latter direction of protection is due to the fact that the protection of certain types of natural objects has a certain specificity within the framework of the general task of ensuring a favorable quality of the environment. This chapter discusses the features of the protection of lands, waters, subsoil, forests, wildlife and atmospheric air.

NOTES

[1] Order of the Ministry of Natural Resources of the Russian Federation No. 323 of April 6, 2004 «On Approval of the Strategy for the Conservation of Rare and Endangered Species of Animals, Plants, and Fungi». In: Legal Reference System «Consultant Plus», accessed September 8, 2021.

QUESTIONS AND TASKS FOR SELF-CONTROL

1. What are the main areas of legal regulation of land protection?

2. List the rules of law regulating forest protection.

3. What measures for water protection do you know?

4. What fauna protection activities are public authorities and users of natural resources obliged to carry out?

5. Specify the main areas of legal protection of subsoil.

6. What are the main measures of legal regulation of air protection?

REFERENCES

Report, S. (2019). *On the State and Protection of the Environment in the Russian Federation in 2018.*

Turbyanov, L.D. (2004). Regulatory Support of Protection of Lake Baikal.

Report of the International Fund for Animal Welfare «Wanted – Dead or Alive: Exposing Online Wildlife Trade» (2014). In: (accessed September 18, 2021). http://www.mnr.gov.ru/upload/iblock/cda/doklad%20IFAW.pdf

CHAPTER 7

Concept and Types of Areas with a Special Environmental Legal Regime

Abstract: The Russian Federation now stipulates the possibility of establishing two special environmental legal regimes in the country, including specially protected natural areas (SPNAs) and ecological disaster zones. The essence of both environmental legal regimes consists of establishing a special procedure for the use and protection of a clearly localized territory different from the regime of using land plots and other natural objects of the country. This manifests itself in establishing features of the management of this territory, the regime of restrictions of civil and corporate rights, as well as additional funding of a range of special nature protection activities. The purpose of the establishment of special restrictions and prohibitions for economic and other use of these territories is to create additional guarantees of the achievement of the main objective of environmental legislation – to ensure a favorable environmental quality.

This means that the establishment of the special environmental legal regime is necessary if the general environmental requirements (licensing, standardization, *etc.*) do not make it possible to preserve and restore specific natural objects and systems in the appropriate state. The list of the relevant prohibitions and restrictions is contained in federal and regional environmental legislation as well as in land, water, forest legislation, legislation on natural and cultural heritage, *etc*. Particular additional measures in the area under consideration can also be adopted at the municipal level with the corresponding legal acts of local government bodies. The legal status of both varieties of areas with a special environmental legal regime (SPNAs and ecological disaster zones) has several similar and different features. The purposes of giving a particular territory a special environmental legal regime are also the same – to ensure everyone's right to a favorable environment. Significant differences between these territories consist in the objective related to them. SPNAs are created to conserve certain ecological systems for present and future generations and to study the unique natural areas; ecological disaster zones are created to restore disturbed ecosystems. In this regard, the access of citizens to SPNAs is not prohibited (it is even encouraged), while they have to obtain a special permit to enter an ecological disaster zone. Consequently, the special regime is established to ensure the protection of two territories that are opposite to their ecological state.

Aleksey Anisimov and Anatoliy Ryzhenkov

Keywords: Arboretum, Baikal, Botanical garden, Cultural heritage, Ecological disaster zones, Fines, Lessee, Natural landscape, Natural monument, National park, Natural system, Nature park, Owner, Privatization, Prohibitions, Recreational activities, Reserve, Restrictions, Specially protected natural areas, Wildlife sanctuary.

CONCEPT AND TYPES OF SPECIALLY PROTECTED NATURAL AREAS

The Russian Federation now stipulates the possibility to establish two special environmental legal regimes in the country – specially protected natural areas (SPNAs) and ecological disaster zones. The essence of both environmental legal regimes consists of establishing a special procedure for the use and protection of a clearly localized territory different from the regime of using land plots and other natural objects of the country. This manifests itself in establishing features of the management of this territory, the regime of restrictions of civil and corporate rights, as well as additional funding of a range of special nature protection activities. The purpose of the establishment of special restrictions and prohibitions for economic and other use of these territories is to create additional guarantees of the achievement of the main objective of environmental legislation – to ensure a favorable environmental quality. In other words, the establishment of the special environmental legal regime is necessary if the general environmental requirements (licensing, standardization, *etc.*) do not make it possible to preserve and restore specific natural objects and systems in the appropriate state. The list of the relevant prohibitions and restrictions is contained in federal and regional environmental legislation as well as in land, water, forest legislation, legislation on natural and cultural heritage, *etc*. Particular additional measures in the area under consideration can also be adopted at the municipal level with the corresponding legal acts of local government bodies.

The legal status of both varieties of areas with a special environmental legal regime (SPNAs and ecological disaster zones) has several similar and different features. The similar feature of the legal regime of SPNAs and ecological disaster zones is that a wrongful act committed in their territory is a characterizing attribute in some sets of elements under the Criminal Code of the Russian Federation (for example, paragraph 2 of Article 250 of the Criminal Code). The purposes of giving a particular territory a special environmental legal regime are also the same – to ensure everyone's right to a favorable environment.

Significant differences between these territories consist in the objective related to them. SPNAs are created to conserve certain ecological systems for present and future generations and to study the unique natural areas; ecological disaster zones are created to restore disturbed ecosystems. In this regard, the access of citizens to SPNAs is not prohibited (it is even encouraged), while they have to obtain a special permit to enter an ecological disaster zone. Consequently, the special environmental legal regime is established to ensure the protection of two territories that are opposite to their ecological state. Despite the obvious difference in the condition of the natural objects and systems in the relevant territories, both are two sides of the same coin and go beyond the standard state of the environment in a locality.

The Russian Federation now has no ecological disaster zones since no special federal law has been adopted on them yet. This is why the practice follows the way of protecting these "especially polluted areas" by developing "targeted" measures for their protection.

SPNAs had more luck in this sense, and the history of their creation in Russia goes back to several centuries. The first information about the creation of conservation areas in Russia belongs to the period of the 14th and 15th centuries. Complete or partial bans on unauthorized hunting, fishing, logging, and visiting certain areas were imposed than in some territories.

These areas were protected based on the tsar's decrees (the Decree of Peter I on the preservation of ship groves, the Decree of Catherine II on the protection of reserve groves). The activity of monasteries, which declared certain areas of forests with their fauna as a reserve (the reserve forest of the Trinity Sergius Lavra, Valaam Island, *etc.*), also contributed to their protection. Though these bans were due to economic, religious, and other state objectives, they contributed to preserving certain natural objects and systems in their natural state.

Now, the following regulations are the legal framework of the organization, protection, and use of SPNAs:

- Paragraph 1 of Article 72 of the Constitution of the Russian Federation, attributing specially protected natural areas to the subjects under the joint jurisdiction of the Russian Federation and its constituent entities;

- Federal Laws "On Environmental Protection", "On Specially Protected Natural Areas", "On Protection of Lake Baikal" and several other Federal Laws;

- Laws and other acts of state authorities of constituent entities of the Russian Federation. Law of Volgograd Region No. 641-OD of December 7, 2001 "On Specially Protected Natural Areas of Volgograd Region" can be mentioned as an example. Similar legal acts are also adopted in other regions;

- Acts of local government bodies aimed at creating specially protected natural areas of local significance according to the procedure established by laws of constituent entities of the Russian Federation. The creation of these areas is a right rather than a duty of municipal authorities.

Specially protected natural areas are parts of land or water space of special nature protection, scientific, cultural, aesthetic, recreational, and therapeutic significance which are completely or partially withdrawn from economical use, according to resolutions of state authorities or local government bodies and have a regime of special protection. Protective zones or districts with a regulated regime of economic activities can be created in the adjacent parts of land and water space to protect some categories of SPNAs (state nature reserves, national parks, *etc*.) from adverse anthropogenic impact. Protective zones are not created around other categories (for example, around state wildlife sanctuaries). Environmental legislation states several features of natural objects and systems for the establishment of a regime of special protection in their relation. As follows from paragraph 1 of Article 58 of the Federal Law "On Environmental Protection", the said natural objects must have a special nature protection, scientific, historical, cultural, aesthetic, recreational, therapeutic, and other value. It appears that the natural objects and systems that include especially valuable natural landscapes, places of growth of certain species of trees or flora, habitats of rare and endangered animal species, water reservoirs to be protected from human economic activities, and other islets of wildlife to be kept pristine for future generations are of conservation interest.

The objects intended for the organization of recreation, tourism, therapeutic, and sports activities of citizens are of recreational significance. Holiday and recreation centers, campsites, tourist camps, sports camps, and other facilities are located on the land for recreational purposes. Natural objects intended for the treatment and recreation of citizens are of therapeutic significance. Objects falling within the scope of legislation on historical and cultural heritage, in particular, historical and cultural monuments (including archaeological heritage sites), landmarks, places of crafts, production, and trade, as well as military and civilian burials, are of historical and cultural significance. Natural objects of historical and cultural significance can be given the status of cultural heritage sites and included in the register based on the findings of state historical and cultural expert reviews and the establishment of protective zones around them.

Legislation provides several measures to ensure the preservation of cultural heritage sites during construction, reclamation, economic and other works, up to the suspension of the activities causing harm. Combined protection of the natural systems possessing features of cultural heritage sites is also allowed. This type of special protection, as a rule, is implemented in the territory of national and nature parks. For example, one of the functional zones of national parks is called the zone of protection of historical and cultural objects; conditions for their preservation are ensured within its boundaries. Almost any, both the abovesaid and other, varieties of natural objects are of scientific and aesthetic significance. At the same time, the current legislation does not establish any somehow objective criteria of the aesthetic value of natural objects.

Environmental legislation now contains no exhaustive list of specially protected natural areas categories. Moreover, paragraph 2 of Article 2 of the Federal Law "On Specially Protected Natural Areas" emphasizes that laws of constituent entities of the Russian Federation can establish also other categories of specially protected natural areas (territories with monuments of garden art, protected coastlines, protected river systems, protected natural landscapes, biological stations, micro-reserves, *etc*.).

For example, the Republic of Sakha (Yakutia) established such a category of specially protected natural areas as resource reserves and Volgograd Region – protected landscapes (of regional and local significance), territories of particular value for the preservation of animals and plants listed in the Larva Red Data Book of Volgograd Region (SPNAs of regional significance) and natural attractions (local SPNAs).

Federal laws made their contribution to the expansion of the list of categories of SPNAs as well. For example, the Law of the Russian Federation "On Protection of Lake Baikal" introduces a new category of SPNAs with their own special environmental legal regime – the Baikal Natural Area. It is understood as the territory including Lake Baikal, the water protective zone adjacent to Lake Baikal, its catchment area within the territory of the Russian Federation, specially protected natural areas adjacent to Lake Baikal, and the area of up to 200 km wide to the west and northwest of Lake Baikal adjacent to it.

This type of special protection is not mentioned in the Federal Law "On Specially Protected Natural Areas"; it is unique and has no other analogs.

There are several classifications of SPNAs.

First, three types of the legal regime of specially protected natural areas are distinguished according to the criterion of sanctity:

1. Absolute sanctity – this regime is inherent in natural reserves and natural monuments, it excludes economic activities in this territory, human

intervention is allowed only in exceptional cases – for research, sanitary felling of trees, firefighting, elimination of predators, *etc*.;

2. Relative sanctity, which is characterized by the combination of absolute prohibition and limited economic activities involving the exploitation of natural resources. Wildlife sanctuaries correspond to this attribute;

3. The combined regime, which means a combination of zones where any economic or recreational activities involving zones used for recreation and tourism are prohibited (national and nature parks and arboretums) (Petrov, 1995).

The following SPNAs are distinguished according to the criterion of organizational structure:

1. SPNAs the management and protection of which are ensured by the nature protection authorities with the same names (non-commercial legal entities), for example, state nature reserves, national and nature parks, arboretums, and botanical gardens;

2. SPNAs for the management of which no legal entities are established; they include natural monuments and many regional SPNAs.

SPNAs of federal, regional, and local significance are distinguished according to ownership of land and other natural resources. For example, the territories of state nature reserves and national parks belong to SPNAs of federal significance. The territories of state wildlife sanctuaries, natural monuments, arboretums, and botanical gardens can be attributed to SPNAs of federal or regional significance. Nature parks are SPNAs of the only constituent entities of the Russian Federation. SPNAs created in compliance with the laws of constituent entities of the Russian Federation can be in municipal ownership. SPNAs of federal and regional significance is created, accordingly, by the Government of the Russian Federation and executive authorities of constituent entities of the Russian Federation. Local government bodies create specially protected natural areas of local significance on land plots that are in the ownership of the relevant municipality. Suppose a specially protected natural area being created will occupy more than 5% of the total area of the land plots that are in the ownership of the municipality. In that case, the local government body coordinate the decision on the creation of the especially protected natural area with the state authority of the relevant constituent entity of the Russian Federation.

Local government bodies settle the issues that are provided for by municipal and environmental legislation and related to the use, protection, conservation, and reproduction of forests of specially protected natural areas located within the boundaries of settlements and urban districts under the provisions on the corresponding especially protected natural areas.

The establishment and change of the legal regime and boundaries or liquidation of SPNAs are implemented based on resolutions of the relevant state authorities of the Russian Federation or constituent entities of the Russian Federation or local government bodies creating these SPNAs. These resolutions required the state environmental expert review findings before, but now the Federal Law "On Environmental Expert Reviews" does not contain this requirement.

Paragraph 5 of Article 95 of the Land Code of the Russian Federation states that to create new and expand the available SPNAs, state authorities of constituent entities of the Russian Federation are entitled to adopt resolutions on the reservation of land, which is to be declared as the land of SPNAs, with its subsequent withdrawal (with payment of the compensation to the owners) and on limitation of economic activities on it. They usually do not withdraw land plots from private owners, but their rights are significantly restricted. However, the creation of SPNAs based on this principle gives rise to three following considerations.

1. The private owners of land plots included in any type of SPNAs (for example, reserves or national parks) are essentially the owners of land plots included the category of land of specially protected areas and sites, and exactly this record must be made in their title documents under paragraph 2 of Article 95 of the Land Code of the Russian Federation. At the same time, paragraph 4 of Article 2 of the Federal Law "On Specially Protected Natural Areas" determines that SPNAs can be of federal, regional, and local significance. SPNAs cannot be in private ownership in principle.

2. Land users land possessors (and in some cases lessees) can claim to acquire private ownership of land plots belonging to the state or municipalities for a fee or free of charge based on a bidding process or without it (Art. 39.3 of the Land Code of the Russian Federation). Paragraph 5 of Article 58 of the Law of the Russian Federation "On Environmental Protection" establishes restrictions of everyone's constitutional right to have a land plot based on the right of ownership, which is quite lawful. This follows from paragraph 3 of Article 55 of the Constitution of the Russian Federation, according to which "human and civil rights and freedoms can be restricted by federal laws only to the extent necessary to protect the foundations of the constitutional order, morality,

health, rights and legitimate interests of other persons, to ensure national defense and state security". In this case, the rights of citizens to privatization of land plots are restricted in the interests of the rights and legitimate interests of other persons, in particular, the right to a favorable environment.

3. According to paragraph 4 of Article 9 of the Urban Development Code of the Russian Federation, state authorities and local government bodies are not allowed to adopt resolutions on reservation of land, withdrawal of private land plots for state or municipal needs, transfer of land from one category to another in the absence of territorial planning documents, except in cases provided for by federal laws. If territorial planning documents do not stipulate SPNAs in a particular place, it will be impossible to reserve and withdraw the land plots to create specially protected natural areas. In its turn, under paragraph 4 of Article 58 of the Law of the Russian Federation "On Environmental Protection", withdrawal of the land of the nature reserve fund is prohibited, except in cases provided for by federal laws.

The existence of any SPNA can cease (with the subsequent redistribution of land) subject to two types of grounds:

1. Complete degradation (destruction) of natural objects included in SPNAs, which, due to this, lose their value and unique character and cannot be restored. In this situation, a land plot of the nature reserve fund can be transferred to another category of land of the land fund (for example, reserve land) based on the resolution of state authority.

2. Withdrawal of a land plot (natural system) to perform international obligations. This conclusion follows from Article 15 of the Constitution of the Russian Federation, according to which generally accepted principles and rules of international law and international agreements of the Russian Federation are an integral part of its legal system. If an international agreement of the Russian Federation establishes rules other than those stipulated by law, the rules of the international agreement apply. The first group of the grounds is sometimes used in practice, and the second group of the grounds of cessation of SPNAs is still purely theoretical.

The state register of specially protected natural areas is maintained for the purpose of assessment of the nature reserve fund. It contains information about their status, geographic location, boundaries, the regime of special protection, users of natural resources, environmental, educational, scientific, cultural, and other values. Russia now has about 12,000 SPNAs of federal, regional, and local significance. The total area of SPNAs is 237.7 million hectares. SPNAs of regional and local significance comprise 97.5% of the total number of SPNAs and 69.9% of their total area. Most SPNAs are located in the Central Federal District. There are 290 federal SPNAs (including 110 reserves), and their total area is 71.5 million hectares (Report, 2019).

The above figures on the area of SPNAs within the boundaries of Russia become even more impressive if we consider the size of some reserves or national parks. For example, Putorana State Reserve occupies an area of 1,887,251 hectares; Ust-Lena Reserve occupies 1,433,000 hectares. Meanwhile, on the millions of hectares occupied by the current SPNAs, there are hundreds of settlements, agricultural lands, roads, forests, and other natural and man-made objects that belong both to public owners (the Russian Federation, constituent entities of the Russian Federation and municipalities) and private owners, who constantly face problems with the sale, lease or privatization of their land plots.

The need to wind down economic activities often leads to social consequences related to poverty, unemployment, and the need to migrate to other regions of the country. The following question arises: how justified is the enormous size of several SPNAs? How do the restrictions and prohibitions imposed because of the creation of SPNAs correlate with the provisions of the concept of sustainable development, which calls for seeking a balance of three groups of interests rather than suppressing one interest with the other one?

It appears that to protect the interests of citizens and businesses, it is necessary to move from the current strategy of gigantomania, when SPNAs of tens of thousands of hectares are created, to a cluster approach, and instead of one enormous SPNA to create several small areas managed by the same directorate and with the same protection regime. This strategy has already been implemented in Orenburg State Reserve, which consists of five isolated areas located in five different municipal districts of the region. The implementation of this approach makes it possible to include into SPNAs settlements, roads, rivers, and territories around villages where the residents grow agricultural products and graze cattle. In fact, while the creation of SPNAs involves the establishment of a regime of increased protection for especially valuable and unique natural systems, what is the point of including into SPNAs villages and pastures, where it is absolutely clear that there cannot be any valuable natural systems in principle?

It is necessary to withdraw from this practice in favor of considering the population's economic and social interests. The creation of clusters will also make it possible to avoid problems related to the need to transfer land from one form of ownership to another one (for example, federal areas of the forest fund that fall within the boundaries of a regional SPNA to the ownership of a constituent entity of the Russian Federation) as well as accusations of misuse of the territory of SPNAs (any road in their territory, settlements, agricultural activities of the reserve's staff, *etc*.). The creation of small SPNAs will also simplify land organization procedures since most SPNAs now do not have clearly fixed boundaries, and it is too expensive to establish them on the ground.

The first step in this direction was taken in 2021 when amendments were made to the Law on SPNAs: now settlements can be included in specially protected natural areas without withdrawal of land plots and other immovable property located in their territory from the right holders (excluding state nature reserves) if it does not contradict the regime of special protection of the corresponding category of specially protected natural areas. In the case of zoning of specially protected natural areas, settlements are included in functional zones, which allows economic activities. The circulation of land plots in the territory of settlements included in specially protected natural areas of federal or regional significance is not limited. The villages included in SPNAs are now not considered to be land of SPNAs; they are attributed to the category of land of settlements.

To sum up, we should note that environmental legislation uses the term “natural heritage”, which raises the question of its correlation with SPNAs. Article 1 of the Federal Law “On Environmental Protection” understands natural heritage sites as natural objects, natural monuments, geological and physiographical formations, strictly limited areas, and natural attractions falling within the criteria of outstanding universal value and defined by the Convention Concerning the Protection of the World Cultural and Natural Heritage. Hence it follows that the first option of the correlation between natural heritage sites and SPNAs is that natural heritage sites are located within the boundaries of SPNAs; they are registered and have a special legal regime. For example, 32 SPNAs of federal and regional significance are already within the jurisdiction of the Convention Concerning the Protection of the World Cultural and Natural Heritage. Other natural heritage sites do not fall within this special regime of national SPNAs and, accordingly, are not located (in full or in part) within the boundaries of specially protected natural areas. This isn't easy to do, especially if this natural heritage site is, for example, the recently added Western Tien Shan (located within the boundaries of three countries – Kazakhstan, Kyrgyzstan, and Uzbekistan), which occupies an enormous area. There are similar problems also in other countries, including Russia.

Hence, in addition to the term “natural heritage sites”, it is necessary to supplement the Federal Law “On Environmental Protection” of January 10, 2002, also with rules on the mechanism of the protection of natural heritage sites both within and outside the boundaries of SPNAs.

STATE NATURE RESERVES

The history of creating reserves in Russia is more than 100 years. The creation of the network of reserves started with the establishment of Barguzinsky State Reserve in the Republic of Buryatia in 1916.

110 state reserves now function in Russia. State nature reserves belong to specially protected natural areas of federal significance. Within the boundaries of state nature reserves, the natural environment is preserved in its natural state, and economic and other activities are completely prohibited, except in cases expressly stated in the law. Natural resources and immovable property located within the boundaries of state nature reserves are federal property, and they are withdrawn from civil circulation unless otherwise provided for by federal laws.

The following objectives are set for state reserves:

a. Protection of natural areas to preserve biodiversity and maintain protected natural systems and objects in their natural state;

b. Organization of research;

c. State environmental monitoring;

d. Environmental education and development of educational tourism;

e. Assistance in the training of scientific personnel and experts in environmental protection.

State nature reserves are established based on Decrees of the Government of the Russian Federation adopted as advised by federal executive authorities in environmental protection. The territories of state nature reserves are expanded according to the same procedure. In the territories of state nature reserves, it is prohibited to carry out any activities contrary to the objectives of state reserves and the regime of special protection of their territories established in the provisions on the relevant state nature reserves, the introduction of living organisms for their acclimatization is not allowed either.

State nature reserves are managed by federal state budget institutions. Land plots (including land plots on which forests are located) within the boundaries of state nature reserves are provided to federal state budget institutions managing state nature reserves for permanent (perpetual) use under legislation of the Russian

Federation.

State nature reserves can include designated areas where any human intervention in natural processes is excluded. The size of these areas is determined based on the need to preserve the entire natural system in its natural state. In their turn, in specially designated areas of partial economic use, which do not include especially valuable ecological systems and objects for the conservation of which the state nature reserve was created, it is allowed to carry out activities aimed at ensuring the functioning of the state nature reserve and the support of citizens living in its territory. The legislator chooses this approach because reserves can occupy thousands of hectares and rural settlements can be located in their territory. Accordingly, to create living conditions for citizens (hayfields, pastures, *etc.*), it is necessary to allocate special least valuable land plots.

Individuals other than residents of the villages located within the boundaries of reserves or officers of the administrations (directorates) of the reserves can stay in the territories of the state nature reserves only with the permission of the federal state budget institutions managing the state nature reserves or the federal executive authority that is in charge of the state nature reserves.

The federal state budget institutions managing state nature reserves charge payments from individuals for visiting the territories of state nature reserves for educational tourism.

Biosphere reserves occupy a special place among reserves; UNESCO includes them in the World Network of Biosphere Reserves that perform global environmental monitoring (for example, the Black Lands Biosphere Reserve in the Republic of Kalmykia).

The territories of state nature biosphere reserves state environmental monitoring (state monitoring of the environment) as well as testing and introduction of methods of rational natural resource management that do not destroy the environment and do not deplete biological resources, can also include biosphere proving grounds, in particular, those with a differentiated regime of special protection and functioning. It is allowed to locate capital facilities and related infrastructure facilities (according to a special list) in the designated areas of the biosphere, proving grounds of state nature biosphere reserves to support the activities stipulated by the provision on these biospheres proving grounds and to develop educational tourism and sports. Land plots necessary for these activities can be leased to citizens and legal entities under land legislation.

The conclusion of intergovernmental agreements for the creation of reserves has become one of the areas of international cooperation in recent decades. For example, according to the Agreement between the Government of the Russian Federation and the Government of the People's Republic of China (Beijing, April 25, 1996), it was decided to create a joint reserve called Lake Khanka in the border areas of Russia and China, its territory includes wetland ecosystems. Lake Khanka Reserve is divided by the line of the state border between Russia and China into two parts – Khankaisky State Nature Reserve in Primorsky Krai (the territory of the Russian Federation) and Lake Khanka Reserve in Heilongjiang Province (the territory of the PRC).

NATIONAL AND NATURE PARKS

Creating national parks emerged more than 120 years ago in the United States. This name of SPNAs was based on the attempt to emphasize that this area belongs to the whole people, the whole nation.

The system of national parks in Russia was established in the 1980s. First national parks were formed in 1983. They are Sochinsky on the Black Sea coast and Losiny Ostrov in the territory of Moscow. Now there are 56 national parks in the Russian Federation.

National parks are education and research institutions for nature protection and environmental education; the territories (water areas) of which include natural systems and objects of particular environmental, historical and aesthetic value, are intended for use in nature protection, educational, scientific, and cultural purposes as well as for recreation and tourism. They are particularly significant because preserving areas of nature as the reserve of national heritage serves as an effective means of education involving nature protection and the spread of environmental knowledge. National parks belong to specially protected natural areas of federal significance. Within the boundaries of national parks, there are zones in which the natural environment is preserved in its original state, and it is prohibited to carry out any activities not provided for by law and zones in which economic and other activities are restricted to preserve natural and cultural heritage sites and to use them for recreational purposes.

The following main objectives are set for national parks:

a. Preservation of natural systems, unique and standard natural areas and objects;

b. Preservation of historical and cultural objects;

c. Environmental education of the population;

d. Creation of the conditions for regulated tourism and recreation;

e. Scientific and research activities in the field of environmental protection for formation of measures aimed at preserving and developing natural and recreational potential;

f. State environmental monitoring;

g. Restoration of disturbed natural, historical, and cultural systems and objects.

The creation of national parks and expansion of the territories of national parks are implemented based on resolutions of the Government of the Russian Federation adopted as advised by the federal executive authority authorized by the Government of the Russian Federation. The zoning of the territories of national parks is carried out as follows for the establishment of the corresponding regime:

a. Reserve zones, which are intended for preservation of the natural environment in its natural state and within the boundaries of which any economic activities are prohibited;

b. Specially protected zones intended for preservation of the natural environment in its natural state and within the boundaries of which guided tours and visits to these zones for educational tourism are allowed;

c. Recreational zones, which are intended for support and implementation of recreational activities, development of sports, and construction of facilities of the tourism industry, museums, and informational centers;

d. Zones of protection of cultural heritage sites (historical and cultural monuments) of peoples of the Russian Federation intended for their preservation, within the boundaries of which the activities necessary for their preservation, including recreational activities, are allowed;

e. Economic zones, within the boundaries of which it is allowed to carry out activities aimed at ensuring the functioning of the federal state budget institution managing the national park and the support of citizens living in the territory of the national park;

f. Zones of traditional extensive natural resource management intended to support small indigenous peoples of Russia, within the boundaries of which traditional economic activities and related types of sustainable natural resource management are allowed. It is not permitted to reduce the area of reserve zones, specially protected zones, and zones of traditional natural resource management.

The correlation of the areas of each functional zone varies notably in different national parks. Reserve zones can occupy the largest area in the national parks like Prielbrusye (73%), Zabaikalsky (41%), Sochinsky (37.5%) or the smallest one, in Meshchyorsky (0.1%), Russky Sever (1%), Nizhnyaya Kama (7%), *etc*.

In the territories of national parks, it is prohibited to carry out any activities which can cause damage to natural systems, animals and plants, cultural and historical objects and which are contrary to the goals and objectives of national parks, including the following activities:

a. Mineral exploration and mining;

b. Activities leading to the disturbance of the soil cover and geological outcrops;

c. Activities leading to changes in the hydrological regime;

d. Provision of land plots in the territories of national parks for gardening and individual garages or individual housing construction;

e. Construction of main roads and pipelines, power lines, and other communications as well as construction and operation of economic and residential facilities (excluding facilities related to the functioning of national parks and the functioning of the settlements located within their boundaries);

f. Wood harvesting (excluding wood harvesting by citizens for their own needs), resin harvesting, commercial hunting, industrial and coastal fishing, harvesting of edible forest resources (food forest resources), other non-timber forest resources (excluding harvesting of these resources by citizens for their own needs), activities leading to the disturbance of the flora and fauna habitation conditions, gathering of biological collections, the introduction of living organisms for their acclimatization;

g. Traffic and parking of mechanized vehicles not related to the functioning of national parks, driving of domestic animals outside public roads and waterways and outside specially designated areas, timber rafting on watercourses and reservoirs;

h. Organization of mass sports and entertainment events, organization of tourist camps, recreation areas, campfires outside specially designated areas;

i. Location of cattle burial grounds, waste disposal sites, *etc*.

The issues of socio-economic activities of economic entities as well as projects for the development of settlements located in the territories of the corresponding national parks and their protective zones are coordinated with the federal executive authorities in the field of environmental protection that is in charge of the national parks.

Individuals can stay in the territory of national parks only with the permission of the federal state budget institution managing the national park or the federal executive authority in charge of the national park. There are several exceptions to this rule related to the stay of residents, staff of national parks, and a range of other categories of citizens in national parks. The federal state budget institutions managing national parks charge payments from individuals for visiting the territories of national parks (excluding areas located within the boundaries of settlements) for tourism and recreation.

Land plots (including land plots on which forests are located) within the boundaries of national parks are provided to federal state budget institutions managing national parks for permanent (perpetual) use. Land plots of other owners and users can also be located within the boundaries of national parks without their withdrawal from economic use.

It is prohibited to withdraw or otherwise terminate the rights to land plots and forest areas provided to federal state budget institutions managing national parks, except in cases stipulated by federal laws.

Federal state budget institutions managing national parks have the right to provide their employees with service lands for gratuitous use within the boundaries of economic zones according to the procedure established by federal laws.

Recreational activities, including therapeutic and sports activities, in the territories of national parks, are organized in compliance with the regime of special protection of national parks. Land plots in the corresponding functional zones can be leased to citizens and legal entities under land legislation to organize recreational activities therapeutic and sports activities.

The legal position of nature parks has features that are similar to and different from the position of national parks. Similar features are the objectives set for national and natural parks, which are to create conditions for recreation (including mass recreation), to develop and introduce effective methods of nature protection, and to maintain ecological balance.

However, there are some differences of nature parks from national parks:

a. Nature parks are nature protection recreational institutions resolutions on the formation of which are adopted by state authorities of constituent entities of the Russian Federation in coordination with federal executive authorities in the field of environmental protection;

b. Nature parks are under the jurisdiction of constituent entities of the Russian Federation, and their activities are financed from the budget of the relevant constituent entities of the Russian Federation;

c. In contrast to national parks, the internal structure of which is established by law, the list of functional zones of nature parks is not compiled as exhaustive, *i.e.*, the settlement of this issue is left to the discretion of state authorities of constituent entities of the Russian Federation. At the same time, in the case of the creation of several nature parks in the territory of constituent entities of the Russian Federation, their internal structure cannot be the same.

STATE WILDLIFE SANCTUARIES

State wildlife sanctuaries are the territories (water areas) that combine the objectives of conservation and restoration of natural objects and systems and limited economic use of certain natural resources. It is allowed to declare territories as state wildlife sanctuaries both with and without their withdrawal from the users, possessors, and owners of land plots. State wildlife sanctuaries can be of federal or regional significance. State wildlife sanctuaries can have a different profile, in particular:

a. Integrated (landscape), intended for the preservation and restoration of natural systems (natural landscapes);

b. Biological (botanical and zoological), intended for the preservation and restoration of rare and endangered species of animals and plants, economically, scientifically, and culturally valuable;

c. Paleontological, intended for the preservation of fossil objects (for example, in Undorovsky Paleontological Sanctuary of Ulyanovsk Region, there are excavations and research of an unknown pangolin that lived there about fifteen million years ago);

d. Hydrological (marsh, lake, river, and sea sanctuaries), intended for the preservation and restoration of valuable water bodies and ecological systems;

e. Geological, intended for the preservation of valuable objects and systems of inanimate nature.

State wildlife sanctuaries of federal significance are under the jurisdiction of the federal executive authority authorized by the Government of the Russian Federation. Federal state budget institutions manage state wildlife sanctuaries of federal significance, and the procedure for the management of state wildlife sanctuaries of regional significance is determined independently by the corresponding state authorities of constituent entities of the Russian Federation.

Sanctuaries of federal significance are created based on resolutions of the Government of the Russian Federation adopted as advised by the federal executive authority authorized by the Government of the Russian Federation. Accordingly, state wildlife sanctuaries of regional significance are created based on resolutions of the supreme state executive authorities of constituent entities of the Russian Federation in coordination with the authorized federal executive authorities in the field of environmental protection.

State wildlife sanctuaries of regional significance can also be created through the transformation of state wildlife sanctuaries of federal significance implemented based on the resolutions of the Government of the Russian Federation as advised by the federal executive authorities authorized by the Government of the Russian Federation and coordinated with the supreme state executive authorities of the constituent entities of the Russian Federation in the territory of which the state wildlife sanctuaries of federal significance are located. These resolutions can be adopted about state wildlife sanctuaries of federal significance located within the boundaries of one constituent entity of the Russian Federation. State wildlife sanctuaries cannot be located in the territories of state nature reserves and national parks.

In the territories of state wildlife sanctuaries, it is constantly or temporarily prohibited or restricted to carry out any activities if they are contrary to the objectives of the creation of sanctuaries or cause harm to natural systems and their components. The objectives and the distinctive features of the regime of special protection of the territory of a specific sanctuary are determined by the provision approved by the federal or regional executive authority in the field of environmental protection. The analysis of the provisions on state sanctuaries leads to a conclusion that the regime of their protection implies a total prohibition of some types of economic and other activities with the permission to carry out other types of activities, to a limited extent and as agreed upon with the sanctuary administration or the Ministry of Natural Resources and Environment of the Russian Federation. For example, in Priazovsky Federal State Wildlife Sanctuary, hunting, waste disposal, logging, and many other types of economic activities are prohibited; however, subsoil use (subject to additional nature protection requirements and the approval by the Ministry of Natural Resources and Environment of the Russian Federation and the sanctuary administration), use of pesticides and agrochemicals in the course of agricultural activities or extraction of aquatic bioresources (subject to the approval by the administration) are permitted.

NATURAL MONUMENTS

Unique, irreplaceable, ecologically, scientifically, culturally, and aesthetically valuable natural systems and objects of natural and artificial origin are declared natural monuments. The main purpose of declaring natural objects and systems as natural monuments is to conserve them in their natural state. Natural monuments can be of federal or regional significance.

There are three grounds for giving a natural object the status of a natural monument: its uniqueness, value (ecological, aesthetic, scientific, *etc.*), and the need for special protection by the state.

Natural monuments can include land and water areas as well as single natural objects – areas of scenic areas, places of growth and habitat of valuable, relict, small-numbered and endangered plants and animals, unique forms of relief and related landscapes, woodlands and valuable forest areas, areas of rivers, lakes or other water bodies, individual objects of living and non-living nature (trees, waterfalls, volcanoes, springs, cliffs, caves), *etc.*

State authorities of the Russian Federation and state authorities of constituent entities of the Russian Federation approve the boundaries and determine the regime of special protection of the territories of natural monuments under their jurisdiction. Transfer of federal and regional natural monuments (or a part of their territory) under the protection of persons (for example, the owners of land plots where these natural monuments were found), registration of the protection obligation, passport and other documents are performed, accordingly, by the federal executive authority in the field of environmental protection and state executive authorities of constituent entities of the Russian Federation.

The passport, which is made for each natural monument, contains the following information: the name of the natural monument and its significance (federal or regional), its location, description of the boundaries and the protective zone, the area, name, and legal status of the owners (users, lessees) of the land of its location, names of the individuals and legal entities that assumed the obligation to protect the natural monument. In the territories where natural monuments are located and within the boundaries of their protective zones, it is prohibited to carry out any activities leading to the impairment of natural monuments. The holders of rights to land plots on which natural monuments are located assume the obligations to ensure the regime of special protection of the natural monuments. Their expenses for ensuring the established regime of special protection of natural monuments of federal or regional significance must be reimbursed from the federal budget and the budgets of constituent entities of the Russian Federation, respectively. The use of natural monuments is allowed for purposes related to science (monitoring of the environment), environmental education, recreation, nature protection, and other purposes that are not contrary to the objectives of the declaration of these natural objects and systems as natural monuments. Natural objects and systems located in the territory of state nature reserves, reserve zones of national parks, historical and cultural monuments, and those that are part of natural systems already declared natural monuments cannot be declared natural monuments.

ARBORETUMS AND BOTANICAL GARDENS

Arboretums and botanical gardens are specially protected natural areas established for the formation of special collections of plants to preserve the flora and its diversity. Natural resources and immovable property located within the boundaries of arboretums and botanical gardens are restricted in civil circulation unless otherwise provided for by federal laws. Arboretums and botanical gardens are managed by federal executive authorities authorized by the Government of the Russian Federation, executive authorities of constituent entities of the Russian Federation and state institutions under their jurisdiction as well as by state scientific organizations and state educational organizations of higher education (for example, Southern Federal University in Rostov-on-Don has a botanical garden).

Land plots and forest areas within the boundaries of arboretums and botanical gardens are provided to state institutions managing arboretums and botanical gardens for permanent (perpetual) use. In the territories of arboretums and botanical gardens, it is prohibited to carry out any activities not related to fulfilling their objectives and leading to the impairment of flora objects.

The territories of arboretums and botanical gardens can be divided into various functional zones, including the following ones:

a. Exposition zones, visits to which are permitted according to the procedure established by the relevant authorities and institutions managing the arboretums or botanical gardens;

b. Scientific and experimental zones, which can be accessed only by the scientific staff of the arboretums or botanical gardens as well as experts from other research institutions;

c. Administrative zones.

The objectives, scientific profile, distinctive features of the legal position, organizational structure, and distinctive features of the regime of special protection of a specific arboretum or a botanical garden are determined in the provisions on them, which are approved by the relevant executive authorities that adopted the resolutions on the establishment of these institutions. Arboretums and botanical gardens are funded from the federal budget as well as the budgets of constituent entities of the Russian Federation.

LEGAL REGIME OF ENVIRONMENTALLY DISADVANTAGED AREAS

Environmentally disadvantaged areas are the land or water areas that significantly degraded as a result of a short-term or long-term negative impact of natural or anthropogenic activities on the ecological systems, which threatens the life and health of citizens and requires the establishment of a special legal regime in this territory for the implementation of urgent measures to restore the quality of the environment. The current legislation of the Russian Federation mentions only ecological disaster zones of all possible types of environmentally disadvantaged areas. These zones are the other side of the same coin of area protection's special environmental legal regime. In contrast to the "positive" regime of SPNAs established for unique and rare natural objects and systems that must be preserved in their natural state, ecological disaster zones have a "negative" legal regime caused by the need for urgent restoration of degraded ecological systems.

Now the area of environmentally disadvantaged areas is 2 million square kilometers, which equals 10-15% of the total land fund of Russia. In these territories, around 60 million residents live in 300 settlements (including such big cities as Ufa and Nizhny Novgorod), and environmental factors cause approximately one-third of their illnesses.

Ecological disaster zones are the areas of the territory of the Russian Federation where economic or other activities result in profound irreversible changes in the environment, causing significant deterioration of the health of the population, disruption of the natural balance, destruction of natural ecological systems, and degradation of flora and fauna. The state environmental expert review report is required to establish this regime for an area (Article 11 of the Federal Law "On Environmental Expert Reviews").

There are a number of objective reasons that impede the process of declaring certain areas as ecological disaster zones:

1. The lack of federal law on ecological disaster zones providing clear legal regulation of the mechanism of creation of these zones and containing distinctive features of the legal regime of the said areas;

2. Financial reasons. Disadvantaged areas must be presumably rehabilitated primarily at the expense of the federal budget, budgets of other levels as well as with the funds of those directly responsible for environmental degradation. However, representative authorities of all levels, first of all, the State Duma of the Federal Assembly of the Russian Federation, do not seek to provide for additional expenses in their budgets, which will be quite significant;

3. The consequences of giving certain areas the legal regime of ecological disaster zones are unclear. The current Federal Law "On Environmental Protection" only mentions ecological disaster zones in Article 57; however, it does not contain any rules regarding the distinctive features of their legal regime. There are no such rules in federal laws either. This is why no areas in Russia have been given the regime of ecological disaster zones yet. The practice of special protection of the environment in numerous environmentally disadvantaged areas in Russia has followed three ways:

1. Several regulations were adopted regarding the elimination of the consequences of the accident at the Chernobyl Nuclear Power Plant. Besides the compensations for affected residents and liquidators of the accident, the list of settlements located within the boundaries of radioactive contamination zones

with different legal regimes was approved, for example, exclusion zones (a part of Bryansk Region); evacuation zones (another part of Bryansk Region); zones of residence with the right to evacuation (Bryansk, Kaluga, Oryol and Tula Regions); zones of residence with preferential social and economic status (Belgorod, Bryansk, Voronezh, Kaluga, Kursk, Leningrad, Lipetsk, Oryol, Penza, Ryazan, Tambov Regions, and some other regions).

2. Besides Chernobyl zone, in the territory of Russia, also other not less hazardous radioactive contamination zones were designated, for example, the city of Chapaevsk, where the special target program "Social and Environmental Rehabilitation of the Territory and Protection of the Health of the Population of the City of Chapaevsk of Samara Region" was implemented for several years for improvement of the situation, the East Ural Radioactive Trace – the zone of the Kyshtym disaster in Chelyabinsk Region; contamination zones resulting from tests of atomic weapons at the Semipalatinsk, Novozemelsk, Totsk Test Sites and underground explosions for peaceful purposes. The regime of restrictions of economic activities and resettlement of citizens with the payment of compensation was individually introduced in these territories.
   However, the environmental conditions in the city of Karabash, Chelyabinsk Region is the most classic case for Russia. The mining and metallurgical facilities, initially not aimed at preserving, conserving, and restoring nature, uninterruptedly operating, and constantly expanding for almost two centuries, had caused an ecological disaster by the end of the 20th century. According to the estimates of researchers, the impact of the Karabash Copper Smelter affects all natural objects. Its emissions, discharges, and solid waste formed the technogenic environment that replaced the original ecosystems. In accordance with the Criteria for evaluating the environmental situation of the territory to identify environmental emergency zones and ecological disaster zones, the territory of the city of Karabash was recognized as an ecological disaster zone in the 1990s.
   However, it was not created because there was no special law.

3. It is mandatory to develop special environmental programs for rehabilitation of radiation-contaminated areas of the territory funded from revenues from foreign trade in irradiated heat-generating nuclear reactor assemblies (Art. 2 of the Federal Law of July 10, 2001 "On Special Environmental Programs for Rehabilitation of Radiation-Contaminated Areas of the Territory"). Radiation-contaminated areas are understood as the areas of a territory that are hazardous to the health of the population and the environment and subject to rehabilitation after radioactive contamination as a result of anthropogenic activities or placement of decommissioned radiation facilities that are especially hazardous.

Emergencies are sometimes understood not so much as environmental but as emergency natural and man-made disasters related to explosions of gas pipelines, trains, fires, earthquakes, droughts, *etc.* The Ministry of Civil Defense, Emergencies, and Disaster Relief of the Russian Federation is involved. It is necessary to have a clear idea of the similarities and differences between emergencies under the jurisdiction of the Ministry of Civil Defense, Emergencies and Disaster Relief of Russia and emergencies leading to the creation of ecological disaster zones and, consequently, to distinguish between the functions of the Ministry of Civil Defense, Emergencies and Disaster Relief of the Russian Federation and the Ministry of Natural Resources and Environment of the Russian Federation, which reflect completely different areas of social relations.

The said emergencies are similar because in both cases, we observe the loss of sustainability of natural areas, which is impossible to eliminate without strict administrative measures that can result in restrictions of the rights and freedoms of citizens (for example, in the area of land use). Moreover, there are adverse changes in the condition of the environment in both cases, *i.e.*, the result of the impact of particular factors on ecosystems is the same.

The difference between the said types of emergencies is the peculiarities of the process that leads to this result.

1. Difference in the time of the emergency. Natural and man-made emergencies usually occur due to short-term catastrophes and natural disasters; the occurrence of ecological disasters is associated with the accumulation of environmental consequences, *i.e.*, with the sustainable impact of anthropogenic factors. There are exceptions, like to every rule: the accident at the Chernobyl Nuclear Power Plant.

2. Difference in the means for elimination of the consequences of the emergency. To eliminate emergencies, the Ministry of Civil Defense, Emergencies, and Disaster Relief of the Russian Federation take urgent actions, while this is not sufficient to eliminate ecological disaster zones. It is necessary to fundamentally change the approaches to the management of economic activities of enterprises and organizations of all forms of ownership in constituent entities of the Russian Federation (municipalities), which will reduce the extent of the adverse impact on the environment, provide conditions for the protection of environmental rights of the population residing in this territory and make it possible to take measures aimed at the gradual

improvement of the environment. This is why eliminating environmentally unfavorable zones requires time comparable to the period of their emergence.

3. Difference in the methods of management of emergency elimination. Mainly administrative methods must be applied during the elimination of natural and man-made emergencies. In addition to administrative methods, the elimination of ecological disaster zones must also involve economic methods since it is possible to overcome this crisis only by resolving economic problems, including conversion of "environmentally dirty" facilities, identification, and elimination of accumulated harm to the environment.

4. Difference in the legal regime of the territory. The regime of ecological disaster zones is established for territories by adopting regulatory legal acts of state-federal authorities with setting the boundaries and distinctive features of the legal regime based on the findings of the state environmental expert reviews. The special legal regime is not given to the territories where natural and man-made emergencies occurred. The abovesaid differences made Article 57 of the Federal Law "On Environmental Protection" ultimately delimit the legal position of the zones under consideration.

CONCLUSION

The chapter notes that the need to give certain territories a special ecological and legal protection regime is to prevent the deterioration of their condition. Such territories include valuable natural objects that need to be preserved for future generations. That is why Russian legislation establishes the peculiarities of the legal status of nature reserves, national parks, and other types of specially protected natural territories. In these territories, human economic activity is prohibited or restricted.

QUESTIONS AND TASKS FOR SELF-CONTROL

1. Define specially protected natural areas. What types of federal and regional SPNAs do you know?

2. What is the distinctive feature of the legal regime of state nature reserves?

3. What are the distinctive features of special protection of national and nature parks?

4. What is the difference of the regime of protection of the territory of state wildlife sanctuaries from other types of SPNAs?

5. What are the distinctive features of the environmental legal regime of natural

monuments?

6. What are the distinctive features of protecting the territories of arboretums and botanical gardens?

7. Describe the legal regime of environmentally disadvantaged areas. Has the regime of ecological disaster zones been established for any territories in the Russian Federation?

REFERENCES

Petrov, V.V. (1995). *Environmental Law of Russia. Textbook for higher education institutions.* Bek.Moscow:

State, Report (2019). *On the State and Protection of the Environment in the Russian Federation in 2018.* Moscow: Ministry of Natural Resources and Environment of the Russian Federation; NPP "Kadastr".

CHAPTER 8

International Cooperation in the Field of Environmental Protection

Abstract: In this chapter, it is stated that the international environmental law is a set of international legal principles and rules governing international relations regarding the protection of the environment from negative impact. These rules and regulations ensure the rational use of environemnt and its components and provide favorable conditions for the life and health of the present and future generations of people. The development in international environmental cooperation was gradual, like the development of national (Russian) environmental law. Some references to international cooperation in this chapter in environmental protection can be found even in the era of the ancient world. However, the full-fledged international cooperation in environmental protection began only in the second half of the 19th century. This can be explained by the fact that the human impact on nature was small before the Industrial Revolution. The negative impact of the neighboring countries on nature arose with the massive construction of plants that release emissions into the air and water bodies. This resulted in the need for governments of different countries to agree on various parameters about the safety of the environment. The development of international cooperation in environmental protection is divided into several stages. It is pointed out that international environmental law is a young branch of law closely interacting with other branches of international law, including international maritime, air, and space law. These branches of law regulate relations regarding the exploitation of the relevant natural resources and are based on the exercise of the rights of sovereign states to use natural resources. According to the authors, international environmental law has an independent subject of legal regulation – international environmental relations, which can be conveniently divided into three groups:

a) Relations for the prevention and limitation of the harmful impact on the environment, which can be resolved only by efforts of the entire world community (pollution of the World Ocean, the air basin, pollution of the environment during military conflicts, *etc.*);

b) Ensuring the rational use of international natural resources (for example, resources of the sea bed);

c) Protection of unique natural objects through their conservation from human economic impact (for example, natural heritage sites, wetlands, rare animals and plants, *etc.*).

Aleksey Anisimov and Anatoliy Ryzhenkov

The subjects of international environmental law include states, international organizations, and international non-governmental organizations. However, states are the main subject of international law.

Keywords: Air, Arctic, Armed conflict, Conventions, Climate, Declarations, International law, Flora, Fauna, International organizations, International non-governmental organizations, Nature, Oil, Refugees, Swamps, State, Tanker, UN, UNESCO, World Ocean.

CONCEPT OF INTERNATIONAL ENVIRONMENTAL LAW

In this chapter, it is stated that the international environmental law is a set of international legal principles and rules governing international relations regarding the protection of the environment from negative impact. These rules and regulations ensure the rational use of environment and its components and provide favorable conditions for the life and health of the present and future generations of people. The development in international environmental cooperation was gradual, like the development of national (Russian) environmental law. Some references to international cooperation in this chapter in environmental protection can be found even in the era of the ancient world. However, the full-fledged international cooperation in environmental protection began only in the second half of the 19th century. This can be explained by the fact that the human impact on nature was small before the Industrial Revolution.

The negative impact of the neighboring countries on nature arose with the massive construction of plants that release emissions into the air and water bodies. This resulted in the need for governments of different countries to agree on various parameters about the safety of the environment. The development of international cooperation in environmental protection is divided into several stages.

1. The first stage of the development of international environmental law began from 1839 to 1913. August 2, 1839, is considered as the beginning of the first stage in the history of the development of international environmental law, when the bilateral Convention on oyster fishing and fishing off the coast of Great Britain and France was adopted. It established the rules of fishing in the English Channel and the North Sea. According to that Convention, the Mixed Commission was created with the duties of developing recommendations regarding the period and areas of fishing. As advised by the Commission, in 1843, Great Britain and France approved the Rules of Fishing outside the three-mile zone of territorial waters. Afterward, the number of bilateral agreements on the protection and use of certain species of animals (the Convention for the

preservation of the fur seal of November 6, 1897) as well as on the protection of other natural objects (the Convention for Navigation on the Rhine of 1868, which regulated the protection of the river from pollution) grew every year. There was still no full-fledged system of international agreements comprehensively regulating environmental protection in that period.

Similar trends took place at the national level. Environmental law of the Russian Empire originated in the second half of the 19th century. Until the 1917 revolution, it focused on the protection of certain natural objects from several types of negative anthropogenic impacts.

2. The second period of the development of international environmental law covers the period from 1913 to 1948. The first attempt in the world to outline an action plan for the international protection of the environment as a whole rather than of its elements was made at the First International Conference for the Protection of Nature held in Bern on November 17, 1913. Representatives of 17 countries, including the Russian Empire, took part in the conference. The Agreement on the Foundation of an Advisory World Nature Protection Committee was signed at the conference. However, the meeting was mainly informational and organizational in nature and did not develop any practical measures to protect the environment. Moreover, all international environmental cooperation ceased after the outbreak of World War I. However, the efforts of the participants of the Bern conference were not void: the International Council for Bird Protection was founded in 1922, and the International Society for the Protection of Bison was founded in 1923. The Standing Committee on Pacific Conservation was created in 1929. The International Office for the Protection of Nature was established in Brussels in 1935 to maintain the register of national nature protection laws and national parks and reserves. Moreover, the Convention Relative to the Preservation of Fauna and Flora in their Natural State (1933) and the Convention on Nature Protection and Wild Life Preservation in the Western Hemisphere (1940) were adopted in the 1930s (Mokhammad, 2011).

3. The third period of the development of international environmental law covers the period from 1948 to 1972. The beginning of this stage in international cooperation in environmental protection is associated with the creation of the United Nations and the first international environmental organization established in 1948, which was originally called the International Union for Conservation of Nature. The African Convention on the Conservation of Nature and Natural Resources was adopted on September 15, 1968. This Convention is an example of a comprehensive approach to the issue of environmental protection, and it highlights two fundamentally new issues: recognition of the need to protect the habitats of endangered species and the requirement of special responsibility for

the states the territories of which are the only habitat of these rare species. At the end of the period under consideration, for the first time in world history, the international conference proclaiming the right of every resident of the Earth to a favorable environment was organized and held in Stockholm in 1972.

4. The fourth period of the development of international environmental law covers the period from 1972 to 1992. At this stage, a system of international legal guarantees of the human right to a favorable environment is enshrined in various international legal acts. The greening of international law takes place, along with the consolidation of the mechanism of guarantees, not only at the universal level within the UN system but also at the regional level within such international bodies as the Council of Europe, the OSCE, *etc*. During this period (1972), the United Nations Environment Program (UNEP) was created as a subsidiary body of the UN General Assembly coordinating the actions of international organizations and states aimed at international nature protection to bring it to a qualitatively new level of the entire UN system.

5. The fifth period of the development of international environmental law covers the period from 1992 to the present day. Its most characteristic feature is the development of the concept of sustainable development. The 1992 United Nations Conference in Rio de Janeiro summed up the results of the cooperation of the countries in ensuring a favorable environmental quality and outlined long-term plans for the future. These plans were specified at the international summit of the United Nations on environmental protection issues, which was held in Johannesburg in 2002, as well as at the international United Nations conference Rio+20 in Rio de Janeiro in 2012. In 2015, the United Nations adopted the Resolution entitled "Transforming our World: the 2030 Agenda for Sustainable Development". It contains 17 global goals (clean water and sanitation, poverty eradication, sustainable cities, and human settlements, *etc*.) and 169 corresponding targets.

All the abovesaid documents made their own contribution to the formation of international environmental law.

International environmental law is a young branch of law closely interacting with other branches of international law, including international maritime, air, and space law. These branches of law regulate relations regarding the exploitation of the relevant natural resources and are based on other priorities – ensuring the exercise of the rights of sovereign states to use natural resources.

International environmental law is based on the use of natural resources subject to restrictions imposed in the interests of international environmental protection. The international level of the issues concerning the regulation of relations regarding environmental protection is due to two main factors. First, the development of scientific and technological progress. Second is the rapid growth of the human population, which leads to the imbalance of the world ecological relationships (today, humanity has no natural enemies capable of regulating its numbers). This rethinking of the role of international environmental law resulted in over 1500 multilateral and over 3000 bilateral international agreements and treaties signed by countries from around the world and related to environmental protection issues.

International environmental law has an independent subject of legal regulation – international environmental relations, which can be conveniently divided into three groups:

a. Relations for the prevention and limitation of the harmful impact on the environment, which can be resolved only by efforts of the entire world community (pollution of the World Ocean, the air basin, pollution of the environment during military conflicts, *etc*.);

b. Ensuring the rational use of international natural resources (for example, resources of the sea bed);

c. Protection of unique natural objects through their conservation from human economic impact (for example, natural heritage sites, wetlands, rare animals and plants, *etc*.)

The subjects of international environmental law include states, international organizations, and international non-governmental organizations. States are the main subject.

It is possible to distinguish several categories of states that are the subjects of international environmental law:

a. Most ecologically vulnerable states and most ecologically prosperous states (for example, island states suffer from global climate change caused by the rising level of the World Ocean that results in their gradual flooding and this is why they initiate the discussion of climate issues);

b. Developed states and developing states, which are independent to a different extent in solving environmental problems and have different subjects of interest in this area;

c. States exposed to the impact of the same natural factors due to their geographic location and states exposed to the impact of different natural factors due to their geographic location, which affects their participation in the adoption of various international instruments Sokolova, N.A. (2000). (for example, northern states participate in the discussion of issues of environmental protection in the Arctic, which are not of interest to more southern states).

Despite the various status and interests of states, international environmental cooperation is based on the same principles. In addition, one of the trends in international environmental law is the increasing importance of international and international non-governmental organizations as subjects of international environmental law.

It should be noted that the issues of environmental protection and rational use of natural resources are regulated primarily by national legislation, which reflects the principles and the main areas of international cooperation in the field of nature. The provision enshrined in Article 15 of the Constitution of Russia, according to which the rules of international law have more legal force than the rules enshrined in the national legislation, fully applies to the area of regulation of environmental relations as well. In connection with the internationalization of issues in the field of environmental protection, the general rules of Russian law become increasingly referential, *i.e.*, they make law enforcement authorities refer to international legislation for the rule to be applied (Law of the Russian Federation "On Environmental Protection", Law of the Russian Federation "On Fauna", *etc.*). Moreover, Russian laws establish the principles of international cooperation of Russia in the field of the environment.

Russian legislation and law enforcement practice distinguish self-executing and non-self-executing international agreements. According to Article 5 of Federal Law No. 101-FZ of July 15, 1995, "On International Agreements of the Russian Federation", provisions of officially published international agreements of the Russian Federation not requiring any domestic acts for their application, are in immediate effect in the Russian Federation. To implement other provisions of international agreements, the Russian Federation adopts the relevant legal acts. Signs of the impossibility of immediate application of provisions of international agreements of the Russian Federation include, in particular, the specification of the obligations of the states that are parties to the agreements to amend their domestic legislation. When courts consider civil, criminal or administrative cases, they directly apply the international agreement of the Russian Federation, which entered into force and became binding on the Russian Federation and the provisions of which do not require any issue of domestic acts for their application and can give rise to rights and duties of the subjects of national law (par. 3 of

Resolution of the Plenum of the Supreme Court of the Russian Federation No. 5 of October 10, 2003 "On the Application of Generally Accepted Principles and Rules of International Law and International Agreements of the Russian Federation by Courts of General Jurisdiction").

The Ministry of Natural Resources and Environment (Minprirody) of the Russian Federation is the main authority in charge of coordinating Russia's activities in the field of international environmental cooperation. The official website of Minprirody contains a list of 20 multilateral treaties, conventions, and agreements for which Minprirody of Russia is the chief agency (for example, the 1971 Ramsar Convention) and more than 10 multilateral agreements to be ratified (subject to adoption, approval or accession). Moreover, Minprirody participates in implementing over 30 bilateral agreements with foreign countries (Belgium, Bulgaria, Brazil, *etc.*). According to several authors, all bilateral agreements signed by Russia can be classified into eight groups: comprehensive environmental agreements (52 percent), in the area of transboundary water bodies (11 percent), on SPNAs (10 percent), on the protection of migratory birds (7 percent), on reduction of radiation hazard (4 percent), on the protection of seas (3 percent), on the protection of animal species (3 percent) and other agreements (10 percent) (Vystorobets and Dolgikh 2012).

OBJECTS OF THE INTERNATIONAL LEGAL PROTECTION OF THE ENVIRONMENT

The objects of the international legal protection of the environment are the natural objects and systems regarding which the subjects of international law have environmental legal relations. Two categories of these objects can be distinguished: international legal objects, which are located within the boundaries of certain states, and objects of international law, which are located in the international areas (outer space, air, the World Ocean, Antarctica).

International objects located in the territories of certain states include land, subsoil, internal waters, flora, and fauna. Internal waters are the waters of the rivers and lakes which can be the objects of international environmental law despite being located in the territory of individual states (for example, Lake Baikal is listed as a UNESCO World Natural Heritage Site).

Rivers are understood as a system of surface and ground water that forms a single whole, attracting the attention of the international community for two reasons. First, some rivers flow through the territory of two or more states (international rivers). Second, the water of rivers somehow enters international waters. The international community tries to protect freshwater of international significance from the following types of pollution: chemicals used in detergents and cleaning agents, chloride used for water disinfection, and discharged oil and petroleum products. An example of the importance of international protection of internal waters is the environmental disaster in Romania in January 2000, when as a result of the accident at the gold mine, almost 100,000 cubic meters of water heavily contaminated with cyanide were released into the Tisza River and after reached the Danube. In just the first two days after the accident, 80 percent of the fish stock in the Tisza died.

Fauna and flora belong to a combined object of legal regulation since the impact on them occur both in the territory of individual states and beyond their borders. International protection covers endangered and rare species of flora and fauna, migratory species of animals, and their habitat in certain regions. The main international instruments regulating the protection of rare animals are the Convention on International Trade in Endangered Species of Wild Fauna and Flora (CITES) adopted in Washington on March 3, 1973, the Bern Convention on the Conservation of European Wildlife and Natural Habitats (1979), the Convention on the Conservation of Migratory Species of Wild Animals (1979), the Convention on Biological Diversity (1992) and several other documents. It is possible to distinguish a range of specific areas of international environmental cooperation of states in the field of protection of flora and fauna:

a. Protection of fauna, including protection of forests and other plants from pests and diseases, protection of tropical timber;

b. Protection of general biological diversity or individual species of animals (Atlantic seals, polar bears, and other endangered and rare species of animals listed in the International Red Data Book).

c. Protection of the habitat of animals – wetlands, habitats of migratory birds. The wetlands protection is covered by the Convention on Wetlands of International Importance, Especially as Waterfowl Habitat (the Ramsar Convention) of February 2, 1971. The main feature of this Convention is that it is based on the ecosystem approach, *i.e.*, it is aimed at conserving birds themselves and recognizes their habitat wetlands as ecosystems that are important for the maintenance of the ecological balance and human well-being.

Air, outer space, the World Ocean, and Antarctica are the objects of international law located within the international areas. Airspace is the common heritage of humankind. The main harmful impact on the atmosphere comes from the territories of certain states due to such activities as sulfur emissions into the atmosphere, which cause acid rain, carbon dioxide emissions, which contribute to the greenhouse effect, the use and leakage of chemicals, which deplete the ozone layer of the Earth, and the release of radioactive substances into the atmosphere. The 2015 Paris Climate Agreement, signed by the Russian Federation, is one of the best-known international instruments concerning the reduction of emissions of harmful gases into airspace.

The World Ocean is an ecosystem occupying more than 70 percent of the territory of the planet, capable of processing a considerable amount of organic matter (we include both the water of the oceans and the water of the seas in the concept of the World Ocean). A sharp increase in the discharge of human waste products (their chemical composition) began to threaten the mechanism of self-purification of the World Ocean, which formed for thousands of years. International cooperation in the protection of the water of the World Ocean is necessary because no single state, even the most developed one, can solve the issues of protecting the water and bioresources of the World Ocean. The World Ocean is a single ecological system that cannot be protected in pieces. This is why it is protected by all members of the world community together.

International environmental law prohibits or restricts the discharge of the following harmful substances into the World Ocean:

1. Oil and petroleum products. The long period of their decomposition and spread over large surfaces are particularly hazardous. For example, the oil tanker Prestige sank off the coast of Spain in 2002 and spilled 64 thousand tons of oil, 500 km of the beach became black, 300 thousand birds died. In November 2007, a severe storm in the Kerch Strait caused damage (including grounding) to more than 10 vessels – bulk carriers, barges, and tankers (one of them was broken in half). About 1300 tons of heating oil and 6800 tons of industrial sulfur were discharged into the sea. Oil spills caused significant damage to aquatic bioresources. The restoration of the normal ecological state of the strait required months and large financial investments. On April 22, 2010, a drilling platform for offshore oil production owned by British Petroleum (BP) sank in the Gulf of Mexico. This disaster resulted in the death of eleven people and the oil spill in the Gulf of Mexico. The company incurred huge losses, which made it start selling some of its assets in many countries worldwide. According to experts, nearly five million barrels of crude oil were spelled into the sea due to this horrible accident.

2. Synthetic products include all types of plastics, including synthetic ropes, fishing nets, and plastic garbage bags. They are hazardous because they are exceptionally buoyant.

3. Poisonous substances, including organochlorine compounds, mercury, cadmium. They can be contained in the discharges of industrial enterprises and production and consumption waste.

4. Radioactive materials. International environmental law prohibits any discharge and burial of radioactive waste at sea.

Outer space is the space outside the Earth's atmosphere. Economic use of outer space is still limited by the technical capabilities of humankind. Nevertheless, space exploration has a negative impact on the environment, since, first, the production of space equipment on Earth entails an additional load on the environment; second, there are several side effects of launching rockets into space from launch sites of any country (related to the emission of harmful substances into the atmosphere when toxic fuel burns), which causes serious health problems for people who live near them. Third, spacecraft pass through the atmosphere, which results in the deterioration of the state of the ozone layer and consequently lowers the level of guarantees of protection of life on Earth from ultraviolet radiation. Fourth, the generation of space debris leads to considerable environmental problems. “Space debris” is a general term that is used to describe all artificial materials in the universe that people do not use for research or other purposes. This waste includes remnants of orbiters or other parts of the spacecraft, which no longer serve useful purposes but leak fuel, coolant and various colorants, blade tips, and other debris left by space expeditions. The expected lifetime of space debris depends on its position: in low-Earth orbit, there is a high probability that most of it burns in the atmosphere, so it is about 25 years. Fifth, the threat of radioactive contamination is closely related to the issue of space debris. The main source of this contamination in space can be an accidental collision and subsequent explosion of satellites, which will produce radioactive space debris and radiation. In case of this collision, contaminated objects can fall to the Earth's surface, thereby posing a serious environmental threat.

The essence of space law is contained in five conventions of the United Nations of 1967-1979 that, unfortunately, insignificantly address environmental issues, which requires their discussion. Meanwhile, international environmental law restricts the testing of nuclear weapons in space, which is a remarkable achievement.

Antarctica is a continent located at the southernmost part of the world, on which no nation-state has been established. The 1959 Antarctic Treaty gave this continent the status of a demilitarized zone, a zone free of nuclear weapons. Any nuclear explosions and disposal of radioactive waste in Antarctica are prohibited. The Convention for the Conservation of Antarctic Marine Living Resources was adopted in 1980, the Commission for the Conservation of Antarctic Marine Living Resources was established in 1982.

At the moment, Antarctica has the largest ozone hole on record. There are no industrial facilities in Antarctica, however, streams of ozone-depleting gases accumulate there, which causes increased ultraviolet radiation. Due to the greenhouse effect, the ice sheet of Antarctica gradually melts, which leads to the rising level of the World Ocean and the flooding of small islands.

PRINCIPLES OF INTERNATIONAL ENVIRONMENTAL LAW

The principles of international legal regulation are generally divided into two groups: general (generally accepted) principles of international law (for example, the principle of non-use of force or the threat of force; the principle of sovereign equality of states, *etc.*) and special principles of international environmental law formulated in the 1972 Stockholm Declaration, the World Charter for Nature (Resolution 37/7, adopted at the 48th plenary session of the UN General Assembly on October 28, 1982), the 1992 Rio Declaration and other documents.

They include the following principles:

1. The principle of the sovereignty of states over their natural resources means their sovereign right to exploit their own natural resources according to their policy in the field of natural resource management, environmental protection, and development. This principle is not absolute.

2. The principle of rational use of natural resources. This principle obliges states to manage and use their natural resources without damaging the integrity of ecological systems as well as to carry out a series of measures for the reproduction and recovery of natural resources (the United Nations Convention on the Law of the Sea of December 10, 1982, the Forest Principles adopted at the United Nations Conference on Environment and Development in 1992 and other documents are dedicated to this).

3. The principle of prevention of transboundary harm to the environment was formulated in the 1972 Stockholm Declaration and the 1992 Rio Declaration. This principle means particular limits for the sovereignty of states over natural resources. It results in the requirement for the states to make sure that the activities carried out under their jurisdiction or monitoring do not cause harm to the environment of other states or districts. In addition, even probable armed conflicts do not exempt the parties from this requirement. The implementation of this principle constantly gives rise to many theoretical and practical problems. In the doctrine of international law, pollution is understood as deterioration of the

environment as a consequence of economic and other human activities. However, pollution can also be caused by natural factors, for example, an earthquake in Iceland polluted the airspace with ash, which paralyzed air traffic several years ago. An accident at the Fukushima Daiichi nuclear power plant in Japan occurred due to another earthquake. This is why this principle and the rules of international law following from it are violated if a state where a natural disaster occurred deliberately failed to take any action to prevent the spread of its adverse effects to the territories of the neighboring countries.

4. The principle of liability of states for violation of the requirements of international environmental law. Criminal or administrative liability are not applied in the system of liability under international law. The main type of liability for international environmental offenses is the compensation for property damage. Damage can be caused to both national ecological systems of another state and objects located within the boundaries of the international areas (the World Ocean, air).

Compensation for damage caused in case of marine oil pollution (Convention on Civil Liability for Oil Pollution Damage, Brussels, November 19, 1969), as well as liability for damage caused by the use of nuclear installations (Convention on Civil Liability for Nuclear Damage, Vienna, September 12, 1963), are the most developed and frequently applied types of liability.

Since disputes between states regarding property damage are inevitable, a special chamber considering intergovernmental disputes in the field of environmental protection was established by the UN International Court of Justice for the purpose of implementation of this principle in July 1993. One of the first cases heard by the court concerned compensation for environmental damage caused by land degradation on Nauru island in the period when Australia administered the island. The court accepted this case for consideration on June 26, 1992, despite the fact that the claims for the damage compensation related to a period of 70 years. Afterward, the parties reached a friendly settlement of their dispute, though.

Another option for resolving international environmental disputes is the consideration of cases by the International Court of Environmental Arbitration and Conciliation, which was established as a non-governmental organization in November 1994. The cases are considered according to the principle of arbitration, *i.e.*, the parties agree in advance that the decision is binding on them.

5. The principle of environmental protection in the period of military conflicts.

There are enough cases of using the environment for military purposes in the history of world wars. The below environmental wars can be cited as an example.

Over 100,000 tons of napalm were used in Vietnam between 1965 and 1973 as part of a strategy of devastation carried out by the American armed forces. This strategy included defoliation of forests and plantations, destruction of rice paddies, incendiary bombardments, and razing entire areas by fire and bulldozers. During the Iran-Iraq war, no fewer than 447 oil tankers were attacked in the Persian Gulf between May 1, 1980, and December 31, 1987, and in 1984 alone, 2,035,000 tons of oil were spilled into the sea. None of either country's oil-producing facilities was spared. This is why the two belligerent States can therefore reasonably be considered to have caused widespread, long-term, and severe damage to the environment (Antoine, 1995). The same methods were used by the belligerent parties during the 1991 war in Kuwait. The total amount of oil spilled into the Gulf ranged up to eleven million or more barrels of crude. By May 1991, over 400 kilometers of the Saudi coast and the southern Kuwaiti coast were affected. There was damage to coastal marshlands, wildlife (over 15,000 birds killed), coastal flora, fishing, and offshore oil operations. The effects of the destruction of the oil installations in Kuwait proved to be serious. The flood of oil from the wells formed lakes and reportedly affected aquifers. The fires involved huge waste of a valuable natural resource and spewed many gases, including the "greenhouse" gas carbon, dioxide into the atmosphere. In Kuwait, in the months after the war, there was heavy atmospheric pollution, causing an increase in respiratory illnesses. The smoke had adverse effects on the environmental situation in neighboring countries. There was black rain in Turkey, Iran, and the Himalayas. Fortunately, soot from the fires does not appear to have risen high enough to cause the global environmental effects some feared (Roberts, 1995).

The 2003 Iraq war also had negative environmental consequences, with the damage to nature from burning and oil spills as well as the use of some types of weapons (increased seismic activity as a result of bombing). The environmental consequences of the war in Syria ongoing since 2015 are not yet exactly known. Nevertheless, the missile and bomb attacks on the oil fields and the oil storage tanks are known to have caused fires and soil contamination as well as harm to the health of the population. As a result of the war, several reservoirs dried up (because no one supervised them), which provoked a shortage of drinking water. Since the centralized oil production in Syria ceased, the population began to produce and sell oil by themselves, which increased the risk of accidents and environmental pollution due to uncontrolled oil spills.

The said negative consequences of the impact on nature during local wars led to the emergence of a special principle in international environmental law specified in the Convention on the Prohibition of Military or Any Other Hostile Use of Environmental Modification Techniques (ENMOD) of December 10, 1976. This Convention contains the prohibition of anthropogenic impact using the deliberate intervention of one state in the natural processes of another state. Members of the Convention undertake not to use environmental modification techniques for military or any other hostile purposes as means of destruction or damage. "Hostile" impact is understood as the impact with widespread, long-lasting and severe effects. Accordingly, the responsible state is obliged to compensate for damage to the environment of the affected country. For example, Iraq compensated for the consequences of its 1991 hostile interference in Kuwait's natural processes.

6. The principle of sustainable development. Sustainable development is the socio-economic and environmental development aimed at preserving peace in the world, satisfying the needs of people reasonably while improving the quality of life of the present and future generations, using the planet's resources economically and preserving the natural environment, developing the economy in a way not accompanied by hazardous pollution and destruction of the natural environment.

7. The principle of environmental impact assessment. In recent years, there has been an increase in the number of principles of international environmental law of a preventive nature, *i.e.*, not related to compensation for damage already caused but aimed at certain preventive measures. The principle under consideration was formulated in the 1991 Convention on Environmental Impact Assessment in a Transboundary Context, the 1982 UN Convention on the Law of the Sea as well as in the regional agreements – the 1982 Regional Convention for the Conservation of the Red Sea and Gulf of Aden Environment, the 1983 Convention for the Protection and Development of the Marine Environment in the Wider Caribbean Region, *etc*. This principle means that environmental impact assessment (including public hearings) of projects that are potentially hazardous to the environment must be carried out at the early stages of planning, both inside states and in the neighboring countries, which can be affected by the impact of the planned environmentally hazardous activities.

8. The polluter pays principle. Two types of implementation of the said principle are distinguished in practice. In the first, most common option, it is applied by establishing a certain type of taxes and the use of funds accumulated as a result for nature protection purposes. In the second option, which has begun to develop recently, there is a liability for damage to the environment established for the state, the activities which lead to this damage. In particular, these are hazardous activities that are allowed since they bring certain benefits to society (for example, nuclear power plants).

9. The principle of natural heritage protection. The 1972 Convention Concerning the Protection of the World Cultural and Natural Heritage understands natural heritage as natural features of outstanding universal value from the aesthetic or scientific point of view. They can consist of geological formations and other areas which constitute the habitat of threatened species of animals and plants of outstanding value from the point of view of science and requiring conservation, natural sites requiring conservation of their natural beauty, *etc*. These objects are to be included in a special register; they are under special protection.

SOURCES OF INTERNATIONAL ENVIRONMENTAL LAW

Sources of international law are understood as the corresponding legal forms of international law – international customs, general principles, international agreements, judgments of international courts, and international doctrines. Sources of international environmental law can be classified on several grounds. Within the first classification, all sources of international environmental law are divided into two groups according to their legal force. First, these are sources containing rules and regulations recognized by states as mandatory rules (international agreements occupy the main place among them). Depending on the number of parties, there are multilateral and bilateral agreements; according to the territorial scope, international agreements are divided into local, subregional, regional, and global. Local agreements are aimed at resolving local issues of protection of the environment of border areas; subregional – at protecting certain ecological systems; regional – at protecting seas, rivers, and adjacent regions; global – at protecting of the Earth's ozone layer, the World Ocean, *etc*.

Second, these are sources containing recommendations for protecting the environment (so-called rules of international soft law). States follow these recommendations voluntarily due to their high moral value and authority. They include resolutions of the UN General Assembly and recommendations of international conferences. The Resolution “Economic Development and Nature Protection” of December 18, 1962 (with the attempt to direct the international community to search for a combined economic and economic interests of society, understanding environmental protection as a system of actions but not as the protection of specific natural resources) as well as the World Charter for Nature, Resolution 37/7, adopted by the UN General Assembly on October 28, 1982 (focusing on the planning of use and protection of natural resources) should be mentioned among the best-known Resolutions of the UN General Assembly. The Declaration of the 1972 UN Stockholm Conference, the Declaration of principles approved at the UN Conference in Rio de Janeiro in 1992, the Johannesburg Declaration on Sustainable Development, and the Declaration of the 2012 United

Nations Conference on Sustainable Development, Rio+20, should be mentioned among the outcomes of the UN international conferences.

The second classification of international agreements uses the connection between the subject of agreement regulation and nature protection issues as the criterion. According to this ground, there are the following types of agreements:

a. Agreements regulating their branch (not nature protection) relations, which do not contain nature protection rules, however, objectively contribute to the protection of natural objects and systems (the 1985 South Pacific Nuclear Free Zone Treaty, the Agreement Establishing the WTO, *etc*.);

b. Agreements regulating relations in the use of certain natural resources but also containing some provisions on their protection as part of the environment (the 1982 Convention on the Law of the Sea);

c. Agreements totally focused on regulating environmental protection. These are the 1998 Convention on Access to Information, Public Participation in Decision-Making and Access to Justice in Environmental Matters (Aarhus Convention), the 1992 Framework Convention on Climate Change, the 1992 Convention on Biological Diversity, *etc*.

The third classification is based on the degree of states' delegation of their sovereign rights for settlement of environmental issues.

a. Framework conventions containing only general principles specified in detail in other international instruments or national legislation (the 1992 Framework Convention on Climate Change). States waive their sovereign rights to the least extent in this case.

b. Agreement regulation related to states' acceptance of voluntary restrictions on economic or other activities in several neighboring countries at once for settlement of regional environmental issues. For example, the Convention for the Protection of the Marine Environment of the Baltic Sea Area (the Helsinki Convention) was signed in 1992 by several countries of the Baltic region, which voluntarily assumed several restrictions to reduce discharges, pollution from ships, waste dumping at sea, environmental impact assessment, *etc*. In this case, the states waived part of their sovereign rights.

c. Adoption of decisions binding on states by supranational authorities (the EU directives are a typical example). We observe significant restriction of sovereign rights of the states in this case.

In recent years, the number of regional international agreements for environmental protection has increased. The distinctive feature of these agreements within international environmental law is that they establish a stricter protection regime of natural objects in contrast to global international agreements. Regional international agreements include the 1968 African Convention for the Protection of Nature and Natural Resources, the 1976 Convention for the Protection of the Mediterranean Sea against Pollution, the 1973 Convention on Fishing and Conservation of Living Resources in the Baltic Sea, and the Belts, *etc*.

There is an increasingly active bilateral cooperation between the Russian Federation and foreign countries, particularly the United States, Norway, China, Finland, Germany, and other countries.

The Russian Federation cooperates with member states of the Commonwealth of Independent States based on the Agreement on Cooperation in the Field of Environmental Protection of the Member States of the Commonwealth of Independent States of May 31, 2013. According to Article 1 of this document, the parties cooperate in environmental protection: protection and use of land, soil, subsoil, forests, water, air, the ozone layer, and climate, flora, and fauna.

The Parties cooperate in the following main areas: development and adoption of regulatory legal acts, environmental rules, and standards in the field of environmental protection and natural resource management; maintenance of the register of natural resources and implementation of environmental monitoring; enhancement of the system of the state control (supervision) over the condition of the environment; measures for the reproduction of living resources, conservation and restoration of biological diversity; development of the network of reserves, sanctuaries, national parks and other specially protected natural areas and natural systems, measures for minimization of economic and other activities in the zones adjacent to them, *etc*.

The Parties established the Interstate Environmental Council of Member States of the Commonwealth of Independent States to implement the agreement. To coordinate their environmental legislation, at the plenary sessions of the Interparliamentary Assembly, the CIS member states adopt model laws which can be used by their legislative authorities for the development of national environmental legislation.

The analysis of the texts of these laws leads to a conclusion that some of the advisory rules outlined in them have already been implemented in Russian environmental legislation. For example, the text of the model law "On Safe Handling of Pesticides and Agrochemicals" is very similar to the Federal Law of July 19, 1997, "On Safe Handling of Pesticides and Agrochemicals". This could be also said about the CIS model law "On Fauna" and the law of Russia with the same title.

On the other hand, many model laws of the CIS have no analogs in Russia, but they are implemented in other CIS countries and therefore can be of interest to the Russian legislator. They include the Model Law on Ecological Disaster Zones (on the Status of Ecological Disaster Zones and Regulation of Economic and Other Activities in Their Territory) (adopted in Saint Petersburg on December 3, 2009, based on Resolution 33-9 at the 33rd plenary session of the Interparliamentary Assembly of the CIS member states) and the Model Law on Environmental Auditing (adopted in Saint Petersburg on November 29, 2013, based on Resolution 39-5 at the 39th plenary session of the Interparliamentary Assembly of the CIS member states).

A number of model laws of the CIS are aimed at regulating the interstate environmental relations of the CIS countries. For example, this category includes the Model Law on Rational Use and Protection of Transboundary Waters (Water Bodies) (Adopted in Saint Petersburg on April 18, 2014, on the basis of Resolution 40-9 at the 40th plenary session of the Interparliamentary Assembly of the CIS member states). The provisions of this law cover the parts of transboundary water bodies located in the territories of the CIS member states.

INTERNATIONAL ORGANIZATIONS AS SUBJECTS OF INTERNATIONAL ENVIRONMENTAL LAW

Now there are over 100 various international organizations in the world that are engaged in environmental protection issues to various extents. All international organizations participating in relations governed by international environmental law can be divided into two large groups: international governmental and international non-governmental (public) organizations. International governmental organizations, in their turn, are subdivided into global (world) and regional.

The United Nations is the most authoritative of global international organizations. The UN General Assembly, which can discuss any environmental protection issues, occupies the central place in the organization of environmental cooperation among the UN member states. The activities of the General Assembly are reflected in the resolutions adopted by it, for example, the Resolution of the UN

General Assembly of December 20, 2018, Protection of Global Climate for Present and Future Generations of Humankind. Reports of the UN Secretary-General reflect the most dangerous environmental threats of modern times. The Report of the UN Secretary-General of July 19, 2017 "Harmony with Nature" suggesting a new philosophy of environmental protection is their typical example. The UN Economic and Social Council (ECOSOC) has broad competence, the functional commissions (for example, the Commission on Sustainable Development) and regional commissions present reports directly to this Council.

Along with the consideration of environmental issues at the sessions of the General Assembly as well as the adoption of various resolutions and the organization of conferences, the specialized agency UNEP (United Nations Environment Program) was established under the United Nations in 1972. By its legal nature, UNEP belongs to subsidiary bodies of the United Nations though it has a certain autonomy in decision-making.

The structure of UNEP includes the Governing Council – the main intergovernmental body guiding its policy, the Committee of Permanent Representatives, and the Secretariat. UNEP is headed by the Executive Director and carries out its activities through its divisions, regional, liaison, and out-posted offices, plus a growing network of collaborating centers of excellence. UNEP is one of the co-founders of the Global Environment Facility. Its main activities aim to coordinate efforts of all countries around the world to protect the atmosphere and marine and terrestrial ecological systems. UNEP pays much attention to the prevention of environmental conflicts between countries around the world, development of nature protection technologies, promotion of interstate cooperation in nature protection, development of draft environmental conventions and agreements, the proposal of measures to protect the environment at the global level, provision of states and population with information about environmental threats and measures to prevent them, *etc*. The most tangible practical result of its work is that it initiated the signing of the 1987 Montreal Protocol on Substances that Deplete the Ozone Layer, which helps to reduce the damage caused by chemicals to the ozone layer of the atmosphere, and the 1989 Basel Convention on the Control of Transboundary Movements of Hazardous Wastes and their Disposal, which is aimed at ensuring control over the international movement and disposal of hazardous waste. Moreover, it was UNEP that organized the international conference in Rio de Janeiro in 1992 as well as other conferences.

There are also other specialized international nature protection organizations within the structure of the United Nations:

a. International Atomic Energy Agency (IAEA). This structural subdivision of the United Nations was created in 1957. Today, it includes 170 countries. Its governing bodies are the annual General Conference of IAEA Member States, the Board of Governors and the Secretariat. The main objective of the IAEA is to promote the peaceful use of nuclear energy. IAEA experts work in all countries that have signed the Treaty on the Non-Proliferation of Nuclear Weapons to monitor the peaceful use of nuclear energy facilities and their non-military purpose. The experts themselves cannot prohibit these activities; however, in case they detect any violations, they submit these data to the United Nations. Moreover, IAEA encourages the studies of the peaceful use of nuclear energy and the discussion of the system of guarantees of the non-use of civilian nuclear programs for military purposes.

b. United Nations Educational, Scientific and Cultural Organization (UNESCO). Its main environmental function is to promote environmental education as well as to register and protect natural objects attributed to the World Heritage Sites;

c. World Health Organization (WHO). The main environmental function of WHO is to study issues of the protection of human health in the context of its interaction with the environment;

d. United Nations Food and Agriculture Organization (FAO). FAO deals with environmental issues in agriculture, in particular, protection and use of land, improvement of its fertility, protection of forests, water, fauna, aquatic bioresources, *etc.*;

e. The International Maritime Organization (IMO) deals with the protection of seas from pollution participates in the development of international conventions for the prevention of pollution of sea by oil and other harmful substances. In recent years, the IMO has been involved in the discussion of mandatory double hulls for oil tankers and protection of seas from harmful microorganisms transported in ballast water and dumped into local alien ecosystems, to which they cause considerable harm;

f. The United Nations World Meteorological Organization (WMO) studies the human impact on nature and the planet's climate by conducting global environmental monitoring. WMO coordinates the free exchange of information on the condition of the environment between states, which contributes to the prevention (mitigation) of the negative consequences of natural emergencies;

g. The International Civil Aviation Organization (ICAO) deals with the issues of reducing the negative impact on the environment from emissions of greenhouse gases into the air in connection with the use of aviation and lowering noise from civil aviation.

Regional international organizations include the European Union. The functioning of each EU institution (Council, Commission, European Parliament, Court of Justice, Court of Auditors) is related to environmental protection issues to various extents. The European Environment Agency, a special environmental institution, was established within the structure of the EU bodies in 1990. The main objective of the agency is to monitor the current and expected state of the environment and inform the EU member states about the dynamics of its change under the influence of anthropogenic factors (including environmental quality, load on the environment, environmental sensitivity).

The role of international non-governmental (public) organizations engaged in environmental issues in international environmental law constantly grows. Today, there are over 200 such organizations around the world, directly specializing in environmental protection issues in general or a single issue of nature protection in particular (for example, environmental education). They include any non-commercial associations established according to the domestic legislation of any country and carrying out nature protection activities in the territory of two or more states.

Greenpeace is the best known environmental association; it is known for its high profile (sometimes illegal) environmental actions, for example, campaigns against commercial whale hunting, GMO products, campaigns for the protection of the ozone layer, and against air pollution. In Russia, it organized a high-profile protest against Arctic oil production; they made attempts to seize the Gazprom-owned Prirazlomnaya oil platform from inflatable boats.

Besides the Greenpeace Movement in the world, there are some international environmental non-governmental associations as Ecology, Green Cross, and so forth. International environmental non-governmental organizations such as the International Union for Conservation of Nature (IUCN), the World Wide Fund for Nature (WWF), and the International Council of Environmental Law (ICEL) are even better known. States are the main rule-makers in international environmental law; consequently, the role of non-governmental nature protection organizations in international rulemaking is limited. However, the largest of them, the International Union for Conservation of Nature, using its advisory status under some UN agencies and institutions, has the possibility to officially present its views on draft documents considered at international conferences and in intergovernmental bodies.

To sum up, we will try to list the main environmental threats of the international level which are countered in modern international legal acts: the threat to the environment during hostile use of environmental modification techniques in military operations; the threat of environmental terrorism; the threat of nuclear war; global climate change, the pollution of air, water bodies (including the World Ocean), space and Antarctica, the lack of natural resources and the loss of biological diversity.

CONCLUSION

The chapter states that ensuring the quality of the environment on a global scale is impossible without the development of international cooperation. Its implementation takes place on the basis of generally recognized principles of international law. The international acts of mandatory (conventions) and advisory (declarations) are distinguished. The analysis of the activities of international environmental authorities (UNEP, WHO, and others) is carried out. Non-governmental organizations (Greenpeace) play a special role in the international legal protection of the environment.

QUESTIONS AND TASKS FOR SELF-CONTROL

1. Define international environmental law.

2. What are the objects of the international legal protection of the environment?

3. What principles of international environmental law do you know?

4. List the main sources of international environmental law.

5. What international organizations belonging to the subjects of international environmental law do you know?

REFERENCES

Mokhammad, S.A. (2011). International Environmental Law in a Historical Retrospective. *Eurasian Law Journal, 8*, 44-49.

Sokolova, N.A. (2000). International Law: Issues of Specialization. *Siberian Law Bulletin, 3*, 10.

Vystorobets, E.A., Dolgikh, R.I. (2012). *Bilateral Nature Protection Agreements of Russia: the Reading Book on International Environmental Law with a Scientific Paper and a Commentary.*

Antoine, P. (1995). International Humanitarian Law and the Protection of the Environment in Time of Armed Conflict.

Roberts, A. (1995). Environmental Destruction in the 1991 Gulf War. *Environmental Protection in International Humanitarian Law: Collected Works..* Moscow: Publications of the International Committee of the Red Cross.

CHAPTER 9

Legal Regulation of Environmental Protection in Foreign Countries

Abstract: In the era of globalization, international cooperation becomes more important since no country in the world can solve the problem of global climate change or pollution of the World Ocean on its own. However, the interpenetration of the most successful legal rules and institutions of other countries into national legal systems is a no less significant trend. The study of this comparative aspect makes it possible to better understand the advantages and disadvantages of Russian environmental legislation, formulate constructive suggestions for the Russian legislator, and identify possible ways of bilateral cooperation in environmental issues that are understood in the national legislation of two or more countries.

Russian environmental legislation is more closely linked to the CIS countries both for the geographical reason (as neighbors) and because these countries were part of the USSR for many years, and the approaches to the legal regulation of environmental (and many other) social relations that were established during that period of our joint history are still used today. The environmental laws of the Russian Federation, the Republic of Kazakhstan, and the Republic of Belarus can be compared as an example. The criterion for comparison is the content of the main environmental legal institutions included in these laws. The relevant environmental legal institutions in Russia and these countries can coincide completely, partially, or don't not coincide at all. The main focus in this chapter is not so much on comparing the laws of the Republics of Kazakhstan and Belarus with each other but comparing them with the basic institutions of Russian environmental law. The fundamental difference between environmental law of the European Union and the Russian Federation is not only the supranational nature of EU directives but also the fact that the EU almost does not regulate natural resource management issues *e.g.*, in terms of the procedure for the provision of natural resources based on the right of ownership or other rights. This is the scope of national legislation of the member countries.

Both in Russia and the environmental law of the EU, we can observe a trend of ecologization of related legislation: it means environmental rules are introduced into the regulatory acts governing related areas of social relations (transport, power industry, fight against unemployment, *etc.*). Moreover, in this chapter, the authors point out several characteristics of not only the environmental law of the United States but of Russia, China, the European Union, or many other countries and consider the current distinctive features of the nature protection policy of China.

Aleksey Anisimov and Anatoliy Ryzhenkov

Keywords: Acid rains, Agency, Belarus, Experience, China, Directive, Drinking water, Federation, Flint, Government, Greenhouse gases, Legislation, Kazakhstan, Principle, Quotas, Russia, State, Superfund, United States, Waste.

LEGAL PROTECTION OF THE ENVIRONMENT IN THE CIS COUNTRIES

In the era of globalization, international cooperation becomes more important since no country in the world can solve the problem of global climate change or pollution of the World Ocean on its own. However, the interpenetration of the most successful legal rules and institutions of other countries into national legal systems is a no less significant trend. The study of this comparative aspect makes it possible to understand better the advantages and disadvantages of Russian environmental legislation, to formulate constructive suggestions for the Russian legislator as well as to identify possible ways of bilateral cooperation in environmental issues which are understood in the national legislation of two or more countries.

Russian environmental legislation is more closely linked to the CIS countries both for the geographical reason (as neighbors) and because our countries were part of the USSR for many years, and the approaches to the legal regulation of environmental (and many other) social relations that were established during that period of our joint history are still used today. The main environmental laws of the Russian Federation, the Republic of Kazakhstan and the Republic of Belarus can be compared as an example. The criterion for comparison is the content of the main environmental legal institutions included in these laws. The relevant environmental legal institutions in Russia and these countries can coincide completely, partially or not coincide at all. Below we will pay attention not so much to comparing the laws of the Republics of Kazakhstan and Belarus with each other as to comparing them with the basic institutions of the Russian Federal Law "On Environmental Protection" of January 10, 2002 (hereinafter "the Law of the Russian Federation"). It should be noted that Kazakhstan carried out codification and uses the Environmental Code of the Republic of Kazakhstan of January 2, 2021. In the Republic of Belarus, as well as in Russia, there are numerous environmental laws, the Law of the Republic of Belarus "On Environmental Protection" of November 26, 1992 is the main of them.

Let us compare the environmental legal institutions of the said three countries.

I. Complete Coincidence

1) The name and the general principles of most state regulation measures in the field of environmental protection generally coincide in Russia, Kazakhstan and

Belarus. While comparing with Kazakhstan we observe a number of significant differences in the implementation of some of these state management measures (for example, in terms of economic regulation), there is much more in common between the Russian Federation and the Republic of Belarus, both in form and content. In particular, the institutions of standardization, monitoring, requirements for certain types of environmentally hazardous activities, regulation of issues of environmental control and environmental education coincide in many aspects in the Russian Federation and in the Republic of Belarus. Like Russia, the Republic of Belarus maintains the Red Data Book, based on the same principles and having the same goals and objectives.

2) The lists of environmental rights and duties in the Russian Federation, Belarus and Kazakhstan coincide almost completely. In all three countries, citizens have the right to environmental information, compensation for harm, rallies, processions, demonstrations, *etc.* The right of citizens to participate in environmental decision-making is expressly stated in Kazakhstan and Belarus but cannot be found in Article 11 of the Law of the Russian Federation, however, this right is enshrined in other Russian laws (the Urban Development Code of the Russian Federation). The lists of environmental duties coincide in Russia and Kazakhstan not word for word but in the meaning. The list of environmental duties is broader in the Republic of Belarus than in Russia and Kazakhstan. Meanwhile, these duties are not something fundamentally new (for example, the duty to fulfill requirements in the area of waste management). These duties are just set forth in other federal laws in Russia.

3) Like the Russian Federation, the Republic of Kazakhstan has its own main nature protection authority, the Ministry of Ecology, Geology and Natural Resources of the Republic of Kazakhstan, an analogue of the Russian Ministry of Natural Resources and Environment. In Belarus, this authority is called the Ministry of Natural Resources and Environmental Protection of the Republic of Belarus.

4) In Russia, Belarus and Kazakhstan, the lists of environmental expert reviews coincide – there are state and public expert reviews.

II. Partial Coincidence

1) The Environmental Code of the Republic of Kazakhstan contains no special article dedicated to environmental legal terminology, though some definitions are given throughout the text of the law (for example, what environmental information or environmental safety are). In general, the terminological understanding of the issues of waste management, environmental monitoring, specially protected natural areas, state environmental control (supervision) and

environmental standardization coincides in the Russian Federation and the Republic of Kazakhstan. As a result of comparison of the terminology in Russia and the Republic of Belarus, it is also possible to find terms that coincide and do not coincide with each other. For example, the terms biotope, biosphere reserve and national ecological network are not used in Russia. At the same time, most terms of the Russian Federation and the Republic of Belarus are almost the same (components of the natural environment, monitoring, quality of the environment, *etc.*).

2) The principles of environmental law coincide in the Environmental Code of the Republic of Kazakhstan and the Law of the Russian Federation only partially, for example, in terms of the polluter pays principle. A number of principles of the Environmental Code of the Republic of Kazakhstan are absent in the Law of the Russian Federation (for example, the principles of proportionality, integration, remediation, *etc.*). Accordingly, many principles of the Law of the Russian Federation are absent in the Environmental Code of the Republic of Kazakhstan (for example, the principle of the organization and development of the environmental education system and the formation of environmental culture), and there are more environmental principles themselves in the Russian Federation. If we compare the principles of environmental legislation of the Russian Federation and Belarus, most of them are the same word for word. The other principles are different to some extent in their wording, coinciding in the sense. The principles of Belarusian environmental legislation that are of interest to the Russian Federation include the principle of the prevention of combining the functions of state regulation, management and control in the field of environmental protection, rational use of natural resources and natural resource management functions.

3) Kazakhstan develops the institution of ecolabeling, which is still underdeveloped in Russia. According to Article 47 of the Environmental Code of the Republic of Kazakhstan, ecolabeling is understood as the declaration informing about environmental aspects of the products, works or services in the form of text, signs or graphics on the labels of products or their packaging, in the accompanying documentation, technical description, advertising brochures, public information leaflets or in other forms. The purposes of ecolabeling are as follows: informing consumers about environmental aspects of the products, works and services purchased by them, promoting the growth of the purchase and consumption (use) of green products, works and services in order to reduce the negative anthropogenic impact on the environment, preventing or minimizing the negative anthropogenic impact on the environment during the life cycle of products, contributing to export and increasing the competitiveness of domestic products. Ecolabeling is stipulated in Russia only by Article 7 of Federal Law No. 280-FZ of August 3, 2018 “On Organic Products and on Amendments to Certain

Legislative Acts of the Russian Federation" and has not been further developed yet. The main law on nature protection in the Republic of Belarus does not mention ecolabeling.

4) Separate Chapter 10 of the Environmental Code of the Republic of Kazakhstan is dedicated to the mechanisms of economic regulation of environmental protection and natural resource management. These mechanisms in the Republic of Kazakhstan include the payment for negative impact on the environment, market mechanisms of emission management, environmental insurance, economic incentives for activities aimed at environmental protection, market mechanisms of reduction of emissions and absorption of greenhouse gases and extended producer (importer) obligations. In the course of comparison of these economic regulation elements with Russian ones, enshrined in Chapter 4 of the Law of the Russian Federation, it is easy to find that there are only three elements distinguished in Russia: payment for negative impact on the environment, state support of economic and (or) other activities carried out for the purpose of environmental protection as well as environmental insurance (and the latter has not yet been significantly developed in Russia). It is not mentioned directly but nature protection activities are funded annually from the budgets of all levels of the Russian Federation.

The Republic of Belarus also has more elements of the economic mechanism of environmental protection than Russia. In particular, there are development of state estimates and programs of socio-economic development of the Republic of Belarus in terms of the rational (sustainable) use of natural resources and environmental protection, funding of programs and activities for the rational (sustainable) use of natural resources and environmental protection, foundation of nature protection funds, establishment of payments for natural resource management, economic assessment of natural objects, economic assessment of the impact of economic and other activities on the environment, environmental insurance and so forth.

In the Republic of Belarus, republican and local environmental protection funds were established to fund the state programs of the rational use of natural resources and environmental protection, regional sets of measures and other purposes in the field of environmental protection, these funds are state target budgetary funds. Similar funds operated also in Russia in the 1990s but they were closed.

5) Both Kazakhstan and Russia monitor the state of the environment. The general understanding of goals and objectives of state environmental control coincides in the Russian Federation and the Republic of Kazakhstan. It is interesting that the Environmental Code of the Republic of Kazakhstan stipulates three forms of

control: preventive control without visiting the subject (object), preventive control with visiting the subject (object) and checks. In addition, Article 176 of the Environmental Code of the Republic of Kazakhstan specifies the determination of the amount of the economic benefit derived as a result of violation of environmental legislation of the Republic of Kazakhstan during state environmental control, which is not found in the Law of the Russian Federation.

6) In the Republic of Kazakhstan and Russia, the understanding of goals and objectives of environmental monitoring completely coincides but the understanding of its subsystems is different. According to Article 154 of the Environmental Code of the Republic of Kazakhstan, the Unified State System for Environmental and Natural Resources Monitoring includes the following monitoring systems: environmental monitoring, natural resources monitoring, special monitoring, meteorological and hydrological monitoring and monitoring of the state of the environment. In addition, for example, the objects of environmental monitoring are as follows: the quality of ground water, the impact of facilities of categories I and II on the environment, the state of ecological systems and ecosystem services provided by them, specially protected natural areas, the impact of climate change, waste and waste management. In this sense, there are particular differences between the Environmental Code of the Republic of Kazakhstan and the objects of monitoring in the Russian Federation, where the observation of the impact of climate change is not expressly regulated by law, and there is no category of "ecosystem services" in environmental law of the Russian Federation.

7) It is necessary to point out a range of common and different approaches to environmental requirements for economic and other activities that are hazardous to the environment in the Russian Federation and the Environmental Code of the Republic of Kazakhstan. The Russian Federation distinguishes these requirements in the power industry, agriculture, transport, *etc.* (a similar approach is used in the Law of the Republic of Belarus), and the Republic of Kazakhstan – environmental requirements for the design and construction of gas and oil pipelines, environmental requirements for navigation, in the field of the use of ozone depleting substances, in the field of waste management, design of buildings, for military and defense facilities, genetic engineering activities, *etc.* Hence it follows that all the three countries use the framework of requirements for certain types of economic and other activities, however, in Russia and Belarus this area includes a wider range of requirements than in Kazakhstan. At the same time, some areas as, for example, genetic modification activities, are not appropriately enshrined in any regulations in Russia.

8) The Environmental Code of the Republic of Kazakhstan includes special Section 19, Waste, which contains a number of interesting innovations related to waste restoration (*i.e.*, reuse), waste destruction, neutralization, transportation, energy recovery, *etc.* The following principles of the state environmental policy in the field of waste management are quite interesting: hierarchy, proximity to the source, responsibility of the waste generator and extended producer (importer) obligations. According to Article 339 of the Environmental Code of the Republic of Kazakhstan, waste is a subject of real rights and waste generators are the owners of the waste produced by them. Particular attention is paid to the management of ownerless waste. A special Chapter is dedicated to hazardous waste and the features of its management by the state.

Many waste management provisions coincide in the Russian Federation and Kazakhstan, while many rules of waste handling introduced in Kazakhstan are not sufficiently clarified at the legislative level in the Russian Federation (though they can be found in bylaws), for example, those related to the functioning of landfills that receive different types of waste.

9) Section 18 of the Environmental Code of the Republic of Kazakhstan is dedicated to climate and the ozone layer of the atmosphere. Accordingly, Chapter 20 of the Environmental Code of the Republic of Kazakhstan describes in detail the state regulation of greenhouse gas emissions and Chapter 21 of the Environmental Code of the Republic of Kazakhstan is dedicated to the protection of the ozone layer of the atmosphere. Russia took the first steps to reduce greenhouse gas emissions in Federal Law No. 296-FZ of July 2, 2021 "On the Limitation of Greenhouse Gas Emissions", however, the extent of the regulation of this issue in Russia is much more modest than in Kazakhstan. In addition, we should note that Article 54 of the Law of the Russian Federation, like in the Republic of Kazakhstan, mentions measures for the protection of the ozone layer, however, climate is not considered in Russia as an independent object of legal protection.

10) In contrast to Russia or Kazakhstan, the Republic of Belarus establishes the environmental powers of the President of Belarus, the Council of Ministers, the Ministry of Natural Resources and Environmental Protection, local councils of deputies, their executive and administrative bodies in special Articles. Russia uses another legal technique approach: environmental powers of the federal, regional and local levels are formulated without specifying which particular authority exercises them. Accordingly, the Law of the Russian Federation does not regulate the powers of the main federal executive authority for nature protection. These powers are determined by the Decree of the Government of the Russian Federation. The legislator of Kazakhstan takes a compromise position on this

issue, having determined the competence of the specially authorized authority in the field of environmental protection in Article 27 of the Environmental Code of the Republic of Kazakhstan, but without specifying its exact name.

11) In Kazakhstan, there are mandatory public hearings on a number of important environmental issues, for example, in relation to draft reports on possible impact (Article 73) or in case of strategic environmental assessment (Article 60). In the Republic of Belarus, a similar institution is called "public discussions of projects of environmentally significant decisions, environmental impact assessment reports and environmental statements on strategic environmental assessment". Russia holds public hearings in relation to a number of types of urban planning documentation, and environmental legislation stipulates them only in terms of EIA and hearings held by the Public Chamber in case of creating forest green belts around urban settlements. Therefore, the list of the grounds for public hearings in the Republic of Kazakhstan as well as Article 15-2 of the Republic of Belarus "On Environmental Protection" are much broader.

III. Complete Non-coincidence

1) In the Russian Federation, environmental impact assessment is formal and it is not regulated in the Law of the Russian Federation of 2002. Article 49 of the Environmental Code of the Republic of Kazakhstan stipulates four types of environmental assessment depending on the assessment subject: strategic environmental assessment, environmental impact assessment, assessment of transboundary impact, environmental assessment according to a simplified procedure.Accordingly, Articles 64-79 of the Environmental Code of the Republic of Kazakhstan thoroughly describe the stages of EIA, the procedure for its application, types of impact that are subject to consideration in the course of EIA, *etc.* All this is still not observed in the Russian Federation.

2) The Environmental Code of the Republic of Kazakhstan pays much attention to activities aimed at reducing the level of greenhouse gases, introducing international standards, describing the powers of nature protection authorities in this field, *etc.* For example, greenhouse gas emissions are understood in Kazakhstan as the release of greenhouse gases into the atmosphere as a result of anthropogenic processes. The absorption of greenhouse gases is understood as the removal of greenhouse gas from the atmosphere resulting from any natural process or activity. Amounts of emissions and absorption of greenhouse gases are measured and calculated in tons of carbon dioxide equivalent. The potential of global warming is determined by the authorized authority in the field of environmental protection according to the provisions of international agreements of the Republic of Kazakhstan in the field of climate change. The Republic of

Kazakhstan aims to reduce the carbon balance of the Republic of Kazakhstan at least by 15 percent compared to the carbon balance level of 1990 by December 31, 2030 (Articles 282-283 of the Environmental Code of the Republic of Kazakhstan).

In the text of the Law, we can find also other rules related to restrictions of greenhouse gas emissions. Russia, like Kazakhstan, has also assumed a number of obligations to reduce greenhouse gas emissions by signing the Kyoto Protocol and then the 2015 Paris Climate Agreement. Russia has been carrying out work to fulfill their requirements for a long time, Federal Law No. 296-FZ of July 2, 2021"On the Limitation of Greenhouse Gas Emissions" was adopted, new bylaws are developed.

3) Despite the fact that both the Environmental Code of the Republic of Kazakhstan and the Federal Law "On Environmental Protection" are built according to the "narrow model" and dedicated only to environmental protection but not natural resource management, this parameter is observed in the Russian Federation more clearly. In the Environmental Code of the Republic of Kazakhstan, we can find separate rules on the maintenance of cadasters of natural resources (Article 155 of the Environmental Code of the Republic of Kazakhstan), which is absent in the Law of the Russian Federation. State cadasters of natural resources are mentioned also in Article 72 of the Law of the Republic of Belarus "On Environmental Protection" (in addition, the "climate cadaster", which has no analogs in the Russian Federation, is mentioned among them).

4) Special Chapter 4 of the Environmental Code of the Republic of Kazakhstan is dedicated to environmental information (including issues of access to it, the term and the procedure for its provision, *etc.*). The right of citizens to environmental information is also enshrined in the Russian Federation, however, the relevant rules are included in different laws and bylaws. In a similar manner, a number of Articles of the Law of the Republic of Belarus is dedicated to the content, sources and types of environmental information, forms of its provision and distribution, access and restrictions for its receipt.

5) In contrast to the Russian Federation, in the Environmental Code of the Republic of Kazakhstan, special Section 21 is dedicated to the legal regime of environmental emergency zones and ecological disaster zones. The Environmental Code of the Republic of Kazakhstan clearly regulates the order and the consequences of their creation.

The legislator of the Republic of Belarus regulates these issues not less clearly. The Republic of Belarus distinguishes ecological risk zones, ecological crisis zones and ecological disaster zones. The formation of a differentiated system of environmentally disadvantaged areas can be attributed to the successful innovations of the legislator also from the perspective of legal technique.

6) Chapter 19 of the Environmental Code of the Republic of Kazakhstan is dedicated specifically to measures for protection of water of the Caspian Sea (a reserve zone is established in the northern part of the Caspian Sea), which cannot be found in the Law of the Russian Federation (in relation to any seas).

7) Article 403 of the Environmental Code of the Republic of Kazakhstan stipulates a number of environmental requirements for genetic engineering activities as well as the application and distribution of products obtained with the use of biotechnology. Genetically modified products are understood as the products, including agricultural products, foods and feed the production technology of which involves using genetically modified organisms at any stage. The use of genetically modified products is allowed in the Republic of Kazakhstan only within the list approved by the authorized authority in the field of environmental protection and the state authority in the field of the sanitary and epidemiological well-being of the population. Genetically modified products are included in the register (list) of genetically modified organisms and products. All foods, feed and feed additives containing or consisting of or obtained from genetically modified organisms are subject to marking according to the technical regulations. In Russia, products with the use of GMOs are completely prohibited. The legislator's approach in the Environmental Code of the Republic of Kazakhstan appears more balanced and thoughtful.

8) Paragraph 2 of Chapter 7 of the Environmental Code of the Republic of Kazakhstan as well as Article 58.1 of the Law of Belarus mention the category of “strategic environmental assessment”, which has no direct analogs in Russian legislation. It is carried out for the items from the statutory list established in the field of state environmental expert reviews, strategic environmental assessment and environmental impact assessment.

9) The Republic of Belarus distinguishes the legal regime of SPNAs (Article 62) and natural areas subject to special protection (Article 63). The latter include resort zones, recreational zones, parks, public gardens and boulevards, water protective zones, riversides and coastal strips of reservoirs, protective zones of specially protected natural areas and a number of other areas. All of them differ in their regime of protection from both SPNAs and common land, in relation to which no additional protection measures are taken. Russia has such areas, however, all of them together are not mentioned in any law and their common parameters of additional protection are not established. Certain types of economic activities are prohibited in these areas.

10) The Republic of Belarus uses the legal framework "national ecological network" and it has no analogs in Russia and Kazakhstan. The national ecological network is a system of functionally interconnected specially protected natural areas and natural areas subject to special protection established to preserve natural ecological systems, biological and landscape diversity as well as to ensure the continuity of habitats of animals.

The scheme of the national ecological network is approved by the President of the Republic of Belarus. The national ecological network consists of core areas, ecological corridors and protective zones. For example, core areas include certain SPNAs (their parts) and (or) natural areas subject to special protection (their parts) ensuring preservation of natural ecological systems, biological and landscape diversity.

Summarizing the conducted comparative analysis of environmental legal institutions of the main environmental laws of the three countries, we can note that the main feature of the Environmental Code of the Republic of Kazakhstan is a very high level of legal technique, thoroughness and interconnectedness of all Chapters of the Law. Some Chapters and Articles of the Environmental Code of the Republic of Kazakhstan somewhat resemble sections of a textbook on environmental law, they are not so much regulatory as informational, explaining the position of the legislator.

Among the analyzed provisions of the Laws of the three countries, the Environmental Code of the Republic of Kazakhstan is the most comprehensive and detailed, followed by the Russian Law on Environmental Protection, and the Belarusian Law is the least detailed.

What is the reason for these coincidences or differences? It appears that the draft Law of the RSFSR "On Protection of the Natural Environment" of December 19, 1991 was initially based on provisions of European environmental laws of the second half of the 1980s. The concept of this Law of the RSFSR of 1991 became the basis of both the current Federal Law "On Environmental Protection" of December 10, 2002 and the Law of the Republic of Belarus "On Environmental Protection". The Republic of Kazakhstan drafted the Environmental Code in the second half of the 2000s on the basis of the environmental laws which were in effect in European countries at that time and those laws had changed dramatically since the late 1980s. This is why the concept of the Environmental Code of the Republic of Kazakhstan is considerably different from the concepts of the main Russian and Belarusian environmental laws, both from the perspective of the names of the main environmental legal institutions and from the perspective of their content.

LEGAL PROTECTION OF THE ENVIRONMENT IN EU COUNTRIES

The European Union is an economic and political association of 27 European states established as a result of the Maastricht Treaty of 1992. The EU is an international entity that combines features of an international organization and a state. It can be said that it is a particular type of confederation as a form of state structure. The adoption of universal legal acts that are in force in all EU countries resulted in the establishment of a common market, free movement of people, goods and services as well as common requirements (standards) for the protection of the environment. The main governing bodies in the EU include the European Council (setting the strategic areas of the EU development), the European Commission (government), the Council of the European Union, the Court of Justice of the European Union, the European Court of Auditors, the European Central Bank and the European Parliament.

The EU adopts regulatory legal acts that determine the common policy of all countries of the EU in the field of the environment. The uniqueness of the European Union consists in the fact that environmental legislation of EU member states is not part of EU law. Each country has its own environmental legislation, which is closely related to regulatory acts of the EU and cannot be in conflict with them. Regulatory legal acts adopted in the EU include constitutional acts the adoption of which resulted in the emergence of the EU itself and regulatory acts aimed at solving various daily issues in the EU. The latter are adopted on the issues of the exclusive or shared competences of the EU. Within the exclusive competences, regulatory acts are adopted only by the EU (for example, regarding the general agricultural policy). The environmental policy is within the joint jurisdiction of the EU and EU member states, which allows these countries to adopt environmental acts. The system of EU regulatory acts includes directives, regulations and resolutions (the latter are addressed to individual countries of the EU rather than to all, they are related to local issues). EU member states are obliged to include the provisions of environmental directives in their national legislation irrespective of whether they are an act of the parliament or an instruction, whether they are adopted centrally or with subsequent specification at the regional level. The only fundamental rule is that directives must be implemented in the entire territory of the country.

Several bodies of the EU perform environmental functions. For example, the Directorate General for the Environment is the European Commission department responsible for EU policy on the environment. It protects, preserves and improves the environment for the present and future generations by proposing and implementing the policy that ensures a high level of environmental protection and the quality of life of EU citizens. It also guarantees that member states correctly apply EU environmental law and represents the European Union with respect to environmental issues at international meetings. The Directorate General for Climate Action leads the European Commission's efforts to combat climate change at the EU and international levels. Its objectives include the implementation of the EU climate policy and strategy, participation in international climate negotiations, introduction of the emissions trading system, promotion of low-carbon technologies, *etc.*

The European Environment Agency (EEA) was created in the EU in order to implement the European Union Regulation of 23 April 2009 on the European Environment Agency and the European Environment Information and Observation Network. Agencies in the EU are decentralized governing bodies that are not included in EU institutions (the European Council, the European Parliament, *etc.*). Agencies are established to accomplish certain objectives. As for the EEA, the objectives are to observe the state of the environment and provide reliable environmental information. The main objectives of the EEA include the assistance for the EU and its members in making substantiated decisions to improve the environment and to integrate environmental requirements into the economic policy to achieve sustainability as well as the coordination of the operation of the network of national nature protection bodies established to assist the agency.

The EEA heads the European network of environmental observation, which includes more than 300 institutions. For this purpose, the EEA works closely with national (coordinating) structures in the corresponding countries. To support the collection, study and analysis of the data, the EEA establishes special European centers covering major environmental issues.

The fundamental difference between environmental law of the EU and the Russian Federation is not only the supranational nature of EU directives but also the fact that the EU almost does not regulate natural resource management issues, for example, in terms of the procedure for the provision of natural resources on the basis of the right of ownership or other rights. This is the scope of national legislation of the member countries.

Both in Russia and in environmental law of the EU, we can observe such a trend as ecologization of related legislation, when environmental rules are introduced into the regulatory acts governing related areas of social relations (transport, power industry, fight against unemployment, *etc.*).

In contrast to Russian regulatory acts, EU directives contain detailed instructions as to which issues must be regulated by national legislation, within which period and in what manner. EU law does not have bylaws in the Russian understanding, their function is performed mostly by acts of national legislation (Krasnova, 2008).

In contrast to, for example, the Republic of Kazakhstan, where the largest part of environmental issues is codified in a single regulatory act, the EU does not have such a code, there are several hundreds of regulatory acts governing certain issues of environmental protection in the EU.

All practical activities in the EU for environmental protection are based on so-called Action Programmes. Each Programme is a political legal act setting the EU priority activities for the medium term as well as specific goals and objectives.

The 7th Environment Action Programme is currently in effect in the EU. It establishes three key objectives: to protect, conserve and enhance the Union's natural capital, to turn the Union into a resource-efficient, green and competitive low-carbon economy, to safeguard the Union's citizens from environment-related pressures and risks to health and wellbeing. Four so-called "enablers" help to deliver on these goals: better implementation of legislation, better information, wiser investment for environment and climate policy, full integration of environmental requirements and considerations into other policies. Within the framework of the 7th Environment Action Programme, the EU adopted action plans for more local environmental issues, for example:

1) The Circular Economy Action Plan was adopted by the European Commission on March 11, 2020. This Action Plan is one of the main building blocks of the European Green Deal, Europe's new agenda for sustainable growth. This Action Plan announces initiatives along the entire life cycle of products, promotes circular economy processes, encourages sustainable consumption and aims to ensure that the resources used are kept in the EU economy.

This Action Plan suggests empowering consumers and focusing on the sectors that use most resources and where the potential for circularity is high such as: electronics, batteries and vehicles, packaging, plastics, textiles, construction and buildings, food, water, *etc.* Moreover, the Plan aims to ensure less waste. The European Commission adopted its first Circular Economy Action Plan in 2015. All 54 measures of the Plan have been implemented or are in progress.

2) The European Strategy for Plastics was adopted by the European Commission on January 16, 2018. This strategy is part of the transition of Europe to a circular economy and it will contribute to the achievement of the Sustainable Development Goals, global climate commitments and industrial policy goals. This strategy will help to protect the environment, to reduce the amount of marine litter, greenhouse gas emissions and the dependence of Europe on imported fossil

fuels. It will support more sustainable and safer consumption and production patterns for plastics. In May 2018, the European Commission proposed new EU-wide rules to target the 10 single-use plastic products most often found on Europe's beaches and seas, as well as lost and abandoned fishing gear. Together these constitute 70% of all marine litter items.

The Directive of the EU of June 5, 2019 on the reduction of the impact of certain plastic products on the environment was adopted for the purpose of implementation of this strategy. For example, according to Article 4 of this Directive, EU member states must take the necessary measures to achieve a reduction in the consumption of the single-use plastic products listed in the Annex to the Directive in their territory by 2026 compared to 2022.

EU member states must ensure that each single-use plastic product listed in Part D of the Annex placed on the market bears a conspicuous, clearly legible and indelible marking on its packaging or on the product itself informing consumers of the waste management options for the product.

In general, all EU directives can be classified into four groups:

1) Directives of a general nature (for example, the EU Directive of December 13, 2011 as amended on April 16, 2014 on the assessment of the effects of certain public and private projects on the environment or the Directive of the European Union of April 21, 2004 on environmental liability with regard to the prevention and remedying of environmental damage);

2) Directives setting the requirements for certain types of activities (for example, the EU Directive of April 26, 1999 as amended on May 30, 2018 on the landfill of waste, the EU Directive of June 25, 2002 relating to the assessment and management of environmental noise, the EU Regulation of November 25, 2009 on the EU Ecolabel, the EU Directive of April 23, 2009 on the promotion of the use of energy from renewable sources, *etc.*);

3) Directives aimed at protecting certain natural objects (for example, the EU Directive of November 30, 2009 on the conservation of wild birds, the EU Directive of November 3, 1998 on the quality of water intended for human consumption, the EU Directive of October 23, 2001 on national emission ceilings for certain atmospheric pollutants);

4) Directives aimed at giving a special legal regime to unique and valuable natural areas (for example, the Directive of May 21, 1992 on the conservation of natural habitats and of wild fauna and flora).

The Court of Justice of the European Union administers justice in the EU (also with respect to environmental issues). For example, in April 2016, the European Commission referred Poland to the Court of Justice of the EU for failing to ensure that the environmental impacts of exploratory mining drillings are properly assessed. Under Polish law, it is possible to drill down to depths of 5000 meters without assessing the potential impact on the environment beforehand. The high threshold introduced under Polish law does not take into account all relevant criteria and standards established by the Environmental Impact Assessment Directive (2011), which should be used when determining whether certain types of projects require an assessment. Under EU law, deep drillings need to be assessed, in particular for the waste they produce, their effects on water and soil, use of natural resources, the risk of accidents, and any cumulative effects.

LEGAL PROTECTION OF THE ENVIRONMENT IN THE UNITED STATES

In the American legal system, environmental law as an independent branch began to actively develop from the 1960s, although even before that period there had been some regulatory acts governing the procedure for the use of natural resources and their partial protection.

It is possible to point out several features characteristic only of environmental law of the United States (but not of Russia, China, the European Union or many other countries):

1) The historical formation of the American state has led to the construction of a federation in which its constituent entities (states) are endowed with a fairly substantial range of environmental and other powers;

2) The system of sources of environmental law of the United States consists of legislation and acts of common (case) law, and these two components of the American legal system complement each other well;

3) The environmental policy of the United States depends significantly on the political affiliation of the US president. For example, the Democrat B. Obama signed the Paris Climate Agreement, while Republican D. Trump withdrew from the Paris Agreement and reduced funding for environmental programs (Garusova and Kuryanova 2019).

4) In the United States, as nowhere else in the world, we can observe well-developed public opinion and activity in the judicial protection of citizens environmental rights. Therefore, economic entities polluting the environment act

not only according to the law but also with consideration of the public opinion and the potential risk of claims from the environmental community.

Let us study the first two trends more thoroughly.

The Constitution of the United States determines relations between the federal government and 50 constituent entities, states. The fundamental principle of American constitutional law is that Congress and the US Government have limited powers, which follows from the doctrine of the separation of powers and their mutual limitation (restraint). This is why the US federal government has no power to take any actions that it considers to be in the public environmental interest.

One of the most important powers of Congress is the right to regulate the issues related to interstate commerce. Anti-pollution laws are frequently adopted on the basis of this law. Pollution often has consequences affecting different states. Moreover, the regulation of the industry as well as emissions from vehicles and other pollution sources is considered to have significant consequences for interstate commerce. Another important area of environmental lawmaking for the US Congress is its power to manage property owned by the United States (almost 73 million hectares of land which are covered by laws and other regulations on the protection of the environment and natural resources).

Since the United States is a federation, its states have the right to adopt their own laws on environmental protection, however, these laws must meet the following requirements:

1) They must not burden interstate commerce. This prohibition manifested itself when the Supreme Court of the United States (the highest court) protested the law of the State of New Jersey that prohibited the importation of most waste which originated outside the territorial limits of the State (City of Philadelphia v. New Jersey, 1978).

2) Environmental laws of states cannot be in conflict with federal laws. For example, if a state adopts a law on air protection which establishes pollution limits below those stipulated by the corresponding federal law, this law of the state will be abolished by the court since it would be in conflict with stricter nature protection requirements adopted at the federal level.

3) Being equal to each other, states of the United States established effective horizontal cooperation in environmental protection. For example, in 2004, the governors of three states of the United States approved thirty-six recommendations in five areas of action jointly developed by all three states. The

goal of this project was to achieve greenhouse gas reductions. These five areas included the adoption of standards to reduce greenhouse gas emissions from vehicles, expansion of the markets for energy, development of renewable resources and alternative fuels, *etc.* Therefore, these three states moved ahead in large part to fill the vacuum that has been left by the US federal government (Olmsted, 2008).

4) States fully use their right of anticipatory rulemaking, *i.e.*, they fill gaps in federal legislation. For example, the United States have not managed to adopt a federal global warming law, however, the States of California (2006) and Massachusetts (2008) adopted global warming laws approving a greenhouse gas emissions reduction program, thereby setting nature protection regulations and requirements for economic entities that are stricter than those stipulated at the federal level (Broslavsky, 2019).

This is the main feature of the American federation – executive authorities of the federation and its states function on the basis of mutual cooperation and partnership rather than subordination, which is called "cooperative federalism".

Like constituent entities of the Russian Federation, states participate in the implementation of federal programs in which they are included and work under their own environmental programs, in particular, they monitor the state of the environment, issue permits for emissions and discharges as well as control the compliance with environmental rules and programs. The governments of states bear the main responsibility for the fulfillment of both federal and their own programs. States can pass nature protection laws independently. They must supplement or specify provisions of federal laws. Federal environmental authorities and states work closely together and every year they also jointly determine what nature protection activities they will implement next year.

The environmental management system of the United States includes the below authorities.

1) The Council on Environmental Quality within the Executive Office of the President of the United States performs coordinating functions. The Council interacts with various executive authorities, issues an annual report for the President on the state of the environment, controls the work of the EPA and serves as an arbiter when certain authorities come into conflict regarding standardization issues or other aspects of environmental protection.

2) The Environmental Protection Agency (EPA) is the main nature protection authority of the United States. This agency was established in 1970 for general management and unified control over the state of the environment. It is headed by

the Executive (Administrator), who is subordinate directly to the President of the United States, nominated by the President of the United States and approved by the Senate, like all persons appointed to a political position. The structure of the EPA includes 11 offices, including the Office of Air and Radiation, the Office of Chemical Safety and Pollution Prevention, the Office of Land and Emergency Management and a number of other offices. The Agency has 10 regional agencies located in 10 key cities in various parts of the country, each of them is responsible within 3-8 states.

Regional offices work directly with states, tribes and local authorities in order to enforce and ensure the compliance with regulatory requirements, control and supervise activities related to subsidies and contracts concluded with states, ensure that states exercise their powers according to nature protection legislation. Programs of the Environmental Protection Agency are highly decentralized. Around 90 percent of checks are carried out by governments at the state or local (municipal) levels. For many years, the budget of the EPA has been about 500 million dollars and it has about 2800 employees. The work implemented is the result of joint efforts of its employees working at the national, state and local (municipal) levels.

The EPA takes enforcement measures within the framework of most laws dedicated to environmental protection, including the Clean Air Act, the Safe Drinking Water Act, the Endangered Species Act, the Comprehensive Environmental Response, Compensation, and Liability Act and many other acts.

According to most federal nature protection laws, the EPA has the powers to use administrative enforcement measures. It can issue emergency orders to prevent threats to the health of people, to ensure the cleaning of polluted natural objects, to issue instructions for compliance with legal rules, *etc.* It is important to note that in many cases of harm caused to the environment enforcement measures can be taken both by the government of a state and by the EPA.

Let us mention the main environmental laws in effect in the United States.

1) The modern environmental legislation of the United States begins with the National Environment Policy Act (NEPA) of 1969, which has become the main law in the environmental area of the United States, outlining the basic principles, institutions and mechanisms of the state environmental policy. The Act stipulates mandatory analysis of the environmental consequences of activities of various economic entities and the need to prevent and eliminate environmental damage and establishes the right of citizens to a healthy environment. The importance of the NEPA consists in the fact that it emphasizes the need to inform the population of all significant projects that are to be implemented at the federal level and

capable of having a negative impact on the environment. The population should know about the consequences of this impact. The Act regulates not only the work of many federal agencies (for example, developing programs and managing property) but also the activities that require federal permission or use public funding. This Act is significant because it requires that environmental factors be considered along with other relevant factors in selecting one of the alternative projects. A common sanction for a violation of the NEPA is a court decision on prohibiting a federal agency from participating in a project, developing it, licensing or funding a private organization until all the requirements of the Act are met. The claimants are usually individuals. Beginning from the NEPA, each subsequent federal nature protection act of the United States includes its own system of sanctions but Congress of the country has never adopted one common regulatory document for all types of environmental offenses (Khoia, 1994).

2) The Safe Drinking Water Act was adopted in 1974. This Act protects the health of the nation and regulates the drinking water supply system. It was amended in 1986 and 1996. National standards for drinking water for 83 certain contaminants were established in 1986 and a particular significance was attributed to social participation and the right of the society to receive information (annual reports) in 1996. The United States have primary and secondary drinking water standards. Primary standards establish legally binding maximum allowable concentrations of contaminants in drinking water and mandatory methods of contamination elimination.

Secondary standards have no legal force, they regulate visual (aesthetic) characteristics of water rather than its impact on human health (for example, color, taste, odor). Primary drinking water standards are established in three stages:

a) The Agency (EPA) identifies contaminants that can have impact on human health.

b) The Agency establishes the threshold of maximum allowable concentrations for contaminants in drinking water;

c) The Agency sets the highest level of contaminants allowed in drinking water and mandatory methods of purification.

As a result of the establishment of these standards, all stationary sources of contamination that discharge contaminants into the US territorial waters must obtain permits issued on the basis of calculations of the maximum amount of a contaminant permitted to be discharged into the US water reservoirs so that the water bodies would comply with water standards for that specific contaminant.

Russia uses a similar principle, when the values of regulations of permissible discharges into water bodies for specific economic entities are calculated in the manner preventing any excess of the specified environmental quality values.

The case of Flint, Michigan is the best known case in the US judicial practice regarding harm caused to the health of citizens by contaminated drinking water. Flint is located along the Flint River, approximately sixty miles northwest of Detroit, Michigan. Flint is considered a poor city in terms of the United States, since 41.6 percent of its population has a standard of living below federal poverty thresholds.

In 1967, for the purpose of ensuring high quality of drinking water, Flint agreed to a long-term contract with the Detroit Water and Sewerage Department (DWSD) for supply of drinking water from Lake Huron. The water coming to the city from the lake was treated to combat corrosion. Flint took a hard heat from the 2008 financial crisis, having driven Michigan Governor to declare a financial emergency in the city. Trying to save money, Flint started using water from the Flint River as a temporary solution. Meanwhile, in contrast to the high-quality water of Lake Huron, the Flint River had been used for discharge of industrial wastewater for decades, its water had high concentrations of chloride and other harmful substances and was nineteen times more corrosive than the water from Lake Huron (Lado, 2017).

The decision to use the water from the Flint River had catastrophic consequences. Just a few days after water users began to complain that their water was unpleasant in appearance, taste and color. Flint citizens expressed their concerns also in the next eight months. However, the authorities of Flint did not take any actions and refused (in order to save money) to provide connection to the water supply from Lake Huron. Soon scientists tested nearly 300 drinking water samples in Flint, and approximately thirty samples indicated excess lead levels. The authorities of Flint and Michigan did not take any actions for additional purification of water in Flint up to the moment when doctors confirmed the facts of lead poisoning of twelve thousand children aged from one to 18 years that resided in the city. The state of health of adults was not better. New research also discovered a link between water contamination and a range of diseases (for example, pneumonia) which likely spread through the city's drinking water. As a result, ten people soon died from these diseases. Studies showed that Flint water was completely unsuitable, both for drinking or cooking food and for using for hygienic purposes. The EPA inspection established that the water was contaminated to the extent that it could be classified as toxic waste, however, the utility service providers of Flint continued to demand full payment in the amount of 200 dollars per month in connection with its supply. Lead contamination of water, which could have been prevented by anticorrosion water treatment, became a political scandal, when the public knew about emails and documents which proved that the authorities of Michigan tried to hide the problem for several months. The US president had to introduce a state of emergency in Flint. The Flint water crisis is a story of unpreparedness, inaction and incompetence of regional and local authorities that failed in their fundamental responsibility to supply the population with high-quality drinking water. The Michigan Department of Health failed to take adequate measures to protect health of the population. The authorities of the state and the city persistently denied all the attempts of the civil society to raise their awareness of the problem of unsafe water, the fact of its contamination with lead and increased cases of diseases among the citizens. The consequences of this tragedy for Flint will be long-lasting. This story deeply affected the city's public health, its economic future, and residents' trust in authorities, since the environmental crisis was not caused by actions of only one person or institution. The Flint water crisis resulted in a great deal of litigation, which still continues today. The number of residents who have been exposed to the contaminated water is in the tens of thousands. Perhaps the most troubling fact is that the current environmental legislation of the United States should have prevented such an environmental crisis, stipulating measures for water purification, monitoring of water bodies, notifying the public about the environmental situation in a given area, *etc.* However, these measures gave no effect, which requires further study of these events in Flint (Weiser-Burton, 2019).

3) The Clean Air Act of 1963 is one of the examples of how the states implement a federal program. Though the Clean Air Act is a federal law which covers the territory of the entire country, states carry out considerable work to comply with it. The EPA establishes federal standards of maximum allowable concentrations for pollutants in the air that pose risk to the health and well-being of the nation. To comply with the Clean Air Act in the territory of the states, the states must develop a plan for the implementation of the program for the achievement of compliance with the values of the maximum allowable concentration of harmful substances in the air of the states and submit it to the EPA. The program implementation plans include regulatory documents which will be used by the states to clean the air in the territories where the values of the maximum allowable concentration for harmful substances in the air are not achieved or which will provide the possibility to continue observing this Act in the territories where the values of the maximum allowable concentration for harmful substances in the air are already achieved. Giving states the main role in developing plans for the achievement of the values of the maximum allowable concentration for harmful substances in the air, the Act recognizes the fact that the fight against air pollution in different parts of the country requires knowledge of local industries, geographic

and weather conditions, patterns of housekeeping, *etc.* The most important condition for the approval of the programs is the availability of quick and practically feasible measures for the achievement of the values of the maximum allowable concentration for harmful substances in the air. As soon as the Environmental Protection Agency approves the plans of the states, they have a legal force not only as acts of the states but also as federal acts.

4) The Endangered Species Act of 1973 is to protect endangered species of plants, fish and animals as well as their habitats from extinction. Their list is made exclusively on the basis of scientific data. Critical habitats are identified with consideration of all factors, including economic ones. No federal agency can take any action that would jeopardize the existence of endangered species or destroy their habitats. Acts prohibiting activities of federal agencies in compliance with this Act stipulate quite impressive sanctions. The case of Tennessee Valley Authority v. Hill, 1978, is a typical example of the effect of this Act. The Authority had been building the dam on the Little Tennessee River for ten years. The dam was almost completed when it turned out that one of the biological species, small fish that inhabited upstream, was endangered. If the dam were completed, the reservoir would change the habitat of this fish, causing extinction or considerable reduction of its population. Environmental groups filed the case to enjoin completion of the dam and impoundment of the reservoir on the ground that those actions would violate the environmental legislation of the United States by directly causing the extinction of the species. The Supreme Court of the USA reversed the lower court and granted a permanent injunction to halt completion of the dam, having found serious evidence of the violation of the environmental legislation in that the Tennessee Valley Authority had failed to take necessary action to avoid jeopardizing the natural habitat of the fish. The Court also relied on the intention of Congress to halt species extinction, whatever the cost, since the value of the species was incalculable and damage irreparable.

The immense significance of the decision is evidenced by the following words of the Court: it may seem curious to some that the survival of a relatively small number of three-inch fish among all the countless millions of species extant would require the permanent halting of a virtually completed dam for which Congress has expended more than $100 million. The paradox is not minimized by the fact that Congress continued to appropriate large sums of public money for the project, even after congressional Appropriations Committees were apprised of its apparent impact upon the survival of the snail darter. We conclude, however, that the explicit provisions of the Endangered Species Act require precisely that result. It is clear from this statement that the Supreme Court afforded the highest of priorities to creating a remedy that would prevent the environmental harm. Tennessee Valley Authority was a defining moment for the environmental legal world because of the case's high public profile and because of its utmost support for an injunction to prevent environmental harm, even in the face of immense social costs (Axtell, 2011).

5) The Comprehensive Environmental Response, Compensation, and Liability Act (CERCLA) of 1980 provided for the creation of the Superfund. The federal Superfund program is managed by the EPA, it is designed to investigate and clean up sites contaminated with hazardous substances. Part of the identified sites are included in the National Priorities List based on the level of environmental risks. The EPA seeks to identify parties responsible for hazardous substances emissions (discharges) to the environment and either compel them to clean up the sites, or it may undertake the cleanup on its own using the Superfund and seek to recover those costs from the pollutants. This is a typical case of the implementation of the polluter pays principle. Approximately 30 percent of the time the polluter cannot be found and then taxpayers pay for the cleanup. Today the Superfund programs suffer from under-funding.

Therefore, in the United States, for many decades, there have been various acts of environmental legislation setting a sufficiently effective mechanism of environmental protection. Meanwhile, federal environmental programs often suffer from under-funding and the implementation of environmental requirements can be ignored at the local level, which leads to negative consequences for the environment and the health of citizens.

LEGAL PROTECTION OF THE ENVIRONMENT IN CHINA

The People's Republic of China is one of the most economically developed states. Over the past 70 years, China's GDP has grown tenfold and the use of natural resources in the economy has increased 40-fold. The state of the environment has worsened significantly as a result of the industrial production in China. About a third of China's land is affected by erosion and desertification is a very acute problem. There is still a shortage of fresh water as well as the problem of its pollution (about 25 percent of the population consumes poor quality drinking water). However, the most acute problem in China is the quality of air. China ranks first in the world for many types of pollutant emissions. As a result, about one third of the population have to breathe polluted air, which has a negative impact on their health. China has the second highest level of greenhouse gas pollution in the world after the United States, which leads to constant acid precipitation. Coal-fired power stations and transport make the largest contribution to air pollution. Environmental pollution has a negative impact on the state of fauna of China and causes the extinction of rare species (for example, giant pandas and South China tigers are at risk of no longer existing).

Therefore, China's environmental problems have a complex nature, affect all major components of the biosphere and take a toll on the environment of some neighboring countries including Russia.

In this situation, the Chinese authorities make enormous efforts to reduce the negative impact on the environment. The said measures are organizational, economic and legal.

First (organizational) set of measures. The National People's Congress is the legislative authority in China. This is the highest body of the country's state power adopting laws including those on environmental protection. The State Council of the People's Republic of China is the highest state executive authority. The State Council consists of also ministers, including the head of the main nature protection authority of the PRC.

This executive authority of China is called the Ministry of Ecology and Environment of the People's Republic of China. The Ministry traces its history back to 1974, when the Environmental Protection Leadership Group was established under the State Council to develop environmental principles, plans, and draft regulations. Now the Ministry includes over 20 Departments, the most important functions are given to the Central Supervision Office of Ecological and Environmental Protection, the Department of Water Ecology and Environment, the Department of Atmospheric Environment, the Department of Climate Change, the Department of Solid Wastes and Chemicals, *etc.*

The main powers of the Ministry are as follows:

1) Development and implementation of the national environmental policy, interaction with other authorities with regard to environmental issues, development of draft laws and departmental acts;

2) Initiation and coordination of the investigation of offences that cause significant pollution of the environment and damage to it, coordination of the settlement of environmental disputes between the regions;

3) Environmental supervision, issue of permits for emissions (discharges), development of environmental regulations;

4) Development of proposals for fixed assets investments in the area of environmental protection, development of a circular economy;

5) State environmental monitoring, provision of environmental information;

6) Protection of nature reserves, protection of wildlife, wetlands, protection against desertification, protection of biodiversity;

7) Nuclear and radiation safety;

8) Environmental impact assessment;

9) Development of strategies, plans and policy in the area of climate change and greenhouse gas emissions;

10) Organization of educational campaigns for nature protection, *etc.*2

Therefore, we observe that many powers of the Ministry of Ecology and Environment of the People's Republic of China and the Ministry of Natural Resources and Environment of the Russian Federation match (environmental supervision, environmental impact assessment, issue of permits for emissions and discharges, *etc.*). At the same time, a number of environmental powers in Russia are provided to other executive authorities (for example, Rostekhnadzor ensures nuclear and radiation safety). The issue of desertification and climate change is not so clearly expressed and the development of a circular economy is not mentioned in any way in Russia. These differences are due to objective natural and climatic conditions and the character (and amount) of environmental pollution in Russia and China as well as the policy of state authorities in the environmental field.

If we consider the recent examples of the Ministry's work, its activities for the execution of a resolution adopted at the height of the coronavirus pandemic are of some interest. The PRC believes that the virus is widespread not only among humans but also among wild animals. This is why the highest legislative body of China adopted a resolution on a complete ban on consumption of wild animals throughout the country. Its resolution requires severe punishments for hunting, trade and transportation of wild animals from a special list (it does not include fish, livestock, poultry, *etc.*). A number of orders were given to the Ministry to combat illegal trade in wild animals. These measures are due to the fact that, according to China's data, the coronavirus first appeared in a seafood market in Wuhan (Hubei province), where, as follows from reports of Chinese media, wild animals were often sold illegally.

It should be noted that China is a unitary state (in contrast to Russia or the United States), consequently, it has no independent regional administration. It has either no local government bodies in the Russian or European understanding. People's Congresses and the People's Governments are bodies of state power in provinces and at the local level.

The second (economic) set involves the China's establishment of the payment for environmental pollution, the system of compensation for environmental damage and financial incentives (income tax benefits) for the transition to greener technologies (for example, incentives for the purchase of systems for treating air emissions and wastewater discharges). There were attempts to calculate the environmental GDP of the country taking into account the economy losses from pollution, however, this practice has not been developed.

We should point out the rule of one of the PRC's environmental laws which stipulates that income received from the payment charged from excessive emissions of pollutants must be used to prevent and combat pollution and must not be used for other purposes. Moreover, China provides tax preferences for industrial activities that promote the development of a circular economy and supports the import of technology, equipment and products that save the consumption of energy, water and other resources through such measures as tax reduction and the restriction of the export of products the production of which requires the consumption of much energy and generates significant pollution.

The third set of nature protection measures is of a legal nature, which manifests itself in the adoption of numerous laws on environmental protection.

The 1982 Constitution of the People's Republic of China states (Article 9) that mineral resources, waters, forests, mountains, grassland, unreclaimed land, beaches and other natural resources are owned by the state, that is, by the whole people, with the exception of the forests, mountains, grassland, unreclaimed land and beaches that are owned by collectives in accordance with the law. According to Article 26 of the PRC's Constitution, the state protects and improves the living environment and the ecological environment, prevents and controls pollution and other public hazards. If we compare provisions of the PRC's Constitution and the Constitution of the Russian Federation, we can find out that the regulation of environmental rights and duties in Russia is more detailed.

Environmental Protection Law of the PRC of December 26, 1989 (revised on April 24, 2014). The main environmental law of China performs the same function as NEPA in the United States, it is a corpus of general provisions, principles and mechanisms of legal regulation of environmental protection, which are set forth in detail in other acts of Chinese environmental law.

It is noteworthy that this law is built according to the "narrow model" of the understanding of the subject of environmental law, *i.e.*, it deals only with environmental protection but not with the use of natural resources (in a similar manner, the main Russian nature protection law is focused only on the issues of environmental protection but not the organization of natural resource management). The comparison of the two main environmental laws of the Russian Federation and the People's Republic of China makes it possible to draw the following conclusions:

a) The comparison of their terminology makes it possible to conclude that in the PRC (Article 2 of the Environmental Protection Law of the PRC) the term "environment" refers to all natural elements and artificially transformed natural elements affecting human existence, which includes the atmosphere, water, seas, land, minerals, forests, grasslands, wildlife, nature reserves, historic sites and scenic spots, *etc.* In Russia, we can observe the same principal terminological approach. However, there are also a number of differences in the understanding of protection objects. China purposefully distinguishes grasslands and wildlife as such objects, which cannot be said about Russia. At the same time, Article 1 of the Law of the Russian Federation "On Environmental Protection" presents a detailed terminology, which is absent in the basic Environmental Protection Law of the PRC.

b) Article 4 of the Law of the PRC states that the plans for environmental protection must be incorporated into the national economic and social development plans, which is a manifestation of China's implementation of the concept of sustainable development. We observe the same trend also in Russia.

c) Russian and Chinese Laws use different legal techniques to formulate environmental rights of the citizens. Article 6 of the Law of the PRC specifies that all organizations and individuals have the obligation to protect the environment and have the right to report on or file claims against organizations or individuals that cause pollution or damage to the environment. Despite the capacity and persuasiveness of this wording, we note that the Russian law contains a more comprehensive list of environmental rights of the citizens, including the right to environmental information, association, appeal, environmental rallies, pickets and processions, *etc.*

The list of environmental duties is also detailed in Russia. Moreover, the Russian legislator specifies in detail not only the rights and duties of citizens but also those of public associations created by them.

d) Article 16 of the Law of the PRC is quite noteworthy as according to it the local people's governments are responsible for the environmental quality of areas under their jurisdiction and take measures to improve the environmental quality. Russia has also enshrined environmental protection powers of authorities of all levels, however, their responsibility for their work is not directly expressed in the laws.

e) The mechanism of bringing citizens, officers and legal entities to responsibility for environmental offenses is quite efficient in China. For example, 186,000 administrative punishments were imposed on citizens and legal entities for environmental offenses in China in 2018 and 83,000 – four years before. The total amount of the imposed penal sanctions comprised 15.3 billion yuan (about 2.15 billion dollars).3 As for criminal liability, in the People's Republic of China (as well as in the United States), there is liability of legal entities for environmental crimes, which is absent in the Russian Federation. Environmental crimes in China are punished more severely than in the Russian Federation (if we compare similar sets of elements, for example, illegal hunting or cutting of forest plantations), however, there are less sets of elements of offenses themselves in China and they are more of a framework nature than in Russia. In 2018, people's courts in China handled 250,000 criminal cases related to crimes in the field of environmental protection. Since the successful settlement of cases related to nature protection requires special knowledge, China set up 296 specialized environmental divisions, 617 collegiate panels and 43 circuit tribunals in May 2017 (Xin, 2019).

The whole system of environmental protection measures in the Russian Federation can be divided into measures of a general nature (environmental supervision, liability, *etc.*) and measures of a special nature (requirements for certain types of activities; creation of areas with a special environmental legal regime; special measures for the protection of certain types of natural objects).

We can observe this model in general also in the environmental legislation of the PRC. Besides the above-mentioned measures of a general nature, the PRC has measures of a special nature as well. According to Article 13 of the Law of the PRC, organizations constructing projects that cause pollution to the environment must observe the corresponding state provisions concerning environmental protection. This group includes measures for environmental protection in agriculture (Article 20 of the Law of the PRC), protection of sea waters against pollution (Article 21), consideration of environmental requirements in urban planning (Article 22), introduction of special requirements for the production, storage, transportation, sale and use of toxic chemicals and materials containing radioactive substances, *etc.*

We find similar requirements also in the Law of the Russian Federation. The only difference is that these rules are described in more detail in the Russian Law and there are more of them than in the PRC.

The second variety of the measures of a special nature observed in environmental laws both in Russia and in China is the creation of areas with a special environmental legal regime. There are two types of these areas: specially protected natural areas and ecological disaster zones. They have a special status because they are not ordinary, therefore, the condition of the natural systems within their borders either much better than usually (reserves) or significantly worse (ecological disaster zones). The latter variety of the areas is absent in practice (though mentioned in the Law) in Russia and it is not mentioned in any way in the Law of the PRC.

The situation about the regulation of the legal position of specially protected natural areas is much better in both countries. In Russia, these territories are called reserves, national parks, sanctuaries, natural monuments, *etc.* China also has reserves and other specially protected natural areas, moreover, the administrations of different levels are obliged to take measures to protect the areas that include various types of natural ecological systems, rare and endangered species of wild animals and plants, geological structures of major scientific and cultural value, karst caves, traces of glaciers, volcanoes and hot springs, traces of human history, ancient and precious trees (Article 17).

It is not surprising that the measures for the protection of these valuable areas also coincide, for example, in terms of the prohibition of construction of industrial facilities there or mandatory reduction of the amount of disposed waste.

The third set under Russian environmental legislation includes rules on the protection of certain natural objects. These rules can be found both in the basic Law of the Russian Federation on environmental protection and in laws on natural resources (the Forest Code of the Russian Federation, the Water Code of the Russian Federation, *etc.*). The PRC's legislator has similar views. For example, Article 21 of the Forest Law of the PRC stipulates a series of measures for the protection of forests from fire and Article 22 regulates the organization of forest pest control measures. Measures with a similar content are provided for also by the Forest Code of the Russian Federation.

It should be noted that China has adopted a number of environmental laws that have no analogs in Russia, which requires separate consideration.

1) Circular Economy Promotion Law of the People's Republic of China of August 29, 2008. In the world practice, this is one of the rare cases of adoption of a special law that creates a mechanism for the implementation of an economic theoretical concept. This Law is aimed at reducing resources consumption and waste generation in production, circulation and consumption. It contains a number of measures for the promotion of the direct use of waste as products or the use of waste after its repair, renovation or reproduction as well as the use of waste fully or as a part of other products. The contribution to the development of a circular economy is an important strategy of China's economic and social development.

China encourages a circular economy because it is technologically feasible, economically reasonable and helps to save resources and protect the environment. Waste processing in China requires measures guaranteeing production safety, ensuring the compliance of the quality of products with the national standards and preventing repeated pollution of the environment.

The state encourages and instructs citizens to use and process products saving energy, water and other resources and contributing to environmental protection and reduction of waste generation and disposal. Citizens have the right to report activities of wasting resources and destroying the environment, to access official information on circular economy development and to give opinions and suggestions regarding this issue (Article 10 of the Law).

China works out the National Circular Economy Development Plan, which includes the goals, scope, main content, key objectives and measures for their achievement as well as a range of indices, in particular, efficiency of resources, rates of waste processing and utilization. It purposefully develops the system of circular economy assessment indices and approves the list of technologies, processes, equipment, materials and products encouraged, restricted or liquidated by the government. It is prohibited to produce, import, sell or use the equipment, materials and products included in the lists.

2) Renewable Energy Law of the People's Republic of China of December 26, 2009. The Law aims to support the development and use of renewable energy sources, increase offered energy, enhance the structure of the power industry, ensure energy security, protect the environment and ensure sustainable economic and social development. The term "renewable energy" is used in the Law with respect to non-fossil energy (wind and solar energy, hydropower, bioenergy, ocean energy, *etc.*).

The energy department of the State Council together with other departments works out the national renewable energy development and utilization plan. The plan must include development goals, main objectives, regional plans, key projects, work procedures, construction of associated energy networks and maintenance systems, *etc.* The State guarantees the purchase of all electricity generated with the use of renewable energy sources. The State supports the construction of independent renewable power systems in areas not covered by the power grids to provide power service for local production and living.

A number of Chinese laws are adopted on environmental issues that are similar to those in Russia, therefore, they are also interesting for legal comparison.

1) Law of the People's Republic of China on the Prevention and Control of Atmospheric Pollution of April 29, 2000. This Law is intended to prevent and restrict air pollution, protect and improve the state of the environment, protect human health and promote the sustainable development of the economy and society.

The State takes measures to control or gradually reduce, in a planned way, the total amount of the major atmospheric pollutants discharged in different areas and in general in the country. The local authorities are responsible for the quality of the atmosphere under their jurisdiction, make plans and take measures to ensure that the quality of the air under their jurisdiction meets the established standard.

Like the Russian Federation, the People's Republic of China implements the system of the standardization of the negative impact of industrial and other facilities on air. In case of commissioning and operation of constructed facilities their treatment facilities must be checked and approved by a specially authorized body for environmental protection. Economic entities that emit atmospheric pollutants must report the current emissions of pollutants and the treatment facilities as well as the categories, quantities and concentrations of the pollutants discharged under normal operation conditions to the local authority for environmental protection and submit the relevant technical data concerning the prevention and control of atmospheric pollution to the same department. No industrial production facilities that cause environmental pollution must be built within scenic spots or places of historical interest, natural reserves, areas close to historical or cultural sites under protection and other places that need special protection, as designated by the State Council or the people's government of provinces, autonomous regions and municipalities directly under the Central Government. Enterprises must give priority to the adoption of production techniques that are instrumental to the highly efficient use of energy and to the reduction of the emissions of pollutants so as to decrease the generation of atmospheric pollutants.

The State must eliminate backward production techniques and equipment that seriously pollute the air.

The competent department for comprehensive economic and trade affairs under the State Council publishes a catalog of the techniques which seriously pollute the atmospheric environment and their use must be prohibited within a time limit. It must also make a catalog of the equipment which seriously pollutes the air and its production, sale, import and use must be prohibited within a time limit (Article 19 of the Law).

Motor vehicles and vessels are not allowed to emit atmospheric pollutants in excess of the established emission standards. No legal entity or individual may manufacture, sell or import motor vehicles and vessels that emit atmospheric pollutants in excess of the established emission standards. Where motor vehicles currently in use do not meet the standards for pollutant emissions, they may not be driven on the road.

The State encourages and supports the production and use of substitutes for substances that deplete the ozone layer and gradually reduces the production of substances that deplete it up to the cessation of their production.

2) Law of the People's Republic of China on the Protection of Wildlife of November 8, 1988. Considering measures for the protection of animals and birds, it is impossible not to notice that the PRC has very sad experience of irrational attitude to animals. For example, in 1958 Chinese exterminated almost all sparrows and other small birds at the initiative of Mao Zedong. This decision was justified by the fact that the birds ate too much grain and, if they were killed, the saved grain could feed several million people. There were also opponents of this solution proving that besides grain sparrows and other birds ate insect pests, consequently, there were more benefit from them than harm (in addition, urban birds do not eat grain in the fields). The revenge of nature was not long in coming – already the next year insect pests multiplied and ate significant part of the agricultural crops and even the leaves on the trees. The population was sent to the fields to kill the pests but this gave no effect.

As a result, a famine began in the country and the Chinese government had to ask the USSR for help. Several freight cars with sparrows were sent to China. They reduced the population of insect pests over time.

The abovementioned Law is adopted to protect rare and endangered species of wildlife, protect, develop, use rationally the wildlife resources and maintain the ecological balance. Wildlife is understood as the species of terrestrial and aquatic wild animals which are rare or endangered and the species of terrestrial wild animals which are beneficial or have an important economic or scientific value. It is prohibited to hunt and catch wild animals that are under special protection. Anyone who intends to domesticate and breed wildlife under special state protection must obtain a license. The sale and purchase of wildlife under special state protection or the products thereof shall be prohibited.

Besides the Laws specified above, it is possible to mention also the Law of the People's Republic of China on Promoting Clean Production of June 29, 2002, the Law of the People's Republic of China on Water and Soil Conservation of June 29, 1991, the Law of the People's Republic of China on the Prevention and

Control of Environmental Pollution by Solid Waste of December 29, 2004, the Law of the People's Republic of China on the Prevention and Control of Water Pollution of February 28, 2008 and some other Laws.

Therefore, nature protection legislation of China and Russia is built on the basis of similar models, according to which environmental law regulates environmental protection issues and natural resources law – issues of using natural resources (including ownership issues). The intersection point of the scopes of legislation on the environment and legislation on natural resources is ensuring the rational use of natural resources. Many methods of environmental protection in Russia and China coincide significantly with each other. Regarding a number of issues, environmental legal regulation in Russia is more comprehensive, however, there is a number of environmental measures used in legislation of China that require further study for the enhancement of environmental legislation of Russia, in particular:

1) China's experience is of interest to the Russian legislator in terms of the regulation of renewable energy sources and the development of a circular economy, which reduce the amount of generated waste;

2) In the Russian Federation, authorities of any level are not responsible for the quality of the environment in their territory (the entire Russian Federation, constituent entities of the Russian Federation, municipalities). Environmental legislation only obliges them to take particular measures to ensure the appropriate quality of the environment. The corresponding officials do not bear any (neither legal nor political) responsibility for the efficiency of these measures. In China, local administrations are responsible for the quality of the environment in the areas under their jurisdiction and they take measure to improve the environmental situation. This experience is very interesting and useful to Russia.

3) In China, the income received from fines charged for emissions or discharges of harmful substances in excess of the specified values must be used for the prevention and monitoring of pollution and must not be used for other purposes. There is a long-term fight for the introduction of this rule in Russian environmental legislation. Today in Russia all environmental payments (or fines) coming to the budget are not accumulated for the settlement of nature protection issues but dissolved in other budget revenues.

Despite different periods in the history of the two countries, Russia and China are neighbors for geographical reasons and pollution in one country has negative consequences in the other one. This leads to the active bilateral international cooperation in the field of environmental protection, which has a long history. Both countries have the objective of ensuring sustainable development and building a green economy. This strategy manifests itself in the electricity production increase as a result of the use of wind, solar panels and thermal springs, in the growth of production of environmentally friendly vehicles (electric vehicles) and in the creation of ecocities. In addition, while there are just preliminary talks about these areas in the Russian Federation, China takes decisive measures supported by significant funding.

Given the difficult environmental situation in the immediate vicinity of the state border, in the future the Russian Federation and the People's Republic of China could create an ecological disaster zone according to the principle used in Lake Khanka Reserve, where two halves of that area are within the jurisdiction of different countries but they have a common and coordinated environmental action plan. This type of polluted areas can be created along the banks of the Amur River.

It is impossible not to mention a whole range of other promising areas of the cooperation between the two countries related to the development of ecotourism and environmental entrepreneurship (production of organic agricultural products), the cooperation in the field of climate and the ozone layer protection, conservation of biological diversity, fight against desertification, formation of ecological culture and education, fight against environmental diseases and environmental migration.

The approval of this list of measures would make it possible to mitigate the acuteness of environmental problems in Russia and China, create guarantees against the deterioration of the quality of life of the population, lower the level of international tension from transboundary pollution of water reservoirs and the air of both countries. The settlement of these and many other issues will require mutual understanding and cooperation from state authorities, entrepreneurs and civil society of both Russia and China.

CONCLUSION

The chapter examines the world experience of environmental protection. It is noted that such experience is formed under the influence of unique national natural, climatic, economic and other features. However, every country in the world has a successful experience in solving environmental problems that is of interest to other countries. The peculiarities of national environmental legislation are shown on the example of Kazakhstan, Belarus, the EU, the USA and China.

NOTES

[1] Environmental Protection Agency (EPA) // https://www.epa.gov/aboutepa/epa-organization-chart (accessed September 18, 2021).

[2] Ministry of Ecology and Environment of the People's Republic of China // http://english.mee.gov.cn/About_MEE/Mandates/ (accessed September 18, 2021).

[3] Environmental Law in the PRC Recognized as the Most Stringent in China's History // https://regnum.ru/news/polit/2734353.html (accessed September 18, 2021).

QUESTIONS AND TASKS FOR SELF-CONTROL

1. What are the main environmental laws of the Republic of Kazakhstan and Belarus? What environmental legal institutions of these countries have similarity and differences with Russia?

2. What are the names of environmental management bodies in Kazakhstan and Belarus?

3. What are the main areas of the EU environmental policy? What environmental directives of the EU do you know?

4. What are the distinctive features of environmental protection in the United States? What are the similarity and differences in environmental legislation of Russia and the United States?

5. What are the distinctive features of environmental protection in China? What Chinese experience in environmental protection is of interest to Russia?

REFERENCES

Axtell, S. (2011). Reframing the Judicial Approach to Injunctive Relief for Environmental Plaintiffs in Monsanto Co. v. Geertson Seed Farms. *Ecol. Law Q, 38*, 329-330.

Broslavsky, L.I. (2019). *Foreign Environmental Law: Nature Protection Legislation of the United States: Textbook.* Moscow: INFRA-M.

Garusova, L.N., Kuryanova, U.Yu. (2019). Policy and Legislation of the USA in the Environmental Field.

Krasnova, I.O. (2008). Introduction to the Environmental Law of the European Union. *Agrarian and Land Law, 3*, 130.

Khoia, T.U. (1994). Environmental Legislation in the United States: What Its Violation Costs. *Environmental Law: Reading Book / Contributor V.Yu. Reznichenko.* Moscow: Izvestia.

Lado, M.E. (2017).

Olmsted, J.L. (2008). The Global Warming Crisis: An Analytical Framework to Regional Responses. *Journal of Environmental Law and Litigation, 23*, 125-189.

Weiser-Burton, K. (2019). Clean Drinking Water: A Stream of Success and Opportunity for Reform. *Utah Law Rev, 2*, 514-518.

Xin, M. (2019). Criminal Responsibility for Environmental Offences as a Tool for Prevention of Environmental Harm in China. *Proceedings of the Institute of State and Law of the RAS,* 14-3.

SUBJECT INDEX

A

Aleksey Anisimov and Anatoliy Ryzhenkov

B

C

D

E

F

M

N

R

S

T

www.ingramcontent.com/pod-product-compliance
Lightning Source LLC
LaVergne TN
LVHW070947210926
848482LV00002B/125
9789815049183